IDENTITY AND PEDAGOGY

ERIK H. COHEN

Jewish Identity in Post-Modern Society

Series Editor: Roberta Rosenberg Farber – Yeshiva University

IDENTITY AND PEDAGOGY

Shoah Education in Israeli State Schools

Erik H. Cohen

School of Education, Bar-Ilan university

Boston 2013

This publication has been supported by a grant from a Conference on Jewish Material Claims Against Germany.

Library of Congress Cataloging-in-Publication Data:
The bibliographic data for this title is available from the Library of Congress.

ISBN 978-1-936235-81-0 (cloth)
ISBN 978-1-61811-065-7 (electronic)

Book design by Adell Medovoy
One the cover: Yad Vashem museum, photograph by Debbie Hill.

Published by Academic Studies Press in 2013
28 Montfern Avenue
Brighton, MA 02135, USA
press@academicstudiespress.com
www.academicstudiespress.com

To Einat
and to our children Adam, Itamar and Avner

TABLE OF CONTENTS

List of Tables

List of Figures

Appendices

Acknowledgements

This research would not have been possible without the participation of many people. In particular I would like to extend thanks to:

The Steering Committee

Dr. Yael Barenholtz: Director of Research, Youth and Society Administration, Ministry of Education
Aryeh Barnea: Principal of a state high school
Zvi Inbar: Conference on Jewish Material Claims against Germany
Dr. Zeev Mankowitz: Hebrew University of Jerusalem and Yad Vashem
Professor Dan Michman: Bar Ilan University and Yad Vashem
Dorit Novak: Director of the Central School for Shoah Education at Yad Vashem
Adina Shudofsky: Assistant to the Senior Advisor on Allocations in Israel, Claims Conference
Sarah Wieder: National Supervisor of history education in religious state schools, Ministry of Education
Hanyeh Weintrov: Shoah teacher in a religious state school
Michael Yaron: National Supervisor of history education in state schools, Ministry of Education

Experts and Associations

The School of Education of Bar-Ilan University and in particular Prof. Zemira Mevarech (previous Head, currently Dean of Social Sciences Faculty), Prof. Shlomo Romi (current Head), Dr. Shimon Ohayon, Mr. Moshe Salomon, Ms. Ayelet Kahalani;
The E. Stern Institute of Religious Education Research at Bar Ilan University, and in particular, Prof. Yisrael Rich (Head);
Professor Sydney Strauss, Chief Scientist of the Israeli Ministry of Education and Rabbi Irving Greenberg for their warm recommendations;
The experts who were interviewed at length for the study (see detailed

list in Appendix A). The importance of the contribution of these experts to the present research and its design cannot be exaggerated.
Dr. Avi Zifroni, who agreed to help us in distributing our questionnaires in the ORT network;
The principals, the teachers and the students who participated in the survey;
The team of the Chief Scientist of the Israeli Ministry of Education;
Dr. Yitzhak Weiss for his statistical advice;
Dr. Yael Klein for her input on the history of Shoah teaching in Israel;
Dr. Arielle Rein for her input on the historiography of the Shoah in Israel;
Philippe Boukara for his input on the Shoah teaching in Jewish day schools in France;
Shira Breuer, principal of the Pelech School for girls at Jerusalem for her input on the Journey to Poland
Dr. Shlomit Levy and Orit Elbaz Jacobson for their assistance in the interpretation of some of the cognitive maps
Claude Richard for his comments on the scientific report

Contributors to the Field Research

The Conference on Jewish Material Claims against Germany (Claims Conference)
The Mandell L. and Madeleine H. Berman Foundation
The Ruderman Family Charitable Foundation
The Paul & Margaret Feder Family Trust
The Argov Center for the Study of Israel and the Jewish People at Bar Ilan University
The Jacob Ginzburg Foundation
The E. Stern Institute of Religious Education Research at Bar Ilan University
Bank Hapoalim
Bar Ilan University
The Israeli Foundation for Advancement of Man
The Moshkovitz Ya'acov and Vladislava Foundation
The Abe & Ibolya Schwimmer Holocaust Educational Fund

Contributors to the preparation of the book and its publication

For their generous grant supporting, I extend thanks to:

The Conference on Jewish Material Claims against Germany (Claims Conference)

The School of Education of Bar Ilan University

The Fund of the Vice President for Research, Bar-Ilan University

The Mandel Foundation – Israel

Special thanks to Allison Ofanansky for her contribution in editing the manuscript and Itamar Cohen for the graphic design of the maps.

Last but not least, this research could never have been completed without the numerous anonymous people who took part by answering our questions. We hope we have been true to their view of the world in the interpretation of their responses.

PREFACE:
On the Shoah as a Major Educational Topic

Dan Michman

Professor of Modern Jewish History; Chair, The Arnold and Leona Finkler Institute of Holocaust Research, Bar-Ilan University; Head of the International Institute for Holocaust Research; Incumbent of the John Najmann Chair in Holocaust Research, Yad Vashem

Professor Erik Cohen's survey and study on the place of Shoah education in Israel, the attitudes towards it, the challenges it faces, and its impact is an eye-opener. It provides for the first time a firm and comprehensive picture of the state of affairs, and will thus serve many future studies and probably also decision-making procedures in the field. Such a study should be followed up by similar studies on extra-curricular Shoah education in Israel, and on Shoah education—whether curricular or extra-curricular—in Jewish and non-Jewish settings outside Israel. Prof. Cohen provides a first framework for the evaluation of Holocaust education outside Israel in chapter two, indicating directions for future research to be done.

There is some documentation on Shoah education in other countries, particularly via Yad Vashem, which receives groups of teachers and students from around the world and, moreover, advises and trains teachers involved in Shoah education in schools around the world. Nevertheless, comprehensive and in-depth pictures of the state of affairs are not at hand. Shoah education outside Israel would certainly be served by a comprehensive and in-depth study, paralleling the survey conducted in Israel.

Prof. Cohen gives a picture of the enormous extent of Shoah education, and varying ways of teaching it which are currently employed. This very fact of its scope and magnitude, as well as the impressive level of interest in the subject expressed by teachers and students (shown in the data from the survey), provoke a major question: what made this historical event so important to be turned into a widely embraced national *and* international "educational event"? To my knowledge, there is no similar event in human history which currently has a similar status. This deserves an explanation.

Nowadays it seems self-evident that one can speak about the Holocaust or Shoah. Yet the very fact that we use such terms to indicate the tragic fate of Jews and Jewry during the Nazi era is *not* self-evident. Mass murders were carried out in the past—and though they were described, they were not preserved in memory and history with a special name and did not turn into educational topics worldwide. As for the Nazi regime's mass murder, brutalities and persecutions: such acts were carried out to some extent or another towards other groups, such as Roma ("gypsies"), homosexuals, retarded and handicapped Germans, political opponents in general and Communists in particular, members of certain Christian sects, and more. Therefore, the fate of the Jews could have remained one part of a larger picture of atrocities. Even within the context of Jewish history, persecutions and pogroms happened in many instances before. Consequently, the Shoah/Holocaust could have been integrated into a long-standing chain of Jewish agony without achieving the status it has today.

And indeed this was the case in the first attempts to comprehend what had happened: It was not immediately attributed a special meaning and name. Among survivors, mainly those who spoke Yiddish and came from Eastern Europe—and especially among religious Jews—the leading term in the immediate period after liberation was *Churbn*, literally *destruction* (or *Churban* as pronounced in Hebrew). This term associates the event in Jewish imagery with the destruction of the first and second temples in Antiquity, destructions which signaled a fundamental turn for the worse in the course of Jewish history. In its English translation, *Churbn* found its way even into one of the fundamental comprehensive studies of the Holocaust produced by the first post-1945 generation of scholars, Raul Hilberg's *Destruction of the European Jews* (1961). As for the non-Jewish discourse, in the proceedings of the International Military Tribunal of the major German war criminals held in 1945-1946 (commonly known as the Nuremberg Trials), and in subsequent immediate post-World War II trials of war criminals in Nuremberg and elsewhere, the harsh fate of the Jews was recognized. The number of murdered Jews was estimated at between 5.7 and 6 million. This was perceived as part of a larger phenomenon of "Nazi Conspiracy and Aggression" (the title of a series of eleven volumes of documents from the Nuremberg Trials, published in 1946 by the Office of the United States Chief of Counsel for Prosecution of Axis Criminality).

From this perspective, no special term was needed specifically for the Nazi destruction of European Jewry. Rather, in 1943 a term was coined to express the universal "lesson" to be learned from it—the recognition of a phenomenon of wholesale murder of a specific group: genocide. This term was coined by the Polish-Jewish lawyer Raphael Lemkin (who had made his way to the United States at the beginning of the war, and whose relatives perished in Europe) in response to the reports about the extensive mass murders carried out by the Nazis of Jews and others. Lemkin's intention was to extract a universal lesson from the Nazi extensive murder campaigns in order to establish a legal concept and analytical pattern which could be used in preventing such crimes in the future.

However, in both the Jewish and non-Jewish worlds the comprehension of the event gradually altered—though in a relatively short period. This conceptual change was expressed through the emergence of a specific terminology which defined it as a separate event, which in turn was a precondition for inclusion in the curriculum. In what follows I will explain the importance of this development.

In Hebrew, the language spoken in the pre-state Yishuv (and since 1948 in Israel), the biblical word *shoah*, meaning (sudden) catastrophe, had been used since 1933—in its traditional meaning—in regular reporting (in newspapers and reports of organizations) on the situation of the Jews under Nazi rule. It was understood as indicating a deteriorating situation which affected in essence the legal and economic status of the Jews and dismantled their emancipation. Yet, with the accumulation of information about the atrocities, culminating in the knowledge of the wholesale murder of European Jewry from 1942 through 1945, the term became much more loaded and changed its semantics as compared to its traditional one. And so, at the end of World War II, we find the term *Ha*-Shoah, i.e. *The* Catastrophe, as relating to what had happened specifically during the Nazi regime. Eventually the term became sanctified to a certain extent, and its traditional use in reference to any other "catastrophe" was avoided. The updated comprehension and the accompanying semantic alteration of the word *shoah* turned it into a *terminus technicus*. It came to define the atrocities of the Nazi era as a separate event within that era, also as essentially different from former destructions, especially those of the two temples. By dissociating it from the destructions of the temples, the term could more easily be integrated into the discourse of secular, contemporary Hebrew; consequently, it marginalized the term *Churban* (and the Yiddish *Churbn*), which had been found in the Yishuv's discourse in the years 1943-1945. Indeed, this very fact of competing terminologies caused Rabbi Yitzchok Huttner, a leading spiritual authority of Agudath Israel in the United States in the 1970s, to principally oppose the use of the term Ha-Shoah, insisting that what had happened was a Churban/Churbn, i.e. an event which should be comprehended in a Jewish Torah-predicted framework.

The very emergence of a concrete term for this event paved the way for the possibility to relate to it in education. This happened through the commemorative venue, which by itself was institutionalized first in the 1950s through *Yom Hazikkaron la-Shoah vela-Gvura* (Holocaust Remembrance Day), and in the wake of it through educational materials (first and foremost historical information) in high schools—an issue elaborated on at length by Prof. Cohen in chapter one. In Israel, the Eichmann Trial (1961) consolidated "the face" of the Shoah, both in terms of documented historical knowledge and of the personal aspect as presented in the eyewitnesses accounts. In understanding this book, it is important to emphasize that for Jewish education, the Shoah, an event which happened relatively recently in terms of Jewish history, represented the destruction of a multifaceted past in which different segments of society could (and still can) find sources of inspiration. It highlighted the fragility of Jewish existence in general and in Europe in particular. Therefore, the Shoah could—and still can—be used as a very concrete vehicle to mobilize Jews and especially Jewish youngsters: the loss caused by the Shoah poses a challenge for Jewish survival to be met by the younger generation(s).

In the non-Jewish world, no special term for the Shoah was used until the end of the 1950s, and the Hebrew/Israeli term did not enter the discourse until 1985, when Claude Lanzmann launched his impressive nine-hour film under that title. It was apparently François Mauriac who for the first time used the Greek word for a sacrifice which is entirely burnt—*holokauston* (in French *holocauste*)—in his introduction to Elie Wiesel's novel *La Nuit* (1958). The English translation of the book (*Night*, 1960), which became among the most widely read novelized memoirs about the Holocaust, served as a vehicle for the spreading of this term. It should be emphasized that "Holocaust" presents a Christian view of the event: such an understanding ("sacrifice") did not come up in Jewish interpretations of the Shoah, and the term itself had been used in the past, before World War II, in Christian contexts by Christian speakers.

In any case, a Christian understanding of the specificity of the event met the Jewish one. Indeed, Mauriac was very knowledgeable about the Shoah, as he had previously read and written a foreword to the first comprehensive history of the Shoah, *Bréviaire de la haine* (*Harvest of Hate*), authored by Léon Poliakov (1951).

Yet the term Holocaust would not have caught on if research on Nazi Germany, carried out first and foremost by German scholars in the 1950s, did not show and emphasize the centrality of the "Jewish" ingredient in the Nazi *Weltanschauung*, which served as the driving force for all aspects of Nazi policies, or in other words: that Nazism viewed the world through the lens of an all-embracing anti-Semitism. Thus the comprehension of the special nature and imminent importance of "the Jewish Question" in the Nazi era coincided with the (accidental) use of an interpretational term in the foreword to a literary work. From then on the term caught on in English, and from this so dominant language in modern affairs "Holocaust" made its way into many other languages, not the least through the vehicle of popular culture (the 1978 TV-series *Holocaust* played a major role in this process).

It became clear that Nazi anti-Semitism was not only all-embracing, but that its nature was also different from that of former stages of anti-Semitism, because it resulted in wholesale murder, something which had not happened before. The enigma of deadly anti-Semitism within the context of a variety of murderous activities and enormous conquests committed by a highly competent regime that existed for only twelve years and 98 days—this fact made the Third Reich in general, and the Holocaust as its core evil act in particular, a source of interest, which has not faded over time. The first scholarly and educational question to be asked was: how could a modern regime in a developed society do such a thing? The initial focus of the answers was on Hitler and the top echelon of the Nazi regime, but gradually it was understood that it could not have been carried out without the inventive creativity of the bureaucracy, nor could this have happened without a widespread complicity of German society. However, as from the 1960s attention turned also to the bystanders: Pope Pius XII, the American president Roosevelt and other leaders of the free world. And after the deep social and political changes that took place in western Europe in the wake of the students' revolts and demonstrations in 1968, the questions were directed also to the societies of occupied and Axis countries: how had they allowed their Jewish co-citizens to be arrested, deported, and murdered, or even, in some cases, actually participated in the murder campaign? Thus, the Holocaust became a touchstone and case-study for the possibility to uncover more general deficiencies of societies, for the need for watching human rights, for opening up to cultural diversity, and more. The well-documented and described Holocaust, with some of its survivors still being alive and being able to talk to the younger generations, could serve as the ultimate case for liberal education. But there was more: the fact that Yad Vashem, in 1962, launched the project of recognizing "Righteous Among the Nations," i.e. non-Jews who had acted vis-à-vis evil and saved Jews on the basis of noble considerations, served as a positive educational example.

On the background of these developments, the Swedish Prime Minister Göran Persson took the initiative in 1997 to use the Holocaust as an educational tool to counter the alarming finding of widespread racism among Swedish high school students. He went further to convey this as a tool to other countries too—which led to the Stockholm Conference in January 2000 and the ensuing establishment and worldwide activity of the Task Force for International Cooperation on Holocaust Education, Remembrance and Research (ITF). In the wake of the general atmosphere regarding the Holocaust in the beginning of this millennium, the United Nations decided in 2005 to institutionalize an International Holocaust Remembrance Day on January 27 (the day Auschwitz was liberated in 1945) and to create a special office to further commemoration and education on the Holocaust among its members.

The Holocaust, because of the fact that it presents extreme evil carried out by many, on the one hand, but also because it brought forth shining examples of humanism on the other, and that it bears important significance for the struggle for the continuity of Jewish existence, has thus become the ultimate "usable" historical case for both universalist-humanist *and* Jewish educational ends. Sometimes these differing ends collide, often they can be—and are—combined. In any case, the Shoah has become a central ingredient of present-day awareness, which is reflected in culture and education. I hope that the comprehension of the historical causes that led to this situation, which is presented in such an illuminating mode in Prof. Cohen's study, will enable educators and policy-planners to do their work in a better informed way.

Note to the reader on terms used in this book

Shoah

Throughout this book the word *Shoah*, Hebrew for 'disaster' or 'catastrophe', is used instead of the English word *Holocaust* (except in direct quotes). The term *Shoah* has gained widespread usage throughout the Jewish world and is considered preferable for several reasons. The term *holocaust* comes from a Greek word *holokauston*, referring to religious sacrifices. In an early English translation of the Bible, the word *holocaust* was used for the Hebrew word *olot* (offering) in a passage referring to human sacrifices to a pagan god.[1] The implication that the victims of the Nazis were analogous to religious sacrifices is inherently problematic. Additionally, prior to World War II the English word *holocaust* and the French *holocauste* were used to refer to a wide range of catastrophes such as fires and battles. Gradually, the word *Holocaust* (capitalized) came to be understood as referring to the Nazi mass murder of Jews and other targeted groups such as the Sinti and Roma people (Gypsies), homosexuals, traitors and opponents, mentally retarded and physically disabled people, etc. Recently, the word *holocaust* has been invoked in protests against any number of social and political issues, some of which have no relation to genocide (i.e. environmental problems, crime, abortion, animal slaughter, assimilation and intermarriage, deaths from tobacco use, etc.). The word *Shoah* may be understood as referring to the Nazi's institutionalized mass murder, particularly of the Jews of Europe.[2]

Ashkenazi, Sephardi and Mizrahi

As Jews moved throughout the world during centuries of Diaspora, several sub-groups developed. Though they remained linked as a unified

---

1 In the Rheims Douai Bible (1582-1610), the Hebrew word *olot* in Jeremiah (19:5) was translated as "holocaust." This is the only use of the word holocaust to refer to the killing/sacrifice of human beings in the Catholic Bible (www.berkeleyinternet.com/holocaust). Other uses of the word *olot* were translated as "burnt offerings." Subsequent translations of Jeremiah have used the word "burnt offerings" in this line also: "... and have built the high places of Baal, to burn their sons in the fire for burnt-offerings unto Baal; which I commanded not, nor spoke it, neither came it into My mind ..."

2 Garber and Zukerman, 1994; Gerstenfeld, 2008; Petrie, 2009.

religion, some distinctive cultural features and religious traditions developed. Their different historical experiences during World War II and in Israel are relevant to the subject of Shoah teaching in Israeli schools.[3]

Ashkenazi comes from the Hebrew word for Germany. It refers to Jews descended from those who settled in Germany, France, and Eastern Europe. The vast majority of Jews who lived in Europe and the Soviet Union during World War II were Ashkenazi (as were most of the Jews living in North America at that time, and still today).

Sephardi comes from the Hebrew word for Spain. It refers to the descendants of Jews expelled from the Iberian Peninsula in 1492 who moved throughout North Africa, the Middle East and parts of the Mediterranean. During World War II, most of the Jews of North Africa, Turkey, Greece, and Bulgaria were Sephardic.

Mizrahi is Hebrew for Eastern or Oriental. The Jews who had settled in North Africa prior to the Spanish expulsion, plus those from the regions of Iraq and Yemen are not Sephardi, and may be more accurately described as Mizrahi.

There were also communities of Jews in Ethiopia and India, who are not Ashkenazi, Sephardi, or Mizrahi.

In this book we will use the more inclusive phrase Sephardi-Mizrahi to refer to non-Ashkenazi Jews, unless specific reference is being made to one of the particular communities.

Shoah teaching refers to the didactics and pedagogy used in the classroom.

Shoah studies refer to curricula or programs in schools.

Shoah education refers to the entire phenomenon through which young people learn about the Shoah. It is not limited to the classroom or even the school, but also activities undertaken with the family and youth movements, independent reading, media exposure, etc.

3 Zohar, 2005.

I. INTRODUCTION

This book looks at Shoah education in Israeli State schools. It is based mainly on a recent national survey, the results of which are interpreted against the historical background and sociological context.

Some of the key issues addressed are:

• The increasing academic attention being paid to the subject of the Shoah, reasons behind this trend, and the process through which it emerged.

• Implicit and explicit linkage of the Shoah and the State of Israel: various ways in which national (Zionist) values are expressed, interpreted and debated through the lens of Shoah education in Israeli schools.

• Universality vs. uniqueness of the Shoah: ways in which Israeli educators navigate the pedagogic and ideological challenges to presenting both universal values regarding genocide and a specifically Jewish narrative of the Shoah.

• Implications of the trend towards psychological analysis of the Shoah, including how teachers in different settings (religious, secular, age level) deal with theological and ideological questions pertaining to the Shoah.

* * * * * *

Individual chapters explore the development of Shoah education in Israel and around the world, draw a data-based portrait of Shoah education in Israeli schools today, including methods and materials, goals and messages, beliefs and attitudes. Students, teachers, principals and experts in the field give their evaluation of Shoah education and their recommendations for its improvement.

This is an in-depth study of education in Israeli schools about the Shoah—the systematic murder of six million Jews by the Nazis during their campaign to wipe out the entire Jewish people. It must be clearly stated from the outset that the Jews were far from the only group to suffer during this terrible chapter in modern history. Millions of others deemed 'undesirable' were imprisoned, tortured and killed by the Nazis; tens of millions died in the war. The Shoah is one part of this tragic legacy;

its commemoration and study in Israeli schools is the subject of this book.

Almost seventy years after defeat of the Nazis and the liberation of the death camps, there is still strong interest in the Shoah. More accurately, the Shoah does not so much *remain* of interest as it has *become* of increasing interest over time. In the first decades following World War II, the Shoah was skipped or glossed over in history classes. It was avoided in the popular and news media. While numerous survivors did document their experiences, many were reluctant to speak about their horrific experiences openly and were discouraged from doing so.

In stark contrast, today the Shoah is taught in school systems throughout the Western world. Dozens of museums and memorials have been established. Survivors are frequently invited to speak at schools, community centers, and events, and their testimonies are being taped for future generations. Numerous books have been published, documentaries and films produced, and TV series aired. Universities have courses and even entire departments dedicated to the study of the Shoah. The Task Force for International Cooperation on Holocaust Education, Remembrance and Research (ITF) provides a forum for member countries (currently numbering 28) to establish and improve educational programs, memorials, ceremonies, and research projects. There are searchable online databases of information on the Shoah and readily available curricula. Educators may take training courses specifically in the teaching of the Shoah. Shoah education has become a widespread and multi-faceted phenomenon.

This is even more pronounced in Israel, where the Shoah has become an issue of consensual concern throughout Jewish-Israeli society across political, religious, ethnic and socio-economic spectrums. Significant effort has been invested by the Israeli government and educational institutes in expanding and improving education about the Shoah. However, there was little empirical data by which progress could be measured, areas needing improvement identified, or its impact assessed. At the same time, the subject of Shoah education in Israel and around the world has raised significant controversy and criticisms in recent years, yet little data existed to support or disprove the various claims made.

This is not an analysis of the historical events themselves, but rather a sociological and pedagogical analysis of how it is taught and learned, particularly in Israeli schools. It is largely based on a nation-wide survey of Shoah education in the Israeli state school system, which I conducted in 2007-2009. In addition to the wealth of empirical data collected, the research process was fascinating in terms of identifying the core perceptions about the Shoah, the areas of agreement and points of departure in framing the subject in various parts of Israeli society and throughout the world. This book presents the first full analysis of the results of the survey. The findings are considered in a broad context of Shoah education in other educational systems around the world, larger trends and events in Israeli society, and issues of Jewish identity in Israel and the Diaspora.

In addition to the practical aspects of Shoah education—methods, materials, evaluation and recommendations—the research process uncovered a number of fundamental questions underlying the issue. In any context, teaching about the Shoah is inevitably fraught with painful and difficult questions and controversies. In Israel, where the subject is of such intimate concern, this is particularly true.

Increasing attention to the subject. Perhaps the first question that must be addressed is: why does the Shoah receive so much emphasis and attention? Why has its memory not faded over time, as has been the case with so many atrocities in human history? In particular, why has the Shoah become a core issue in Jewish-Israeli society? While this last question may seem self-evident, it should not be treated as such. Shoah memory emerged after a period of suppression into a prominent place in the collective consciousness. The initial suppression of discussion about the Shoah was an emergent phenomenon, the cumulative result of thousands of individual decisions. The early Jewish-Israeli pioneers did not want to identify with the victimhood of European Jewry, determined to focus on the task of building new lives, new Jewish communities and a new Jewish society in Israel, rather than putting attention and energy into facing the enormity of the destruction of European Jewry. The survivors themselves were not psychologically prepared to discuss their nightmarish experiences. The change in attitude occurred over a period of decades, punctuated by a few pivotal events, and the place it holds today is also an emergent phenomenon resulting from many individual actions and decisions to actively address the issue of the Shoah. How the Shoah is perceived in Jewish-Israeli society is a fascinating indicator of that community's mood.

Though the consensus to teach about the Shoah is clear, during the course of the research it became apparent that there remain some fundamental questions regarding *how* to address it. Teaching the Shoah presents an extreme situation for teachers. The Shoah epitomizes some of the most difficult philosophical, political, theological, and psychological questions. It is highly emotional. It is linked in complex ways to religious and national identity. Thus, in teaching the Shoah, teachers face acute pedagogic dilemmas.

Linkage of the Shoah and Israel. One of these dilemmas concerns the presentation of the connection between the Shoah and the State of Israel. The idea that an independent Jewish State emerged out of the ashes of the Shoah is a compelling and popular one. This portrays the Shoah as the raison d'être for the State of Israel. However, this is not historically accurate. Jews maintained the dream of the return to Zion since the beginning of the Exile some 2000 years ago. The modern Zionist movement started long before the rise of the Third Reich. Several waves of immigrants had already joined the Jewish Yishuv in Palestine, established kibbutzim and bought land; the city of Tel Aviv was founded in 1909. Leaders of the Zionist movement were engaged in a long process of political and diplomatic efforts to found a Jewish state. The oversimplified linking of the Shoah and the founding of the State of Israel obscures this historical process, with far-reaching consequences. Yet it is common, not only in non-Jewish educational settings, but also in Diaspora Jewish settings and in Israel, to portray the State of Israel as an 'answer' to the Shoah. Themes of Shoah education units such as 'from destruction to redemption' reinforce such a link. It has become almost mandatory for diplomatic visitors to Israel to visit Yad Vashem, the national Shoah memorial museum, again implying that the Shoah represents a foundation of the State.

There are a number of reasons for this position. It shortens and simplifies a long and complex story. This may be attributed at least in part to a lack of time in the curriculum. The teachers themselves may lack detailed knowledge of the history of the Zionist movement and modern Israel. Further, such a presentation offers a compelling reason for the necessity of the State of Israel while avoiding an overt examination of Zionism, a subject which is not politically popular in many settings. However, there are shortcomings and dangers to this approach. As previously stated; it simplifies a complex story, giving students a weak and incomplete picture of the era. Students may be misled to understand, from this type of Shoah education, that the State of Israel would not have been created, and perhaps would not have been necessary, had it not been for the Shoah.

Presenting the Shoah as the foundation of the State of Israel leads to a misperception of the State and its society. This is not to say that there is no connection between the Shoah and the foundation of the State. Notably, the 1947 vote of the United Nations General Assembly of Resolution 181 to partition British Palestine into a Jewish State and an Arab State reflected, among other issues, international concern with finding a solution for the Jewish Shoah survivors and refugees.[1] However, teachers should be aware of the implications of presenting the Shoah as the foundation of the State of Israel. They should be encouraged and enabled to give their students a more sophisticated and historically complete picture. This is particularly applicable in the case of Shoah education in Israel. Given the importance attributed to Shoah education, it should be placed in an accurate historical context. Those teaching the Shoah should not assume that students already know enough about Israeli history that they will accurately understand the place of the Shoah in the history of their country without it being made explicit. Moreover, the political discussion regarding the rights of Israelis versus Palestinians to the disputed land takes on a different tone if the Shoah is the fundamental justification for the existence of the State of Israel; the Palestinians may be perceived as secondary casualties of the Shoah.

Universality vs. uniqueness of the Shoah. One of the most sensitive and difficult issues in Shoah education is whether the Shoah is to be treated as a unique event in human history, or as one example of genocide in the long and bloody history of human civilization. Educators and curriculum designers must address this question, even if there is not one answer accepted by all. It should be seen as a historical, not metaphysical, discussion. On a metaphysical level, one may argue that genocide is genocide, one example no more or less atrocious than another, that any person who is killed for no crime other than their racial, religious, or national identity is an equal tragedy, and that the Shoah is that tragedy multiplied by 6 million. But such an 'individualistic' metaphysical approach misses an important dimension of the Shoah, in that a collective identity was imposed on the Jews in rounding them up for elimination.[2]

Moreover, historically and sociologically all cases of genocide should not be treated as the same. To do so negates the students' ability to

---

1 Haron, 1981; Rauschning, Wiesbrock, and Lailach, 1997; Slonim, 1981.

2 Trigano, 1997.

understand the particular set of circumstances which gave rise to each. To lump all together under a general category of 'racism' is an over-simplification. To teach the Shoah out of its distinctive historical context is to misrepresent it. This is not meant to deny or trivialize other examples of genocide, which should also be learned within their specific historical contexts. What happened to the Tutsis in Rwanda in the 1990s, to Cambodians in the 1970s, or to the dozens of Native American tribes which were wiped out in early US history, each occurred within a specific set of historical circumstances which should be taken into account when learning about those events. Aside from the sheer fact of mass murder, there were certain features of the Shoah which set it apart from other examples of genocide. To answer the question "How could the Shoah have happened?" it is necessary not only to look at human psychology and people's apparently enormous capacity to inflict horror on one another; but also to understand the specific set of circumstances that led to the rise of Hitler and the Nazis and the active participation or passive acceptance of so many Europeans in the Final Solution.

Related to this is the question of how the Shoah is to be treated within Jewish history. Is the Shoah to be treated as a unique national catastrophe, not only in its scope but in its very nature, or as a particularly onerous example of perennial anti-Semitic violence? The Nazis' ideology necessitated completely eliminating the Jewish People—their religion and their culture along with their physical bodies—from the face of the earth. This goal took precedence over even military considerations: for example, trains were used to transport Jews to death camps rather than troops to the front or wounded soldiers to hospitals. In teaching the Shoah, teachers should differentiate between aspects of the Shoah that reflect the long history of anti-Semitism, and elements of the Final Solution which were categorically different.

Emphasis on psychological analysis. In recent decades, there had been a trend toward psychological presentation and interpretation of the Shoah to the point where it has begun to eclipse historical, sociological, political, or economic analyses. One manifestation of this is the goal—largely successful as will be seen—that Israeli youth 'identify with' victims of the Shoah. Following the Shoah, Israelis and many other Jews wished to emotionally distance themselves from the image of the victimized Jew; this has changed. Today, students learning about the Shoah are meant to feel an empathetic emotional reaction. Particularly when visiting sites in

Europe, seeing displays at memorial museums, or hearing survivors speak, it is not only acceptable but even expected that students will express an emotional reaction, such as crying or hugging each other. Director of the memorial museum at Auschwitz-Birkenau, Piotr Cywiński, recommends educational programs of several days in order to allow students time to go through an emotional process of shock and grief.[3]

The emphasis on psychology in Shoah education reflects a larger trend in education and throughout contemporary society. As emotions are powerful tools for unification among members of communities (including 'imagined communities'), "...psychology [is] an increasingly inherent and structural component of modern culture...a cultural resource individuals and organizations mobilize to regain coherence."[4]

It is necessary to consider the pedagogic implications of an emotional and psychological presentation of the Shoah. What are the implications on students' understanding of the Shoah when the questions addressed are mainly psychological? A psychological perspective on the Shoah tends to be universal, focusing on questions such as what motivates people to commit such an atrocity, while glossing over the distinctive historical, political, and even theological factors which are equally important to consider if the event is to be understood in context.[5]

Theological questions. The Shoah presents not only psychological dilemmas ("How could people do such a thing?"), or sociological questions ("How did the Nazis organize and carry out their campaign of genocide?"), but also religious ones ("How could God allow such a thing to happen?" and "Why would God allow such a thing to happen to the Jews?"). This is particularly difficult to address, especially in an educational context. Yet students have theological questions about the Shoah, especially religious students learning in religious schools. There are no easy answers to such questions, with which some of the greatest contemporary Jewish philosophers and writers have struggled. Their "answers" span the full spectrum from rejection of a belief in God to a reaffirmation of traditional religious beliefs, from explanations of the Shoah as punishment for collective sin to the "birth pangs" of the Messianic age. In non-Jewish settings this becomes even more problem-

3 Cywiński, 2011.
4 Illouz, 2003, 240.
5 Lazar et al., 2009 .

atic, as theological explanations of the victimization of the Jews during the Shoah may in fact echo the religious justifications for persecuting Jews at that time and throughout history. Therefore, consideration must be given to how teachers can guide students in their own struggles with theological questions about the Shoah. Teacher-training courses could provide guidelines and tools for teachers faced with students' theological questions.

The analysis presented in this book explores the complex and controversial issues related to the messages imparted through Shoah education and the methods used to teach it. It is not the intention here to make a judgment as to who is right or wrong in the ongoing debates regarding the proper orientation or the best method for teaching the Shoah, but rather to present the issues as they are seen by those involved with it in the educational world in Israel: students, teachers, school principals, and educational experts. This picture should help the reader understand this extremely difficult topic from a range of angles and on the basis of a strong, empirical foundation.

The book opens with an historical overview of Shoah education in Israel, tracing changes in presentation and interpretation from the earliest days of the State until today. The evolution of Shoah education reflects changes in the emerging Israeli society, punctuated by key events which catalyzed a shift in Israelis' perceptions of the Shoah and of their national identity. The chapter describes four main stages, though of course there is overlap between them, particularly in terms of implementation in the classroom. Over time, the initial silence surrounding the Shoah was breached and the sense of disdain and shame many of the pioneer Israelis felt for the victimized European Jew was softened during the country's experiences in its subsequent wars. Parallel to this, identification with the Shoah as a formative event in national identity and a sense of connection with Shoah victims has been universalized across Jewish-Israeli society. The way in which the Shoah has been taught at different times in Israeli state schools is an accurate barometer of national feeling on the subject. Changes in education itself, namely a trend towards greater emphasis on experiential and informal activities affecting students' emotions, identity, and values, have altered the way the Shoah is taught in Israeli schools. The historical account sets the stage for the discussion of the situation today.

In the second part of this chapter, the educational history in Israel is placed in the larger context of Shoah education in Jewish-Diaspora schools, public schools, and the general media around the world. Some of the same pivotal events (such as the trial of Adolf Eichmann and the Six Day War) affected memory, attitudes, and education about the Shoah outside Israel as well. Shoah education in Jewish-Diaspora schools resembles that in the Israeli school system in many ways, though certainly not all. It varies widely in different countries, depending on the characteristics of the Jewish educational system and the dominant society in each. The demographic changes resulting from the Shoah itself (in some cases near total destruction of the community; in other cases influx of large numbers of refugees) continue to impact on the way in which the issue is taught in Jewish educational settings. Jewish-Diaspora communities receive significant pedagogic support from Israeli institutes which provide educational materials, curricula, and teacher training seminars.

Teaching of the Shoah in non-Jewish educational settings varies far more widely. In some places (notably many Muslim countries and communities), there is outright denial that it ever happened or aggressive opposition to teaching about it. Some school systems ignore or gloss over the era in history classes (as in many of the former Communist countries). Many places teach units about the Shoah as part of modern European history classes, with differing emphasis on the targeted genocide of the Jews as a group (as in much of Western Europe). Many also include the Shoah in units or discussions of genocide or racism at large (a common approach in North America). In still other settings (as in Germany), the Nazi genocide of the Jews is taught in depth, as a specific event. Even in the latter case, the perspective is distinct from that in Israeli and Jewish schools; for example, the focus may be on the actions of the perpetrators rather than the experiences of the victims. The history of anti-Semitism and Jewish life before the war are rarely taught in non-Jewish settings. Outside schools, the Shoah has also been the subject of numerous popular movies and television series, which have made the subject widely familiar, although the perspective they give may be skewed; for example focusing on cases of heroism and survival, rather than the far more prevalent persecution and death. How the memory of the Shoah is presented in non-Jewish settings simultaneously affects and is affected by how the issue is treated in Israeli schools.

The third chapter gives an overview of the survey in Israeli schools, which forms the basis for the main part of the book. To give as broad a perspective as possible, the survey used both qualitative and quantitative methods, including interviews, focus groups, observations and the distribution of questionnaires to large populations of students, teachers and school principals in junior high schools and high schools in general and religious state schools across the country. Analysis of the data was guided by a Facet Theory approach, a school of thought which has informed my research, with great benefit, for several decades. Facet Theory offers a way to define hypotheses for a research project and to systematically verify, refute, or modify these hypotheses based on empirical results. Facet Theory data analysis techniques enable the researcher to perceive and portray structural relationships among the data, offering a holistic view of the subject under study. In the current study, initial hypotheses were developed based on extensive literature review and interviews with experts in the field of Shoah education. The vast body of data collected in the schools is analyzed from numerous angles, using sophisticated multi-dimensional techniques, which are briefly described in this chapter.

Based on the data collected, the fourth chapter gives a broad portrait of Shoah education in Israeli state schools. The demographic characteristics of the teachers, their training, and types of involvement in Shoah education at their schools are detailed. The survey population of students represents a cross-section of the student body in general and religious Hebrew-language junior high and high schools throughout Israel. Their exposure to the subject of the Shoah in and out of school was assessed, setting the stage for the subsequent evaluation and analysis. The school, it emerged, is the main venue where Israeli youth learn about the Shoah, far eclipsing the family and youth groups. The main methods and materials used in the schools are explored, highlighting the diversity of educational activities and the interaction between the still-dominant formal classroom lessons and the growing role of informal or experiential activities such as ceremonies, field trips, presentations and testimonies of survivors. The methods and materials reflect the teachers' overall didactic and pedagogic approaches, which represent a wide spectrum from mainly cognitive teaching of historical facts to mainly emotional transmission of memory linked to identity. As students are exposed to numerous teachers over the course of their education, the approach of one is often balanced by the contrasting approach of another.

Chapter five looks at the goals and messages of Shoah education, particularly from the perspective of the surveyed principals and teachers but also considering the objectives of experts in the field, the Ministry of Education, and some key Jewish writers on the subject. This is a central yet sensitive question: what lessons can or should be learned from the Nazis' attempted extermination of the Jewish people? Religious, national, and universal messages are all transmitted, with varying emphases on each in different schools and classrooms. Teachers necessarily bring their own opinions and beliefs into the presentation of the subject, and often touch on fundamental issues such as national identity, religious belief, democracy, human rights, relations between Jews and non-Jews, and more.

Following this, the sixth chapter examines the beliefs and attitudes held by the teachers and students (with emphasis on the latter), comparing those which are predominant in the religious and general school streams, and differences according to age. It gives an overview of students' basic values, not directly related to the Shoah, in order to give a basic orientation into their worldview. Jewish and Israeli identities at large are considered, followed by a look at the specific role of the Shoah in the Israeli worldview.

Chapter seven covers the evaluation of Shoah studies in school according to the principals, teachers, and students. To what extent are they satisfied with the curricula being taught? Do they find the curricula important and relevant? What activities have the greatest impact? What do students know about the history of the Shoah? How does the approach of the teacher affect the students' perception of the subject? What are the impacts of various socio-demographic traits of the students on their understanding of the issues?

Chapter eight looks in-depth at one particular facet of Shoah education, the journey to Poland. This program, which takes groups of students to sites of former death camps, has been offered since 1988. It is widely discussed and debated, from the classroom to the highest level of the Israeli government. The impacts of of the journey are assessed. Various critiques of the program are indicated and analyzed in the context of the data. The journey is a popular and effective activity, leaving a strong impression on participants. By comparing participants and non-participants, it is possible to see that it does have a strong educational role. At the same time, it is but one experience among many influencing students' opinions and identity.

The final chapter offers recommendations for the continued improvement of Shoah education, from the perspective of the teachers and principals as well as experts in the field. There is a general consensus that Shoah education should continue to be emphasized and even expanded. There is greater difference in opinion regarding the direction this should take. Some feel Shoah education should be more strongly Zionist in tone, more religious (particularly in the religious schools), or should focus on universal values.

Taken together, the data and analysis give a broad and rich picture of Shoah education in Israel at the beginning of the twenty-first century. While there are some populations which have not yet been surveyed, namely students in the Arabic language schools and students in the independent religious Jewish schools, this foundational data will hopefully make a significant contribution to an informed discussion and decision-making process regarding the issue of Shoah education in Israel. This study is a pioneering first step in evaluating the nation-wide program of Shoah education. It is hoped that future studies will deepen and broaden our collective knowledge on this important and fascinating subject.

It has been deeply satisfying to me personally as well as a professionally to work on this project. I have long been interested in how the Shoah is collectively remembered and transmitted among the Jewish People. I was made aware of the subject by my parents at a very early age. I was born in Morocco in 1951, less than a decade after Allied forces turned back the Nazi invasion of North Africa. To express their gratitude that Nazis were not able to impose their Final Solution in Morocco, my parents gave me the American-sounding name Erik, a name which was unusual in the French-speaking world. Thus I had a personal link to the Shoah, reinforced through my given name. Though I was not a "survivor" of the Shoah, I grew up with knowledge that, had the Allies' North African campaign failed, my family might have met the fate of so many European Jews. This personal connection with Shoah education was revived during a part of my reserve duty in the Israeli army, when I was assigned to dialogue with soldiers following their visits to the national Shoah memorial museum, Yad Vashem.

Preserving and transmitting the memory of the Shoah in this generation, the last to be able to hear directly from its survivors, is a crucial task. It is my hope that this book offers information and insights which will be useful and constructive in guiding this educational endeavor.

II. A BRIEF HISTORY OF SHOAH EDUCATION

This chapter traces the development of Shoah education in Israel: from the first decades when the emerging State was absorbing a large population of Shoah refugees as well as Jewish immigrants from other countries through changes catalyzed by pivotal events and the changing political situation in Israel. This history gives context for the emergence of the Shoah as a unifying theme among otherwise divergent groups in Israel's Jewish population.

The presentation of the subject in Israel simultaneously impacts and is impacted by that in other educational settings outside Israel, in Jewish Diaspora communities and general public school systems. A brief overview is given of Shoah education around the world, and the differing ideological approaches in countries which were Nazi powers, Nazi-occupied, or part of the Allied countries during World War II, and the Muslim world.

A. Development of Shoah Education in Israel

Israel was among the first nations to address the Shoah in its schools. Early in its history, the Israeli government recognized the need to address the atrocity which so deeply affected its citizens and its roots as a nation. The Israel Ministry of Education and public and private institutes such as Yad Vashem, the Ghetto Fighters' Museum, and others were pioneers in the field of Shoah studies and commemoration. They published some of the first educational materials and texts, established public days of commemoration, organized teacher training programs, and developed other resources for preserving and transmitting the memory of the Final Solution and its ultimate failure. Scholars at Israeli universities conducted historical research and documentation on the Shoah. These early pedagogic efforts have continued and expanded, now reaching virtually every student in Israel and having a ripple effect on how the subject is taught in much of the world.

However, the process of developing a pedagogic approach for addressing such a difficult and painful subject in the framework of the school has not been simple or straightforward. The ways in which the Shoah has been understood and taught are intimately linked with historical and social factors in the country. The evolution of Shoah education in Israel is fascinating, and necessary background to understanding how it is manifest in the schools today.[1]

1. The first stage, 1945-1961: State-building. The Jewish population in the early years of the State was composed of three main elements. The first to arrive were the pioneers who joined the small Jewish population who had lived there during the previous centuries. In waves of immigration (*aliyah*) from Europe and Russia, Jews gradually purchased land and established settlements, kibbutzim, and cities, ideologically motivated, as part of the modern Zionist movement, to create a Jewish state in the Land of Israel. A key point of this ideology was the unfeasibility of Jewish life in the Diaspora. On the eve of independence, the "Yishuv" (Jewish settlement in British Palestine) numbered approximately 670,000, and the Arab population of British Palestine numbered between 1 and 1.2 million.[2]

During and immediately after World War II, a flood of Jewish refugees arrived from Europe. These included survivors of the death and work camps, partisan and ghetto fighters, and those who had been in hiding or fled as the Nazis advanced through Europe and the Soviet Union. They began arriving illegally, as since 1939 the British Mandatory government had limited Jewish immigration into British Palestine, and this applied to those in Displaced Persons camps following the war. Following the declaration of the State of Israel in May 1948, they were able to immigrate under the new State's Law of Return which offered citizenship to all Jews. The magnitude of the immigration of Shoah survivors on the new State was immense. Of the over three quarters of a million Jews who immigrated to Israel between 1946 and 1953, almost half were Shoah survivors and refugees.[3] About two thirds of the total number of Shoah survivors went to Israel. The United States took in

---

1 An excellent historiography of Shoah research in Israel may be found in Rein and Bensoussan (2008).

2 Statistical abstract of the British Government of Palestine, Department of Statistics, 1944/45, p 16; quoted in Kamen, 1991.

3 Hakohen, 2003; Ofer, 1996; Sicron, 1957.

some 140,000 Jewish refugees after World War II; the remainder went to numerous other countries around the world. In each of these countries, of course, the refugees made up a tiny proportion of the population.[4] As Israel took in the majority of the survivors, who at that time made up a significant part of the population, the social link with the Shoah is clear.

In the 1950s and 1960s, waves of immigration from North Africa, Asia and the Middle East brought almost three quarters of a million more Jewish citizens. Due to the conflict between the Arab countries and the new State of Israel, life became increasingly difficult for Jews in Arab and Muslim countries, prompting mass emigration to Israel as well as other countries. Early attitudes towards the Shoah in Israeli-Jewish society emerged in the meeting of these three groups, the intersection of their distinctive yet intertwined histories and identities.[5]

1.1 Shoah survivors in Israel. In the resettlement camps where many of the refugees were housed upon arrival, priority was given to teaching Hebrew, providing basic education for a generation of children which had lost years of schooling, and addressing the most pressing physical and mental health concerns. The situation was even more dire in the Displaced Persons camps in Europe, where members of Zionist youth movements volunteered, helping to encourage and prepare potential immigrants by setting up kibbutz-style training farms. The immediate goal of education in the resettlement and DP camps was to enable survivors to integrate into Israeli society and make a new life for themselves and the next generation. As expressed by a Shoah survivor who moved to Israel (and later worked there in the field of psychiatry), "... the theme of personal, family and community rebirth is central to the survivors' lives in Israel ... the rebirth motif also provided the survivors with a rationale for their escape from extinction as well as a positive self-image as pioneers and builders of a new society."[6]

However, while Israel gave Shoah survivors an opportunity to rebuild their lives, physical refuge, and often significant material aid during their resettlement, in the years immediately following the Shoah, many of the survivors and refugees were reluctant to talk about their experiences and were generally discouraged from doing so, as previ-

4 Helmreich, 1991.
5 Israel Central Bureau of Statistics, 2011; Stillman, 1991.
6 Klein, 1973, 395.

ously noted. Many survivors displayed denial, repression, and survivor's guilt, though these symptoms and syndromes were not yet recognized by mental health professionals. Israeli society "... demanded that they abnegate their former identities, their Holocaust experiences above all, and repress all the emotional problems that the Holocaust created...."[7] While there was a general atmosphere of shocked silence which shrouded open discussion of the Shoah during the early years, this silence was not universal. Some schools taught about the recent destruction of European Jewry. Jewish historical associations were convened in Europe to collect testimonies of survivors, though most of these had disbanded by the 1950s. In Israel, too, survivors published testimonies and memoirs. Institutes such as Yad Vashem and the Ghetto Fighters' Museum conducted important documentation. These primary sources and early works formed an important basis for later educational programs and continued academic research.[8]

1.2 "Veteran" Israelis and Zionist pioneers. If survivors were reluctant to talk about their experiences in the Shoah, Israeli veterans were equally reluctant to hear them. There was a sort of emotional cleavage among Israelis between feelings of connection to and affiliation with the survivors, as fellow Jews, and a simultaneous desire to distance themselves from the survivors.[9] They wanted to shed what they saw as the weakness and perpetual suffering of the Diaspora Jew. The pioneers were striving to create an image of the New Jew, physically strong and collectively organized. The victims of the Shoah were viewed with a degree of disdain because they had not recognized the futility of life in the Diaspora earlier and come to build the Jewish homeland. European Jews were criticized as having gone to the death camps without resisting, "like sheep to the slaughter." Worse, there was some perception that people who survived may have been somehow complicit or selfish. As written in a Labor Party newspaper in 1949, "...we [the veterans] had to transform these dust of men into a new Jewish community; it was an enormous task ..."[10] They expected the survivors and refugees to shed their past and join the work

---

7 Solomon, 1995, 215.

8 On Shoah survivors immediately following the war, particularly in Israel see: Cohen and Cochavi, 1995; Danieli, 1981, 1984; Dror, 1996; Gross, 2010; Jockusch, 2007; Klein and Kogan, 1987; Kochavi, 2001; Mankowitz, 2002; Ofer, 2000; Ofri, Solomon, and Dasberg, 1995; Ouzan, 2004; Yablonka, 1994.

9 Gutwein, 2008.

10 Dan, 1949, quoted in Ofer, 1996.

of building the new nation.[11] Even mental health professionals at that time advocated "forgetting and moving on."[12] The difference between the difficulties and suffering veteran Israelis had undergone during the years of the war and the unimaginable horrors of the Shoah was not fully grasped; it took time to accept that the survivors' gruesome stories were not exaggerated.

Further, as most veteran Israelis had only relatively recently left the countries in which the Shoah occurred, there was some degree of society-wide "survivor guilt." Almost everyone had lost family members, former friends, and neighbors. Though efforts were made to save Jews of Europe (predominantly by trying to convince and enable them to come to join the Yishuv) they were unable, of course, to prevent the six million deaths. Reluctance to address the most painful aspects of the Shoah may have in part reflected their own sense of helplessness and self-blame.[13]

Another, more general aspect of the attitude towards Shoah survivors was that the political elite of veteran Israelis looked down on all newcomers, as was also seen in the case of the Sephardi and Mizrahi Jews discussed in the next section.

1.3 Sephardi/Mizrahi Jewish communities. World War II affected the Jews of the Middle East and North Africa to varying degrees. Until recently this history has been overlooked, overshadowed by the horrors inflicted in Europe.[14] While it is widely assumed that the Jews outside Europe were safe from the Nazis, the Axis powers stretched far into North Africa before they were stopped. As in Europe countries, where the Nazis found willing accomplices among the local populations, so too there were factions and leaders in the Muslim countries who embraced Nazi ideology.

The Jewish communities in these areas were well aware of Hitler's rise to power and the Nazis' virulent anti-Semitism. During the early years of the war some European Jews managed to escape to North

---

11 Ofer, 1996, 7.

12 Dekoning, 1980; Dorst, 1985; Rosenthal, G., 1998, 2002; Segev, 2000.

13 On attitudes of Israeli pioneers towards the "New Jewish identity" and towards Shoah survivors in specific see: Almog 2000; Aviv and Shneer, 2005; Ben-Amos and Bet-El, 1999; Dashberg, 1987; Gelber 1996; Gross, 2010; Porat, 2004; Segev, 2000; Stauber, 2004.

14 Della Pergola (2011) insists that this historical omission must be corrected, and that Jews who suffered physically or financially in any country occupied by fascist regimes should be eligible for compensation.

Africa, where they were taken in the by the local Jewish communities. They brought news of the campaign against the Jews by the Nazis. In Iraq, a pro-Nazi regime led by Rashid Ali al-Kailani came to power in a military coup, and in June 1941 a series of pogroms known as the *farhud* broke out in Baghdad. More than 100 Jews were killed, hundreds were wounded, and Jewish-owned businesses and houses were looted and destroyed. In North Africa, Jews suffered attacks from Nazi sympathizers and anti-Semites among both the local Muslim populations and European colonists. As Axis control stretched into North Africa, conditions for its Jewish communities worsened. Hostility against the Jews was fueled by propaganda from the German and Italian fascist regimes and their supporters in France as well as by Arab nationalism. After Germany occupied France in 1940, Jews in French colonies and territories came under the authority of Marshal Henri Phillip Pétain and the Vichy Regime. Many of the local leaders and officials of the colonial governments in the Middle East, particularly in Syria and Lebanon, preferred the pro-Nazi Vichy regime to the de Gaulle government. Jews of Algeria (an annexed department of France) were subject to the anti-Semitic legislation of the Vichy Regime and lost the French citizenship they had enjoyed since 1870.[15] Similarly, Jews in territories under Mussolini's rule were also subjected to anti-Semitic laws. Thousands of Jews (along with other political prisoners) were conscripted into forced work details, particularly during Germany's brief occupation of Tunisia. Jews in Libya, under Italian control, were subject to fascist laws and restrictions, and hundreds died in concentration and work camps.

Because the war turned in favor of the Allies, the Nazis never succeeded in bringing the full force of the Final Solution to North Africa. These Jewish communities were spared. Like the rest of the world, they were unaware of the extent of the Nazi's extermination campaign until Allied troops (including the Jewish Brigade from British Palestine) reached their countries at the end of the war. Even then, it took time for the full scope of the Shoah to be understood as more than just the latest example of the perennial persecution of the Jewish people, and for the Sephardi-Mizrahi communities to recognize what would have happened to them too had the Third Reich succeeded in conquering

15 Granted in the Crémieux Decree, named for its originator Adolphe Crémieux, first president of the Alliance Israélite Universelle and minister of justice in the French Second Republic government.

the Middle East and North Africa.[16]

Following the end of the war and the founding of the State of Israel, hundreds of thousands of Jewish immigrants made *aliyah* from Middle Eastern and North African countries. The largest waves of immigration took place in the 1950s and 1960s, as tension and fighting continued between the new Jewish state and the Arab countries. In general, the Sephardi and Mizrahi immigrants (like the Shoah survivors and refugees from Europe) were concerned with building new lives and integrating into Israeli society, which expected them to shed their distinctive types of Jewish identity. Sephardi and Mizrahi immigrants faced particular challenges and considerable prejudice in integrating into Israeli society, which at the time was predominantly Ashkenazi, particularly in terms of its political and intellectual elite.[17]

1.4 First steps towards developing Shoah education. Within this complicated environment of conflicting attitudes and divergent experiences, Israeli society began to try to come to terms with what had happened, and the first steps were taken towards public discourse and education about the Shoah. The first official act was the designation of a national day for commemoration. A collective day of ritualized mourning is well-established in Jewish tradition, among "... the most ancient of all traditional Jewish responses to national and communal catastrophe ... part of a national commemorative cycle" that includes recollection of ancient wars and attempted genocides.[18] In 1951, the Israeli Knesset (Parliament) named the 27th of the Hebrew month of Nissan (in the spring) Shoah and Ghetto Uprising Day. The date corresponds to the Warsaw Ghetto Uprising, which lasted from mid-April through mid-May of 1943.[19] The name was later changed to Day for Remembering the Shoah and Heroism (commonly referred to as *Yom HaShoah*). As

16 On the Sephardi-Mizrahi Jews during World War II see: Abitbol, 1989; H. Cohen, 1966; Debono, 2008; De Felice, 2001; Meir-Glitzenstein, 2004; Saraf, 1988; Sarfatti, 2006; Sussman, 2010a, 2010b; USHMM, 2010a; Yablonka, 2009; Yad Vashem, 2010; Zuccotti, 1987. For an analysis of how the period under the Vichy regime influenced subsequent political thinking in the region, see Lewis, 2005.

17 On Sephardi-Mizrahi Jews in early Israeli society see: Ein-Gil and Machover, 2009; Medding, 2008; Shitrit, 2004; Smooha, 2004.

18 Young, 2004, 436

19 The Warsaw Ghetto Uprising began on Passover Eve of 1943. Rather than designate a day for Shoah commemoration on the religious holiday, the Knesset chose to set the date later in the month. Gutwein, 2008; Adina Shudofsky of Claims Conference, personal communication January 2012.

indicated by the name, great emphasis was placed on examples of physical and military resistance. Some Knesset members and religious leaders opposed the idea of a separate day for remembering victims of the Shoah, particularly since it did not correspond to the traditional Jewish calendar. They claimed it was sufficient to remember them on a traditional religious fast day (the tenth of Tevet, in the winter), on which the prayer (*kaddish*) for the deceased may be recited for people whose date of death is not known or who have no living relatives to say the prayer for them.[20] Nevertheless, the observance of a separate day for remembering the Shoah became firmly established in Israeli society and widely observed in schools, as will be discussed in greater detail later. Such communal, ritual commemoration and mourning apparently had some reparative and therapeutic value for survivors.[21]

The next major act of the government in this area was the 1953 founding of Yad Vashem as a national institute for research, education and "the Jewish people's living memorial to the Holocaust."[22] This early initiative had long-lasting and far-reaching impacts. Yad Vashem has become one of the world's leading sites for learning about the Shoah, visited by millions of Israelis and international tourists. Further, Yad Vashem's International School for Holocaust Studies offers programs for students, teacher training seminars, and academic conferences attended by Jewish and non-Jewish educators and researchers from Israel and around the world. It produces study guides and educational materials for use in schools in Israel and abroad, publishes books and a journal, and maintains an extensive archive of documents, photographs, testimonies, and a database of names of victims. Other memorial-museums and research institutes were established around the same time, such as the Ghetto Fighters' Museum in Galilee. These institutions undertook some of the first historical documentation and research of the Shoah. It may be noted that the study of the Shoah in Israel was influenced by a broad approach to Jewish history developed earlier at Hebrew University. Very generally, this approach, as summarized by Professor Michman of Bar Ilan University and Yad Vashem, was characterized by a view of Jewish history as a continuous and unified concept and an

---

20 Keren, 1985.
21 Eitinger, 1980; Klein, 1973.
22 www.yadvashem.org.

assumption of Israel as central in this historical narrative. Unlike previous studies, which viewed Israel from a spiritual perspective, now social, economic, cultural, and political factors were emphasized.[23]

The work of Israeli institutes for the study of the Shoah provided the basis for some of the first textbooks and educational materials. *The Shoah and the Rebellion*, co-published in 1953 by the Israeli Ministry of Education and the Ghetto Fighters' Museum, included photographs, a map and a chart of key events. The Ministry of Education, headed by historian Professor Ben Zion Dinur, developed a two-hour unit called *The Nazis' Rise and the Shoah*, to be studied in 8th grade. Over the next decade, the Ministry of Education and independent institutes published a number of textbooks with chapters on the Shoah, testimonies and memoirs by survivors, and activity guides for use by teachers and counselors.

However, Shoah education was not yet institutionalized, and many schools taught about the Shoah sporadically or not at all. There were no mandatory units on the Shoah, and students taking matriculation exams in history were not tested on that era. Israelis educated in the 1950s recall a sense of alienation from the fate of the Jews in the Shoah. Nevertheless, it had already become common at this time for schools to hold memorial ceremonies and informal activities on Shoah and Ghetto Uprising Day and/or on the tenth of Tevet. Such informal educational activities on the Shoah tended to be strongly Zionist in tone, following a theme of "From Destruction to Revival" and drawing the conclusion that life in the State of Israel is the only viable alternative to ongoing cycles of persecution in the Diaspora.

In the 1950s and early 1960s, several important events took place that impacted the way Israeli society viewed the Shoah. In 1952, the West German government agreed to pay the State of Israel the equivalent of three billion marks, as compensation and reparations for the persecution of the Jews during the Shoah, slave labor, and Jewish property stolen by the Nazi regime. The agreement was highly controversial for a number of reasons. First, there was strongly emotional opposition in Israel to the very idea of any contact with the German authorities. Negotiations were initially conducted through other Western governments, and even this indirect dialogue was distasteful to many Israelis

23 Michman, 2008.

and Jews worldwide. When the Knesset voted to enter in direct negotiations, impassioned protests broke out; some protesters threw stones at the Knesset building. Second, rather than compensating survivors directly, the Federal Republic of Germany agreed to pay the State of Israel to offset the economic burden of absorbing Shoah refugees as immigrants. An additional 450 million marks was paid to Jewish organizations via the Claims Conference.[24] Many Israelis felt that accepting monetary compensation from Germany was tantamount to forgiving the Nazis for their crimes. Others said that the money was necessary to help the new government pay for costs related to absorption of survivors of the Shoah. Despite the controversy, the money was accepted and invested in Israel's infrastructure. Even more shocking to the Israeli public, the Israeli military received weapons from Germany and even sold guns to them. Anticipating the opposition this would inevitably raise, attempts were made to keep the arms deals secret, though they eventually became public in the 1960s.[25]

Another important event was the Kasztner trial, which began in 1954 and lasted four years. Rudolph (or Israel) Kasztner had been a leader of the Zionist Aid and Rescue Committee in Hungary. He assisted Jewish refugees and in cooperation with the Jewish Agency helped many illegally immigrate to British Palestine. In doing so, he negotiated with and bribed Nazi officials, including Adolf Eichmann. Most controversial was a chapter towards the end of the war, after the Nazis occupied Hungary. Kasztner attempted to persuade the Nazis to accept a large bribe in exchange for protecting all of Hungarian Jewry. In the end, after numerous betrayals by the Nazis, Kasztner was only able to arrange passage to Switzerland for some 1600 Jews—including members of his family and many wealthy and influential Jews able to pay extra bribes, as well as common Jews, widows, and orphans. Kasztner himself did not escape on the infamous "Kasztner train." Most of Hungary's Jews were deported to work and death camps.

After the war, Kasztner spent several more years in Europe working with refugees and participating in the Nuremberg Trials, then moved to Israel, where he became a state employee associated with Ben-Gurion's Mapai party. In 1953 independent pamphleteer Malkiel Gruenwald ac-

24 Honig, 1954; Lavy, 1996.
25 Rodman, 2007; Von Hindenberg, 2007.

cused Kasztner of collaboration with the Nazis and preferentially saving people based on favoritism and bribes. Kasztner and the State of Israel brought a libel suit against Gruenwald. Although Kasztner was the complainant, not the accused, the trial quickly became an indictment of him and his actions. The judge rejected the libel suit, stating that Kasztner "sold his soul to the devil." In particular, the judge damned Kasztner for not warning the rest of Hungarian Jewry of the danger they were in. A large segment of the Israeli public agreed with this assessment, and an impassioned public debate was sparked. Could there be any understanding of or sympathy with Jews who negotiated with the Nazi regime? Was armed resistance the only acceptable model of heroism? Did negotiating with the Nazis to save some Jews make Katsztner responsible for the Hungarian Jews who were sent to their deaths? These issues extended beyond Kasztner, encompassing attitudes towards, for example, members of the *Judenräte* (Jewish councils under the Nazi regime), and even Shoah survivors at large. Further, this ideological debate was fueled by a political feud between Israel's political parties. The criticism of Kasztner became an attack from both the left and the right against the ruling Mapai party. The reputation of Mapai and Ben Gurion were tarnished. Kasztner appealed to the Supreme Court, but before the appeal was heard he was shot and killed by Ze'ev Eckstein, a member of a radical Jewish underground movement. The political assassination of a Jew by another Jew in the new State of Israel shocked the public. After his death in January 1958, the lower court decision was reversed by the Supreme Court, which ruled that Kasztner's negotiations to save some Jews did not make him complicit in the Nazis' murder of others. Over time, the Kasztner episode has been re-interpreted, with more sympathy for the complicated nature of the rescue attempt undertaken.[26]

The outcry against making an agreement with the German government for reparations and against Kasztner for negotiating with the Nazis indicated general attitudes towards the Shoah at this time. Correspondingly, Shoah education was strongly Zionist in tone, explicitly imparting the message that life in the sovereign state of Israel was the only meaningful option for Jews following the Shoah. Heroism and resistance by European Jews were emphasized over their suffering and powerless victimization, as the former fit the image of the New Jew be-

26 Chanes, 2009; Mnookin, 2010; Weitz, 1994, 1996a.

ing formulated in early Israeli society. The heroism of the Yishuv settlers and those who fought the Nazi threat in the Middle East were similarly held up as role models. Contemplation of what would have happened had the Nazis conquered British Palestine and the Yishuv was emphatically not part of the discourse.[27]

2. The second stage, 1961-1967: Awareness after Eichmann. A distinct era of Shoah education in Israel opened with the trial of Adolf Eichmann in 1961. Eichmann had been the head of the Race and Resettlement Office of the Nazi government, responsible for organizing the transport of Jews to the death camps. Prime Minister of Israel David Ben Gurion instructed the Israeli secret service (Mossad) to hunt down Eichmann. He was found in Argentina and brought to Israel for trail. Israelis followed the trial, which was broadcast on radio and television, with great interest. Emotionally wrenching testimonies of survivors exposed the horrors of the Shoah to the Israeli public. The broadcasting of the trial was intended to serve as an educational message. The Eichmann trial particularly affected youth and teenagers, breaking down widely held stereotypes and caricatures of European Jewry and Shoah survivors.[28] The image of Eichmann sitting impassively in a glass booth while survivors recounted the horrors they experienced at his hands and his refrain that he was "only following orders" produced a strong emotional reaction. The trial initiated a greater acceptance of the Shoah as a collective legacy, breaking down the gap between survivors and veteran Israelis.[29]

This same year, 1961, the term "concentration camp syndrome" was coined, giving name and legitimacy to what clinical psychologists were beginning to recognize as the long-term and far-reaching traumatic impacts of the Shoah. Additionally, impacts on the children of survivors were becoming apparent.[30]

In response to the heightened level of concern for the subject, in 1963 the Ministry of Education established a public committee to help make decisions regarding the teaching of the Shoah in Israeli schools.

---

27 On early Shoah education see Dror 2001; Firer, 1987, 1989; Gross, 2010; Noy, 1989; Riger, 1958 (quoted in Gross, 2010); A. Rosenthal, 2002; Shapira, 1997; Weitz, 1996b.

28 Deutsch, 1974; Weitz, 1996a.

29 Gouri, 2004; Gutwein, 2008.

30 Eitinger, 1961; Ofri, Solomon, and Dasberg, 1995.

A more comprehensive (but still optional) curriculum was developed for elementary and post elementary schools on the Shoah and Jewish resistance. The second part of the curriculum was added to help combat the negative image of Shoah victims as passive "sheep to the slaughter." In the same vein, an informal educational program for schools with the theme "From Shoah to Revival" was issued. The Ministry put out two new textbooks which dealt with the Shoah. Academic and historical study of the Shoah became important disciplines. The materials produced by the Ministry of Education continued to be supplemented by institutes such as the Ghetto Fighters' Museum and Yad Vashem. To help address the concern that the educational system was not sufficiently prepared to deal with the subject of the Shoah, Yad Vashem initiated a series of seminars for teachers and teachers-in-training. Reflecting attitude of the time, the educational materials of this era emphasized the heroism of the Jews of Europe, such as the uprisings in ghettos and Jewish fighters among the partisans, as can be seen in the title of two books published at the time: *The History of the Shoah and Rebellion* and *The Shoah and the Rebellion: An Educational Subject.*[31] Psychological research examining perceptions of the Shoah in the context of current events found that the new curricula and programs launched during this time were largely successful in making Israeli youth more aware of and sensitive to the subject of the Shoah.[32] A relatively high percentage of students in the Israeli school system during this time were children of survivors. Many of them did not learn about the Shoah from their parents, who were still largely silent about their experiences. It was only beginning to be understood how the psychological perception of the world among the children of survivors was impacted by their parents' unspoken narratives.[33]

3. The third stage, 1967-1981: From war to political turnover. The Six Day War was another watershed in Israeli history which impacted attitudes regarding the Shoah. During the tense weeks of waiting period before war broke out with Egypt, Jordan, and Syria in June 1967, Israelis experienced an existential angst and fear of the possible destruction of the state of Israel. The sense of superiority Israeli veterans had felt to-

31 Farago, 1982; the two books cited were published by Haifa University.

32 Keren, 1985, 174-186.

33 Fox, 1999.

wards Shoah survivors and victims evaporated. However, after Israel's victory, that angst was replaced with a sense of national pride and a reinforcement of the feeling that the existence of a strong sovereign Jewish state had prevented another massacre of Jews. A strong theme that emerged in Shoah education was that the Jewish People must never return to the helplessness that existed prior to the establishment of the State of Israel.

The Israelis' sense of strength and security following the Six Day War was fundamentally shaken by the surprise attack by Egypt and Syria on Yom Kippur of 1973. Despite Israel's eventual victory, they sustained heavy losses. The first days of the war renewed empathy for victims of the Shoah. Pictures of captured soldiers made people re-examine the criticism that European Jews did not fight hard enough against the Nazis. The trauma of the Yom Kippur War broke down the confidence of Israelis and brought into question the Zionist theses of bringing all Jews to Israel as a solution for national survival.[34]

The political shift that brought Menachem Begin into power in 1977 led to further changes in Shoah education. Begin was concerned with the subject of the Shoah. He also had considerable support from Sephardi–Mizrahi Israelis, who by this time had begun to penetrate the mainstream of the society and economy.[35] During Begin's term, there was a personnel change and comprehensive reform in the Ministry of Education. Among other changes, a team of experts was tasked with writing a new high school history curriculum that included a 28-hour optional unit, *Anti-Semitism and the Shoah*. Rather than making Shoah studies mandatory, the Ministry decided to enhance informal education. They issued an activity book called *Jewish Vitality in the Shoah* for use with the informal "From Shoah to Revival" program.

The first mandatory unit on the Shoah was introduced in 1979, with much controversy and debate among researchers and educators. This new curriculum for high schools, launched in classrooms in 1981, consisted of 30 study hours towards the history matriculation exams. Making Shoah education a mandatory part of the history curriculum necessitated many related initiatives. First and foremost, history teachers had to be trained in teaching the subject. Institutes such as

---

34 Liebman, 1993; Pins, 1974.

35 Gorny, 1998; Keren, 1985.

the Ghetto Fighters' Museum, Moreshet, Massuah,[36] and above all Yad Vashem began to offer professional advancement programs and seminars, produced curricula and educational materials, and more. This work has spread beyond Israel as educators from around the world take part in their seminars and conferences, and their publications, translated and often available on the internet, are used internationally.

A comprehensive textbook issued in 1980, *Shoah,* introduced a search for meaning into Shoah education. An important innovation of this book was that it dealt with the German side without demonizing them, exploring historical and psychological reasons to explain their behavior. This approach was taken up in subsequently published books. Also, the issue of the *Judenräte* councils was explored with more subtlety, enabling a discussion of how some members of these councils tried to alleviate suffering by working with the authorities, rather than simply labeling them as collaborators and traitors.

In general, there was a shift away from the insistence on physical, armed revolt as the only type resistance to be acknowledged. A broad concept called "sanctification of life" acknowledged the inherent value of survival over martyrdom, and the myriad ways in which the Nazis were undermined by those who managed to maintain their humanity or help others. Emphasis shifted from knowing about the Shoah to understanding the Shoah. The title of the first official textbook for the new curriculum, *The Shoah and its Meaning* expresses the new emphasis on linking the study of the Shoah with values education.[37]

4. The fourth stage, 1980s–2000: A unifying theme in fragmented times. By this time, the third generation following the Shoah had entered the school system. The "... act of remembering started to shift from the generation that experienced the Holocaust to the generation that heard about it."[38] The grandchildren of survivors and their peers who were not direct descendants together received the legacy of the

36 The Moreshet Mordechai Anielevich Memorial Holocaust Study and Research Center, located in Givat Haviva, between Tel Aviv and Haifa. Moreshet was founded in 1963 by a group of partisan and ghetto fighters who had immigrated to Israel. It highlights the role of youth movements and Jewish resistance fighters (www.givathaviva.org/page/36). The Massuah Museum and International Institute for Holocaust Studies, established in 1969, emphasizes the significance of the Shoah on contemporary culture. www.massuah.org.il.

37 Firer, 1989; this book was authored by professors Chaim Shetzker and Yisrael Gutman in 1981.

38 Yablonka, 2009, 105.

Shoah as a national trauma, which became universally internalized through education, memorial ceremonies and the media.

Political conflicts continued, but while in previous decades threats served to unite the nation, this time period saw growing rifts in Israeli society and a loss of consensus around the Zionist ethos. Public opinion regarding the Lebanon War, which began in 1982, and the Palestinian Intifada, which broke out in 1987, was divisive. This was paralleled by fragmented opinions on a range of religious, economic, and social issues. During the Gulf War of 1991, Iraq launched missile attacks against Israel, but the Israeli army, at the urging of the USA, did not take part in the attack against Iraq led by Coalition Forces. Instead, Israeli citizens equipped with gas masks waited in bomb shelters or in makeshift "sealed rooms" in their homes, with windows taped against gas attacks. The Israeli army took part only in domestic defense measures. The country's passive position recalled for many, the helpless stance of European Jews during World War II, and the threat of attack with chemical weapons or gas further evoked images of the Shoah. During this war the fear was for families in their bomb shelters, rather than for the viability of the State itself; the fear bound citizens together in what Segev describes as a quintessentially Jewish experience.[39]

Preserving the memory of the Shoah emerged as a unifying theme, important to all segments of society: religious and secular, left, right, and center. It became part of a common civil religion. A telling indicator of shifting attitudes was that Israeli mental health professionals, unlike their predecessors, expressed greater sympathy and admiration for Shoah survivors than for combat soldiers.[40] Shoah education continued to be expanded in the public school system. A review of school curricula archived in the Yad Vashem library found that only five were issued in the 1970s, the first in 1975. In the 1980s, following the designation of the Shoah as a mandatory history unit, twenty curricula were developed. In the 1990s, fifty Shoah curricula were issued; twice the number, in a single decade, of the total until that time.[41] The Shoah became a recommended, though not required, subject in junior high schools. Israeli elementary school and even kindergarten teachers began to introduce

39 Segev, 2000; on the Gulf War, see also: Arian and Gordon, 1993; Auron, 2008; Gur Ze'ev, 1999; Resnik, 2003; Zuckerman, 1993.

40 Ofri, Solomon, and Dasberg, 1995.

41 Dror, 2001.

the topic to their students, at least marking *Yom HaShoah*, the national Shoah remembrance day, although educators in other countries have suggested that the topic is too disturbing for young children.[42] Even picture books broaching the subject of the Shoah began to be published in Hebrew, often with the theme of a child talking to a grandparent who survived the war.[43]

At the same time, within this framework of universally recognized importance, opinions regarding the Shoah, the messages to be drawn from it, and the best way to transmit its memory were far from homogenous. Commemoration, memory, and interpretation of the Shoah in Israel became diversified and personalized.[44]

A number of influential plays, films, novels, and scholarly works published in the 1980s and 1990s dealt with the Shoah and its impact on Israeli identity. Children of survivors wrote of the difficulty of growing up with the silence that surrounded their parents' past. Sephardi-Mizrahi authors and directors breached Ashkenazi hegemony regarding Shoah memory. While the economic and political gap between Ashkenazi and Sephardi-Mizrahi lessened over the decades, their sense of distinct ethnic identity has not disappeared (reflecting Israel's character as an 'ethnic democracy' in which boundaries are maintained between ethnic groups within a democratic system).[45] In schools, lessons on the Sephardi-Mizrahi experience during World War II have been added, along with a presentation of the Shoah as the collective heritage of all Jews, regardless of family background.

Discussion of Shoah memory became part of a larger debate surrounding national identity, "post-Zionism" and "neo-Zionism," being played out in the popular media and academic world.[46] From various angles, Israeli writers and scholars began to critique the ways in which Shoah memory was formulated and linked to identity. Use of Shoah symbolism in the nationalist narrative and its relationship to the Israeli-Arab conflict was criticized and debated.

---

42 Brody, 2009; Dagan, 1986, 2007; Goldhirsh, 2008; Nir, 1994; Ritchler, 2006; for critiques of Shoah education among young children, see: Schweber, 2008; Totten, 1999.

43 Darr, 2010; see for example *Grandmother, Why Do You Have a Number on Your Arm?* by S. Weis (1997), and Nili's Story by E. Sharfian (1998).

44 Gutwein, 2008.

45 Smooha, 2002.

46 Auron, 1993a; Linn and Gur-Ze'ev, 1996; Michman, 2000, 2003; Morris, 2004; Ofer, 2009; Pappé, 2010; Segev, 2000; Tlalim, 1994; Vaknin, 1998; Zertal, 1998.

A different type of critique came from some in the *haredi* (ultra-orthodox) leadership, who blamed the Shoah on the secular Zionist movement or attributed the Shoah to Divine punishment for Jews' sins.[47] During this time, forums for Shoah education emerged among the *haredi* population, whose children (particularly boys) often attend independent schools rather than public-religious schools. In the yeshiva system in which many boys from *haredi* families learn, however, the Shoah (or indeed, Jewish history as an academic discipline), was still not taught. However, seminaries for religious women began to teach the Shoah and the main teacher-training institutes for religious women developed a pedagogic approach for teaching the subject in independent religious schools. These present Shoah memory from a religious perspective, striving to strengthen students' faith in a post-Shoah world through stories of Jews who observed religious traditions or helped others during the Shoah. An increasing number of articles and editorials in newsletters and newspapers aimed at the Orthodox community addressed the Shoah. A memorial museum opened in the almost exclusively *haredi* city of Bnei Brak, the *Kiddush Hashem Archives* (Sanctification of God's Name), which, catering to their target audience, did not present the classic Zionist narrative of the main Israeli memorials, emphasizing instead the spiritual life of European Jewry at the time of the Shoah. This institute provides educational units and materials for use in religious schools, youth movements and pedagogic centers.[48]

Debates about Shoah memory and meaning in the public realm reflected the rifts in political and religious ideology in the State. As Shoah education expanded and became institutionalized throughout the Israeli school system, its messages and methods of teaching evolved. The way in which the subject was taught reflected larger pedagogic trends. The tools, activities and techniques for teaching the Shoah expanded and became more sophisticated. In particular, there was an increased emphasis on experiential and informal learning. Field trips to institutes and museums about the Shoah became more common. Survivors were invited to schools to give testimonies in an effort to make Shoah education more human and individual. A program of school journeys to Shoah sites in Europe was launched in 1988 following the fall of Poland's

47 Caplan, 2001; M. Friedman, 1991; Porat, 1992; Yablonka, 2009.

48 Caplan, 2001; Ettinger, 2011; www.ganzach.org.il

Communist regime and the subsequent opening of the country to international tourism.[49] This program, which will be discussed in greater detail later, brings groups of students (mainly 12th graders) to Poland for a week, during which they visit former concentration camps, the Warsaw Ghetto Memorial, and sites of pre-War Jewish communities, such as synagogues and cemeteries.

The goals expanded to simultaneously address issues related to Jewish and Israeli identity, democracy, and universal values. Textbooks explored the causes and ideologies which led to the Shoah, and the consequences following it. Efforts were made to integrate Shoah education with other subjects. Another major shift was that Shoah education was expanded to include the experiences of anti-Semitism against the Jews in North Africa, in an effort to instill a sense of shared fate among Jews from all backgrounds.[50] The cumulative result of these educational efforts and public discourse was that Israeli youth in the 1980s expressed a greater sense of identification with the victims of the Shoah than did the previous generation. New teachers had themselves learned about the Shoah in school, and as a result the Shoah played a significant role in their Jewish-Israeli identity, with far-reaching implications for their students.[51]

5. The next stage: Shoah education at the turn of the third millennium. The next stage, Shoah education in Israel in the first decade of the twenty-first century, is the subject of the current research and the bulk of this book. By this time, there has begun a trend of "deconstructing" the official narratives and collective memory of the Shoah. Shoah education became more epistemological and analytic. There has been a broadening and diversification in the ways in which Israelis relate to the memory of the Shoah. This expanded view of Shoah education is espoused at the highest levels of government, as expressed by Knesset member Zvulun Orlev, chair of the Committee on Education, Culture and Sport, in 2009: "The Education Committee states that Shoah educa-

49 A preliminary version of this program was initiated in the 1960s, following the Eichmann trial, but was suspended due to the break of diplomatic relations between Israel and Poland, which were not restored until 1988 (Gross, 2010; Hazan, 2001).

50 Heinman, 1999; Ofer, 2004; Yablonka, 2009.

51 Aharon, 2001; on Jewish identity in the 1960s and 1980s, see: Fargo, 1989; Ofer, 2009; on college students in education programs, see: Auron, 1993b, 2008.

tion has significant value to the student's education, both Jew and Arab, in all aspects, including the national aspect of the existence of Israel as a Jewish and democratic state and of course the human and universal aspects." Some texts and curricula encourage students to analyze historical sources and deduce their own conclusions. However, such approaches have been controversial, and there is a corresponding countermovement to re-establish the Zionist theme in Shoah education.[52]

B. Shoah Education Outside Israel

Shoah education in Israel does not exist in a vacuum. What goes on in Israeli classrooms is part of a larger story, unfolding on a global scale. The data collected in this survey cannot be fully understood if analyzed as a narrow case study. We must also look at how the issue has been addressed—or not—in other places. It is the hope that this book will be of use to people in the field of education around the world, and therefore it is important to place the case of Shoah education in Israeli state schools in an international context.

On a theoretical level, the subject of the Shoah is inextricably bound up with issues of a global nature: anti-Semitism, universal values, minority rights, national identity, Israel-Diaspora relations, and human nature. Prevailing attitudes on these topics have an impact on how the subject of the Shoah is perceived and taught in each national educational system.[53] Educators in one setting would be better prepared to teach about the Shoah if they had a broad perspective on how their colleagues are teaching it, and how students in other countries perceive it.

On a practical level, educational initiatives in one place affect others, particularly in this age of almost instant communication and mass transportation. There is dialogue and interaction between Israeli and other educational systems on how the Shoah should be remembered and taught. Israeli teachers and students visit Shoah sites in Europe and memorial museums in other countries, noting the similarities and differences in presentation. Teachers from around the world come to training seminars in Israel, bringing home with them an Israeli perspective

52 Gross, 2010; Kashti, 2011; Shtull-Trauring, 2011; Velmer, 2011.
53 Heimberg, 2002.

on the Shoah. Yad Vashem and other Israeli institutes produce educational materials which are used around the world. To give one example, two (non-Jewish) British brothers established an educational center dedicated to study of the Shoah in the UK after visiting Yad Vashem.[54] Students and educators from around the world are brought together by international events such as the March of the Living, a commemorative march from Auschwitz to Birkenau. The Task Force for International Cooperation on Holocaust Education, Remembrance and Research (ITF) provides a platform for comparative evaluation of Shoah education in its 28 member countries.[55] Information, books, films, and curricula are shared across borders. Exhibits prepared at one memorial museum are lent to others. The internet provides an easily accessible forum for teachers and students to exchange educational materials and information (as well as a forum for Shoah denial, anti-Semitism and neo-Nazi sites; issues with which educators in some areas must contend). Discussions and debates on the Shoah and related issues of attitudes towards Israel, anti-Semitism, other cases of genocide, racism, multiculturalism, and more are carried out on an international scale.

Some of the same pivotal moments which catalyzed shifts in attitude in Israel regarding the Shoah also impacted how Jewish communities and the general public in other countries thought about it. News of the capture of the former Nazi Adolph Eichmann and his trial in Jerusalem in 1961 were broadcast internationally, exposing the horrors of the Shoah to many, particularly those too young to remember World War II. The threat posed to the young State of Israel in the Six Day War of 1967 raised the specter of another massacre of Jews. Israel's victory ushered in an era of pride among Diaspora Jews as well, and intensified their sense of affiliation with Israel, as well as increased interest in the Shoah.[56] The opening of Eastern Europe to tourists in the late 1980s

---

54 Round, 2009.

55 The ITF was initiated in 1998 by Swedish Prime Minister Göran Persson. Professor Yehuda Bauer, former chair of the Yad Vashem Research Institute in Jerusalem, currently serves as chairman of the ITF. The 28 member states are the European countries of Austria, Belgium, Croatia, Czech Republic, Denmark, Estonia, Finland, France, Germany, Greece, Hungary, Italy, Latvia, Lithuania, Luxembourg, Netherlands, Norway, Poland, Romania, Slovakia, Spain, Sweden, Switzerland, and the United Kingdom. Four countries outside Europe are also members: Argentina, Canada, Israel and the United States of America. Member states issue reports following a standard questionnaire format on the status of Shoah education in their country. http://www.holocausttaskforce.org/education/holocaust-education-reports/.

56 Cohen, 2008; Horowitz et al., 1971; Lederhendler, 2000.

and early 1990s gave rise to "dark tourism" to former death camps and related sites. The release of documentaries and popular movies dealing with the Shoah, notably *Shoah* by Claude Lanzmann in 1985, and Steven Spielberg's *Shindler's List* in 1993, brought the issue into the wider public's consciousness.

That the Shoah has not faded from memory, that in contrast, it has become indelibly imprinted on humanity's conscience, did not happen by accident. It is the fruit of the concerted efforts of many people around the world who do research, write books, produce films, dedicate and manage memorials and museums, develop curricula and establish educational policies which ensure that the next generation will learn about this tragic but important piece of history.

Therefore, before turning to the research on the current situation in Israel, it is worthwhile to take a brief look at the history of Shoah education in some key regions and countries around the world, both in Jewish settings and in public schools. This overview is not meant to be comprehensive, but rather to provide background and context.

1. Shoah education in Diaspora Jewish communities. Shoah education in Jewish schools outside Israel paralleled in many ways the process seen in Israel. There was avoidance in the first two decades. Interest and discussion increased following the Eichmann trial and the Six Day War. In recent years, Shoah studies have diversified, with a trend towards linking study of the Shoah to discussions of Jewish identity, Israel, and universal values. In addition to teaching about the Shoah in Jewish day schools and Hebrew schools, Diaspora Jewish communities have established Shoah memorial museums and education centers. They organize memorial ceremonies and host other events such as film screenings and testimonies by survivors. Some activities may be done in conjunction with non-Jewish community organizations, such as sponsoring exhibits about the Shoah in local museums or community centers or including information about the Shoah in multi-cultural events.

Only a few European countries have rebuilt their Jewish educational systems to any significant extent after the destruction of their institutions and the murder or exile of their teachers and students in World War II. In many communities, what little educational structure exists is dependent on financial and logistical support from Jewish communities in North America and Israel. Yad Vashem is particularly active in offering support, materials and advice to Shoah education projects around the world and offering workshops for teachers in Jewish day schools. Institutes in Israel such as the L.A. Pincus Fund for Jewish Education in the Diaspora (based in Jerusalem) organize educational activities and materials dealing with the history of the Shoah and rebuilding Jewish life in Europe (among other topics) for use in Jewish Diaspora educational settings.

1.1 Western Europe

a. France. Following the Nazi invasion of France, about a quarter of French Jews were deported, many to their deaths. Most Jewish community and educational systems in the country were destroyed. Equally serious was that French Jews felt betrayed by the collaboration of the Vichy regime and the acquiescence of many French citizens. Their belief in the commitment of the French nation to its professed ideals was shaken. Despite local resistance against the Nazis and the Vichy government, latent anti-Semitism in France was revealed. The Jews had accepted the French Republic's promise equality for all citizens; they were highly acculturated and felt secure in their position as French citizens. The realization that in the eyes of many of their compatriots they were *not* equal struck a hard blow to the French-Jewish world, the psychological impact as painful as the physical. Since World War II, French Jews have been re-assessing their position in the country, as French citizens and as Jews. Issues of identity following the Shoah are intensely discussed in French-Jewish academia. While still strongly patriotic and highly acculturated, the security of their position was cast into doubt, and the repercussions of this reverberate until today, as may be seen in the vast body of philosophical writings on French-Jewish identity.[57]

Gradually, the Jewish education system has been rebuilt and it has revived greatly in the past several decades. By the year 2000, approximately a third of French Jewish students were enrolled Jewish schools. In addition, many French Jewish youth attend supplementary Jewish education or take part in a Jewish youth movement. Jewish youth in France today for the most part are *not* descendants of Shoah survivors,

57 To name only a few key works on this topic: Roger Ikor (1968), Annie Kriegel (1984), Emmanuel Lévinas (1963), André Neher (1962); for an overview of contemporary French-Jewish writers on post-Shoah Jewish identity, see also Cohen (2011a).

but rather children of Sephardi families from North Africa who came to France following the war.[58] Nevertheless, they learn about the Shoah in such a way that they feel a sense of identification with the fate of its victims.[59] This may be illustrated using data from two surveys of French Jews I directed. Auschwitz was indicated as a symbol of Jewish identity by over 95% of a representative sample of French-Jewish heads of households surveyed in 1988, a large majority of whom were Sephardi. (Israel was also chosen as a symbol of identity by over 95% of the respondents; the two symbols of Israel and Auschwitz were the most commonly chosen from a list of 17 symbols). More recently, in a survey of over 1400 French Jewish youth conducted in 2008, 92% said the Shoah affects their worldview.[60]

In addition to the mandatory history unit on World War II, as is taught in the public schools, Jewish schools in France provide some informal activities commemorating the Shoah, particularly on the international and/or the Israeli Shoah memorial days. Some students in Jewish high schools in France participate in the March of the Living (along with Jewish and non-Jewish peers in public and private schools). Schools offer orientation programs for several weeks leading up to the March by bringing speakers, survivor-witnesses and providing other educational materials about the Shoah. Materials prepared by Israeli institutions such as Yad Vashem and Ghetto Fighters' Museum, translated into French, are used in French Jewish schools. In younger grades, students learn about pre-war Jewish culture (European in general and French in particular). In upper grades they hear testimonies of survivors and discuss complex issues such as collaboration and resistance, racism and anti-Semitism, and the role of the Church. Throughout, there is an underlying theme of upholding Republican values of citizenship.[61]

b. United Kingdom. The Jews of the UK were spared the experience

---

58 Some Jewish families in French colonies and departments in North Africa had been granted French citizenship, and thus many were citizens prior to moving to continental France. The 1870 Crémieux Decree granted citizenship to the tens of thousands of Jews living Algeria. Several thousand Jews in the French region of Morocco and in Tunisia applied for and were granted French citizenship. The Crémieux Decree was suspended in 1940 by the Vichy regime, then reinstated in 1943 (Sussman, 2010a; Laskier, 1983; Weil, 2008).

59 On Jews of France, see Cohen, 2011a.

60 The surveyed youth were participants in educational tours to Israel. Not all were students in Jewish day schools, but the majority has received some formal and informal Jewish education (Cohen, 2008).

61 FSJU, 2012; Hazan, 2005.

of being turned over to the Nazis by their government or neighbors, and therefore the basis of their identity was less dramatically called into question by the Shoah. Nevertheless, during the first decades after the end of World War II, British Jews' priority was on fitting into the post-war society and economy. They had little desire to recall, publicize or identify themselves with the victimization of their brethren on the continent. At this time, Jewish education in the UK was weak, with few full time Jewish schools operating. As the UK has become increasingly multi-cultural, and separate ethnic identities more visible and accepted, Jewish identity has also become more open, with a corresponding surge in Jewish school enrollment.[62] Through the Jewish Museum in London and survivors' associations, a curriculum for studying the Shoah has been created for Jewish and general schools. This curriculum gives particular attention to rescue efforts such as the *Kindertransport* which brought 10,000 children to the UK during World War II.[63] The predominant British policy during the war years of severely limiting Jewish immigration to the UK as well as to British Palestine is glossed over.[64] The sensitivity of this subject was seen during the Exodus program, a special segment of Israel Experience tours in which participants travel to Israel by boat with an educational simulation activity reenacting the infamous episode in which the *Exodus 1947*, a ship of Shoah refugees heading for British Palestine, was forced to return to European DP camps. For groups of American participants, the program includes simulations of being searched by British soldiers and leafleted by a British plane demanding they turn back; in programs for youth from the UK, the role of the British in obstructing Shoah refugees' attempt to reach British Palestine is de-emphasized, as it uncomfortably conflicts with their sense of loyalty to their home country.[65]

c. Germany. The fastest growing Jewish community in Europe is (with oft-noted irony) in Germany. The community consists mainly of recent immigrants from the former Soviet Union, who come with little Jewish religious background and little knowledge of the Shoah. There remains essentially nothing of the dynamic German-Jewish culture that existed before the Shoah, with its unique contributions to litera-

62 Alderman, 1999; Miller, 2001

63 www.ajr.org.uk/kinderhistory-packlaunch; www.kindertransport.org.

64 London, 2003.

65 Cohen, 2004.

ture, philosophy, theology, sociology, the arts, and more. Today Jewish educational and cultural programs in Germany are often organized through American or Israeli institutions. On the 50th anniversary of the Eichmann trial, for example, the Jewish Agency organized a program for German-Jewish students to meet with survivors who testified at the trial.[66] The Jews living in Germany today benefit from extensive efforts in their society to address the memory of the Shoah (discussed in more detail below). The political-social context for Jews in Germany, thus, is significantly different than in other former Axis or Nazi-occupied countries in which local citizens' roles (active or passive) in the Shoah are widely ignored.

d. Netherlands. As in France, the memory of the treatment of Dutch Jews during World War II had a lasting impact on the remaining Jewish community and led to cynicism regarding the extent to which Jews could feel truly accepted in multicultural, secular Dutch society. Less than a quarter of the 140,000 Jews living in the Netherlands in 1940 survived the war. Teaching the history of the Shoah and particularly the local history are part of the effort to preserve Jewish identity in private Jewish schools, which are attended by between 15-20% of Dutch Jewish students.[67]

1.2 Soviet Union and Eastern Europe.

The worst of the genocide against the Jews occurred in Eastern Europe and the Soviet Union, where the majority of the Jewish population was murdered by the Nazis, *Einsatzgruppen* (German for "action groups" referring to SS death squads) and local collaborators. Following the war, the remnant Jewish communities were not able to re-build their institutions and essentially no Jewish education was permitted by the Communist regimes. The generation of Jews raised during the Communist era was highly assimilated into the dominant societies, which were based on Marxist ideology that envisioned an end to religion and a merging of ethnicities into a world proletariat culture. Thus Jewish identity was suppressed externally and internally. There were almost no public venues in which Jewish identity could be expressed or developed. In public schools, the history of World War II was taught,

66 Abebe, 2011; Peck, 2006.
67 Rietveld-van Wingerden, 2008.

but the attempted annihilation of the Jews was either ignored or else subsumed as part of the general carnage of the war. Young Jews did not learn about the Shoah unless they heard of it from their families or in their own reading.[68]

Since the fall of the Communist regimes, a large portion of the Jews, particularly those with a strong sense of Jewish identity, emigrated. In all of Russia there are approximately 15,000 students in Jewish day schools and a few dozen in the Ukraine, many of which are under the auspices of the international *Chabad* Hasidic movement. Several projects have been organized to revitalize Jewish life in the former Soviet states; education about the Shoah and commemoration of its victims are both included in this larger goal. Since the fall of the Soviet Union, research centers and memorial museums have been founded in the Ukraine and Russia offering educational activities and seminars for students and teachers in general and Jewish schools with support from Yad Vashem, the Jewish Agency and other international organizations. A Jewish cultural center in Budapest includes education about the history of the Hungary's Jewish community before and during the Shoah—including taping survivors' testimonies—as part of a larger program to build and enhance Jewish identity among the young generation. This project takes an innovative approach by training young Jews as peer-guides who are then licensed to lead educational walking tours through the city to sites of Jewish history.[69]

1.3 North America

The USA is home to by far the largest Diaspora population in the world. The main waves of Jewish immigration to the USA, however, were well before World War II. By the end of the First World War there were some 3.5 million Jews in the US. In response to rising anti-immigration sentiment (not limited to anti-Semitism), the National Origins Act was passed in 1921, which limited the total number of legal immigrants to the USA and set a quota system for various groups. This legislation remained in place until 1965, limiting Jewish immigration throughout the rise of the Nazi regime, the extermination campaign across Europe, and the decades following the war. In 1944 the American government estab-

---

68 Gitelman, 1997.

69 Altman, 1999; Gidwitz, 1999, 2011; Krichevsky, 2005; www.pincusfund.org.

lished a War Refugee Board, credited with helping save some 200,000 European Jews, though not all of these came to the USA. In 1938 and 1939 some 85,000 European Jewish refugees came to the USA. During the years that American troops were fighting Germany, only 21,000 Jews were granted entry into the USA. Fewer than 150,000 Jewish refugees were granted entry into the USA in the 1930s and 1940s and only several thousand to Canada.[70] Therefore, a relatively small percentage of Jewish Americans are Shoah survivors or direct descendants.

During World War II, segments of the diverse American-Jewish community reacted to the crisis in Europe in different ways, such as staging rallies and protests on behalf of European Jewry, organizing boycotts of German goods, assisting rescue attempts of European Jews, raising money to help Jewish refugees who made their way to neutral countries in Europe or to British Palestine, lobbying the US government to change its immigration policy, and working towards the Zionist goal of a Jewish state in Israel.[71]

After the war, despite pride in their country's role in defeating the Nazis, American Jews felt some reluctance in confronting the subject of the Shoah. This reflected a combination of initial disbelief regarding the scope of the genocide, and remorse at not having done—or not having been able to do—more to prevent the catastrophe. During this era, acculturation into the mainstream was the priority. American Jews did not want to identify with the victimization and vulnerability of European Jewry. This was compounded by fear of drawing negative attention to themselves in the political climate of the Cold War with the Soviet Union and McCarthyism. The trial and execution of Jewish-Americans Julius and Ethel Rosenberg as Soviet spies raised fears of anti-Semitism.[72]

Jewish schools wanted to instill a positive sense of Jewish identity among their students, and the helpless victimization of the majority of European Jews was not seen as contributing to this goal.[73] Therefore, as in Israel, early Shoah education in US and Canadian Jewish schools emphasized examples of heroism, although in this case rather than illustrating a collectivist Zionist narrative they were interpreted according to the classic American theme of the triumph of the rugged individual.

---

70 Breitman and Kraut, 1987; Diner, 2009; Friedman, S., 1973; Wyman, 1984.

71 Bauer, 1981.

72 Jick, 1981; Lipstadt, 1996; Novick, 1999; Sheramy, 2003.

73 Sheramy, 2003.

In the early- and mid-1950s, Jewish community associations produced prolific works celebrating 300 years of Jewish life in America, which were full of nostalgia for *shtetl* life, barely mentioning the way in which it had been eradicated, and full of praise for freedom in the US with no critique of immigration quotas which had kept out Jews seeking asylum. Some memoirs of survivors were put out by *Landsmanschaften* associations (groups of Jewish immigrants from the same city or region in Europe), often translated from Yiddish, published with minimal resources, and reaching a very small audience.[74]

In 1964 the American Association for Jewish Education sponsored a conference on teaching the Shoah in Jewish schools. It was found that American-Jewish youth, even those attending Jewish schools, knew little about the Shoah. This conference opened the discussion (still ongoing today) regarding whether the Shoah should be presented along with other examples of racism and genocide, or as a unique and incomparable act of evil. Few educational materials on the Shoah were available for use in schools. One of the few sources was Yad Vashem, which put out high quality scholarly works in English, including its journal *Yad Vashem Studies*, which was launched in 1957.[75]

As in Israel, the Eichmann trial and the Six Day War brought the Shoah into the realm of public discourse among American Jews. The civil rights movement and opposition to the Vietnam War created a social atmosphere in which ethnic identity, demand to redress historic grievances, and criticism of authority were more openly expressed. In addition, by this time American Jews were sufficiently well-established and felt secure enough to raise the issue of the persecution of Europe's Jews without fearing persecution themselves.

Today, the Shoah is taught in virtually every Jewish educational setting. Jewish educators around the world, like their colleagues in Israel, are involved in an ongoing discussion regarding the best way to teach this issue and the messages and values to be imparted. In 2009, for example, the Lookstein Center for Jewish Education in the Diaspora put out a special issue of their journal *Jewish Educational Leadership* dedicated to the subject "Two Generations After: Why, What and How to Teach the Shoah."

---

74 Friedman, 1951; Jewish Black Book Society, 1946; Jick, 1981.

75 Fallace, 2010; Pilch, Feinstein, and Ury, 1964.

Jewish community life in North America is largely organized according to the main denominational streams, and each has developed its own theological stances, styles of commemoration, texts and educational materials for addressing the Shoah. Among Conservative and Reform Jewish communities, awareness of the Shoah has become a focus of solidarity and an impetus to connect with Jewish tradition. Orthodox and *haredi* (ultra-orthodox and Hasidic) communities initially had theological and political barriers to addressing the Shoah, but by the mid-1980s some of the major Orthodox publishing houses were putting out books on the Shoah and today there are numerous Shoah-related novels, biographies, and memoirs directed towards a religious readership. The Shoah is taught even in the most Orthodox settings, although these schools tend to give proportionally less attention to the Shoah, compared to those affiliated with the Conservative or Reform streams, as it is less of a basis for their sense of community and identity.[76]

In the late 1980s, North American Jewish educators launched the March of the Living, an experiential educational program bringing groups of Jewish high school students (and accompanying adults) to Shoah sites in Poland, culminating in a march from Auschwitz I to Birkenau on *Yom HaShoah* in April. During the march, the American participants join with delegations of Israel students, Diaspora Jews and non-Jewish youth. The group spends a week in Poland then continues on for another week in Israel, coinciding with Israeli Independence Day, explicitly linking the study of the Shoah with a connection to Israel. This program has many similarities to the Israeli youth tours to Poland. The stated goal of the program is to convince participants of the importance of making a commitment to Jewish life and strengthening their Jewish identity. Fifteen hundred youth participated in the first tour in 1988, and as of spring 2009 more than 150,000 joined the bi-annual pilgrimage.[77]

Jewish youth, of course, are also exposed to portrayals of the Shoah in popular media. There has been a rapid proliferation of fiction and nonfiction, films, and television programs on the Shoah. Some critics have voiced the opinion that the emphasis on the Shoah may overshadow

---

76 Caplan, 2001; Michman, 1996; Nadel and Frost, 1981; Porat, 1992; Schweber, 2008.

77 Helmreich, 1994, 2005; Kaufman, 1996; Sheramy, 2007, 2009.

other more positive aspects of Jewish identity, and may over-saturate and eventually trivialize the issue.

2. Shoah education in public schools and the public realm outside Israel. How the non-Jewish world remembers the Shoah is far from homogenous. Distinctive national narratives and collective memories of the era have evolved in Germany, in countries that were occupied by the Nazis, in countries that fought the Axis powers and those that were neutral in World War II. The magnitude of the atrocity and that such a thing could occur in the twentieth century in what was perceived as the heart of civilized Europe, presents mankind with difficult questions, and even if many would prefer to sweep the entire era under the carpet of collective amnesia, the issue has not disappeared from public discourse. To the contrary; as in the Jewish world, discussion of the Shoah has increased in recent decades.

There are memorial sites dedicated to the Shoah in dozens of countries, mostly in Europe or the former Soviet Union at sites where specific events occurred or in other public spaces. In the course of daily life, people may come across memorials or plaques serving as reminders of the prisons and concentration camps that once existed in their country. Many of these memorials were established at the initiative of local or national governments and are designed to appeal to an international audience, often using symbols and artwork to portray messages beyond that of simple historic markers. Designing appropriate and meaningful memorials has proven to be a complex and sometimes controversial task. Dozens of educational memorial museums, archives, libraries, and learning centers have been established around the world; in Europe and Russia and also in places geographically removed from the actual events, in Argentina, Australia, Japan, North America, and South Africa. These museums host school groups and field trips which are often part of a curriculum of learning about the Shoah.[78]

---

78 A website cataloguing Shoah memorial sites, associated with the Task Force for International Cooperation on Holocaust Education, Remembrance and Research, lists sites in thirty countries in Europe and the former Soviet Union (Austria, Belarus, Belgium, Bulgaria, Croatia, Czech Republic, Denmark, Estonia, France, Germany, Greece, Hungary, Italy, Latvia, Lithuania, Luxembourg, Macedonia, Netherlands, Norway, Poland, Romania, Russian Federation, Serbia-Montenegro, Slovakia, Slovenia, Spain, Sweden, Switzerland, Ukraine and the United Kingdom), plus six others (Argentina, Australia, Canada, Japan South Africa, and the United States). Some countries have multiple memorials and museums dedicated to the Shoah (see www.memorial-museums.net).

Art, literature, and film have been important in bringing the Shoah into public consciousness. These media reach a wide audience and may emotionally engage people in fundamentally different ways than history lessons do. Particularly when the artists or writers are survivors, their children, or others who were directly involved, art related to the Shoah may be powerful educational tools. At the same time, some popular media related to the Shoah may be inaccurate or sensationalist, or gloss over the realities of the atrocity.

The Task Force for International Cooperation on Holocaust Education was established in 1998 to support and ascertain the state of Shoah education in its member countries, attesting to the level of attention given to the subject. In 2005, the United Nations General Assembly designated an International Holocaust Remembrance Day on January 27, the date of the liberation of Auschwitz-Birkenau. Concomitantly, they passed a resolution urging UN Member States to develop educational programs to transmit knowledge about the Shoah to future generations, with the goal of preventing future genocides. This has been recognized in dozens of countries (primarily European), where ceremonies are organized in schools or by public or private organizations. Despite the laudable concept of an international memorial day, some critics fear that the designated day may become a superficial event, removed from historical context or used to whitewash a country's participation or complicity in the atrocity.[79]

2.1 North America. The American public's first exposure to the Shoah was through photographs and newsreels of Allied troops liberating the death camps in 1945. General Dwight D. Eisenhower invited members of Congress, journalists and army photographers to witness, document and publicize the liberations and the discovery of the mass slaughter which had taken place under the Nazis. Later that year, the Nuremberg Trials of Nazi leaders were covered by international and American press. Both contributed to the sense of national pride in America's role in the defeat of the Nazis.

Other countries may have permanent or traveling exhibits within general history or art museums not included in this list. A list of Shoah museums may be seen at http://www.science.co.il/holocaust-museums.asp.

79 Alphen, 1998; Dreyfus, 2011; Insdorf, 1983; Marcuse, 2010; Stone, 2000; www.holocausttaskforce.org/; www.un.org/en/holocaustremembrance/.

In the years following the war, however, the Cold War with the Soviet Union moved to the front of national consciousness and West Germany was 'rehabilitated' as an American ally. Scholarly documentation and attention in the American academic and media waned.[80] The Shoah was marginalized in mainstream non-Jewish American consciousness for several decades.[81]

Shoah education was introduced into US public schools during the late 1970s and 1980s following the recommendations of a commission established by President Jimmy Carter in 1978, that "...study of the Holocaust should be part of the curriculum in every educational system throughout the country."[82] That same year, the National Council of the Social Studies published a curriculum called *The Holocaust Years: Society on Trial*, which presented the subject as part of a psychological investigation of human nature and moral development.[83] Subsequent units, with names such as *The Holocaust and Genocide: A Search for Conscience*, and *Facing History and Ourselves*, also stressed universal moral and ethical themes. Such curricula reflected the pedagogic environment in the US at that time, which was struggling to make education in general and social studies in particular more relevant to students' emerging concerns with minority identity, multiculturalism, and societal values.

Around the same time, the Shoah re-emerged in American consciousness through popular media, such as the television miniseries *Holocaust* (1978), the *Maus* graphic novels (Spiegelman, 1986, 1991), and movies such as *The Wave* (1981), *Sophie's Choice* (1982) and *Schindler's List* (1993). In 1993, the US Holocaust Memorial Museum opened in Washington DC, near other major national memorials. Its interpretation places the experience of learning about the Shoah within a distinctly American context, which intentionally "...recast the story of the Holocaust to teach fundamental American values ... pluralism,

80 Boden's book and original taped interviews and transcripts have only recently been rediscovered and are now being preserved, analyzed and made available to the public through the Voices of the Holocaust project: see http://voices.iit.edu/voices_project.

81 Arendt, 1951; Baron, 2003; Ben-Bassat, 2000; Boder, 1949; Jick, 1981; Lipstadt, 1996; Novick, 1999; Reichmann, 1951; Rosen, 2010; Sheramy, 2003; Shandler, 2003; Tenenbaum, 1956; Weinreich, 1946.

82 Wiesel, 1979, 12.

83 This curriculum was developed by Massachusettes educators Roselle Chartock and Jack Spenser in conjunction with the Anti-Defamation League and the National Conference of Christians and Jews.

democracy, restraint on government, the inalienable rights of individuals, the inability of governments to enter into freedom of religion."[84] In this way, "What had been a more privately-held Jewish story in the early postwar years was by the end of the twentieth century an integral part of the American narrative."[85]

Today, public schools in most states address the Nazi era, usually as a short unit in junior high or high school history or social studies courses. Available choices of curricula, educational materials, and literature have greatly broadened, although *Anne Frank: Diary of a Young Girl*, with its emphasis on the individual experience, rather than the larger historical context, is still by far the most widely read book about the Shoah. The specificity of Jewish history in Europe is de-emphasized. Presentation of the Shoah reflects an American ethos of democracy and human rights and issues such as the responsibilities of the individual in challenging racism or of governments in intervening to stop genocide may be debated. The link between anti-Semitism and Christianity in pre-World War II Europe is essentially ignored.[86]

During the same years that the national study of Shoah education in Israel was being conducted (2007-2009), I also directed an evaluation of a Shoah education curriculum, *Echoes and Reflections*, used in US public, private, and parochial junior high and high schools, providing an enlightening insight into similarities and differences in presentation of the subject. Even prior to learning this particular curriculum, essentially all the students (99%) had at least heard of the Shoah. Most, but not all of the high school students (83%) had learned about it in school, as had a smaller percentage, though still the majority (64%) of those in junior high. As is common in US schools, the emphasis was on general values such as the dangers of stereotyping and racism, though it also included a unit on anti-Semitism. The curriculum used many primary sources such as photographs, interviews and videotaped testimonies. It encouraged interactive and reflective activities such as classrooms discussions, research projects, and journal writing. Students reported that activities which were most beneficial in helping them understand the subject were the group discussions (85% found them helpful) and

---

84 Berenbaum quoted in Lennon and Foley, 1999, 49.

85 Sheramy, 2009, 11.

86 Ben-Bassat, 2000; Brabham, 1997; Dawidowicz, 1981, 1990; Fallace, 2006; Flanzbaum, 1999; ITF USA country report, 2004; Lipstadt, 1995; Shawn, 1995.

research projects (75%); the journal writing was less effective (rated as helpful by 46%).[87] Students who professed prior interest in the subject, who also were more concerned with related issues such as challenging racism, gave this specific curriculum a more positive evaluation. The link between interest in the subject and reception of its teaching, which pertains to many academic subjects, is particularly relevant in the case of Shoah education. This will be further explored in the case of the Israeli students who almost universally have an interest in the subject.

In neighboring Canada, the situation is similar to that in the US. Although there have been several highly publicized cases of Canadian teachers who promoted denial of the Shoah and Jewish conspiracy theories in their classrooms and/or in public forums, public schools teach the Shoah as part of mandatory history curricula and in other classes, and Canada is a member of the ITF. A survey of teachers in Ontario found enthusiasm for the importance of the subject, but again there is a lack of attention to underlying issues such as the history of anti-Semitism and the role of the Church.[88]

2.2 Europe. Teaching about the Shoah in the countries where it took place is, of course, difficult and sensitive. The extent to which various governments and school systems have broached the subject varies widely. A few common themes may be noted. Teaching about the Shoah has become widespread throughout Europe. Twenty-four European nations have joined the Task Force for International Cooperation on Holocaust Education, Remembrance, and Research (ITF), indicating a commitment to teaching about this era. Many European countries recognize the International Holocaust Remembrance Day and schools often organize ceremonies and informal educational activities for it. Shoah teaching is mainly limited to a small number of classroom hours during junior high school or high school classes on national and European history. Beyond the minimal curricular requirements, there is considerable flexibility between schools and individual teachers regarding the amount of time dedicated to teaching the Shoah as well as methods and materials. Use of films and survivor testimonies to supplement textbooks is widespread. It is not uncommon for the Shoah also to be addressed in classes

---

87 Cohen, 2009a.

88 Cohen-Almagor, 2008; Lipstadt, 1994; Short, 2000a, 2001.

such as literature, art, philosophy, civics and religion.

Lack of teacher training often limits the effectiveness of teaching about the Shoah. In particular, teaching about the Shoah in the framework of religious studies suffers from a lack of oversight, leading to the danger that students may receive distorted information on the role of religious ideology and institutions in the Shoah or problematic theological discourse. To improve teacher training, European Jewish organizations and Israeli institutes (particularly Yad Vashem) offer seminars and materials, organize talks by Shoah survivors and sometimes subsidize school visits to Shoah sites.

In many cases, while history curricula include the Nazi era, most lessons focus on the war in general, not the Shoah specifically. There is some ambivalence among European educators and students about dedicating special attention to the Shoah. As Europe is becoming increasingly multi-cultural, school systems are struggling with how to teach the Shoah (and their countries' history in general) to a student body including immigrant populations who do not share a "common historical heritage" and may not see learning about the Nazi era as relevant to them. Often teaching about the Shoah is integrated into discussions about racism, minority rights, group psychology, and contemporary conflicts including, significantly, the Israel-Palestinian conflict. In some areas, persistent or re-emergent anti-Semitism and racism make it difficult to address the Shoah in the classroom. When Shoah education consists only of a short unit, its messages may be contradicted or overshadowed by attitudes gleaned from the media or received from family and community.

Some of the major concentration and death camps from the Nazi era, such as Auschwitz and Bergen-Belsen, have been made into educational memorials, and receive large numbers of visitors including public school groups. The impact of such visits varies widely depending on the previous education and preparation students receive, as well as whether students voluntarily join the trip or if it is part of a mandatory school program. Making the sites relevant to students and preserving a sense of authenticity is a challenge to educators, curators and organizers. In some cases, visiting "authentic" sites has less of an impact than seeing documentaries, hearing witness testimonies or reading memoirs. While some students find such visits highly moving, with strong cognitive and emotional impacts, others are unimpressed, disappointed or uncomfortable with the visits to renovated sites. A seminar for college level students at Bergen-Belsen includes group and individual work using primary sources and intensive discussions on the transformation of places and the nature of historical memory. Such methods deepen the experience, but may not be appropriate for younger students.[89]

Naturally, the role each country played during World War II impacts the nature of Shoah education in its schools. In the countries which were occupied by the Germans, the local population's helplessness and suffering is often emphasized over the targeted decimation of the Jews. Only recently has the role of popular anti-Semitism been acknowledged. Some include information about pre-war Jewish populations in their region.[90] In Spain, whose government was aligned with Axis powers but never entered the war on their side, schools have only recently begun to address the Shoah through classroom programs, seminars, teacher training, events for the international day of remembrance, and student trips to Auschwitz.[91] In countries which were neutral during the war, their non-aligned status and attempts to rescue or provide refuge for Jews fleeing the Nazis is highlighted. Recently these countries have begun to address some of the complications of the neutral position, such as Swiss financial links to the Nazi regime, turning away of some refugees, and local fascist movements during the war.[92] Additionally, contemporary issues such as the integration of immigrants or perceptions of the Israeli-Palestinian conflict impact how the Shoah is taught and perceived in public schools.

a. Germany. German society has undergone a significant and public national process of *Entschuldigung*—apology or pardon for World War II and the Shoah. The Nazi era is a mandatory subject in schools in the Federal Republic of Germany, and most students are familiar with the Shoah from its prevalence in public discourse. High school history and civics classes cover the rise of the National Socialist movement, Nazi ideology, World War II, and the Nazi persecution of Jews and other groups. The subject is also learned through literature, music, and art. Interestingly, in Germany religion classes do address the role of the

---

89 Doerry, 2011, Grandjean et al., 2011; Holocaust Educational Trust, 2009.

90 Frankl, 2003; ITF country report on Germany, 2006a.

91 http://www.holocausttaskforce.org/membercountries/member-spain.html; Payne, 2008.

92 See ITF country reports at www. holocausttaskforce.org/membercountries/; Frankl, 2003; Mudde, 2005; Short, 2001; Van Driel, 2003.

Church—a topic avoided in most countries' Shoah studies programs. Almost 100 memorial museums for victims of the Nazis have been established at former concentration camps and other sites throughout the country, including a memorial to the Jewish victims of the Shoah which was dedicated in Berlin in 2005. Associations of Shoah survivors serve on advisory boards of many of the memorials, participating in the discussion of the best way to commemorate the victims and remind the public of the history. A large percentage of students and teachers have visited such sites on school trips. These serve as sites for discourse on their country's history and configuration of "new" German identity. Since, Germany has received large numbers of immigrants in recent decades, the nature of "German identity," and thus Shoah education, is undergoing change.[93]

b. Austria. For several decades following the war, Austria maintained an official position of exoneration of guilt in the Shoah stemming from the German invasion of Austria and the *Anschluss* (annexation) in 1938. Popular support of the Nazis was downplayed. Education and research regarding the era was minimal. Only in the 1970s did the Shoah begin to be acknowledged in history classes. The 50th anniversary of the *Anschluss* in 1988 marked a new era of Shoah education and commemoration in Austria. Shortly afterwards, Federal Chancellor Franz Vranitzky officially recognized for the first time Austrian co-responsibility for Nazi crimes, a fund to compensate victims was established, and the Austrian Historical Commission began conducting research and publishing its finding regarding the Nazi era. Neo-Nazi activity and denial of the Shoah became a crime in 1992.

Today history curricula for grades 8-11 include units on National Socialism and the Shoah. Teachers take part in training, including participation in sessions at Yad Vashem in Jerusalem. Schools invite Shoah survivors to speak, or use taped videos of testimonies. School groups visit memorials such as one at the site of the former concentration camp at Mauthausen. In 2008, on the 70th anniversary of the *Anschluss*, Catholic and Jewish student and youth organizations held a joint memorial to victims of the Nazis.[94]

c. Italy. Italy, too, has a conflicted national memory of its role in

93 ITF country report Germany, 2006a; Wegner, 1995.

94 ITF country report Austria, 2009.

World War II and therefore of the Shoah. While Mussolini's fascist government joined the Axis powers and passed anti-Semitic legislation, there was an active resistance movement and even soldiers in the Italian army often ignored orders to deport Italian Jews to death camps or explicitly protected them.

A recent Shoah education conference held in Italy focused on the example of Jewish-Italian Shoah survivor Primo Levi, whose memoirs detail the graphic difference between his experience in an Italian prison camp and when he was transferred to Auschwitz. Another conference considered issues of Shoah education in multi-cultural societies, a challenge facing schools throughout Europe. Over the past decade, Italy has increased teacher training programs, including sending teachers to seminars at Yad Vashem. A national school program invited students to create works exploring the theme of Jewish and non-Jewish children whose friendships were disrupted during the fascist era. Older students may take part in a "voyage of memory," traveling by train from Italy to Auschwitz. Participants undergo a rigorous and lengthy orientation, which includes testimonies by survivors of the deportation as well as by members of the Italian resistance. Such programs enable students to learn the history of their country during World War II while retaining the possibility for pride in their heritage and compatriots.[95]

d. France. In the first decades following World War II, Jewish suffering was subsumed into the general suffering brought on by the war, due to German aggression rather than long-standing anti-Semitism. Again, Israel's Six Day War marked a turning point. The fear that Israel may not survive the war against the neighboring Arab countries prompted a public discussion during which, for the first time, the specific Jewish experience was differentiated from the French nation's struggle against Nazi occupation.[96]

The student strike in France in May 1968 ushered in a political and social environment in which traditional values were questioned and previously taboo subjects, such as the role of the Vichy government and its betrayal of the Republican tenet of equality through citizenship, were brought to light. At the same time, support for Israel had begun to erode

---

95 Fontanesi, 2011; ITF country report Italy, 2011, Zuccotti, 1987.

96 "Jews articulated the Holocaust as trauma: a shock to taken-for-granted structures of meaning in place since France first granted Jews citizenship during the French Revolution; a rupture in Jews' unquestioned faith in the idea and security, of inclusion in the national community," (Wolf, 1999).

under President de Gaulle's pro-Arab foreign policy and the French Left's increasing sympathy for Palestinian Arabs. Use of symbols and imagery from the Shoah began to be used in criticisms of Israel.[97]

Films and documentaries have been important in bringing the subject of the Shoah to the attention of the French public. One of the first was *Night and Fog* (*Nuit et brouillard*), a short film directed by Alain Resnais in 1955. Fifteen years later, Marcel Ophüls made the four-hour documentary *Le chagrin et la pitié*, and in 1985, Claude Lanzmann released a documentary film over nine hours long called *Shoah* consisting of extensive interviews with survivors, ex-Nazis, and other witnesses to the era.[98]

World War II is covered in the national curriculum for history studies in French junior high and high schools. Specific units address Nazi ideology, the genocide against the Jews, the collaboration of the Vichy government and resistance against the regime. This is usually covered in several class hours each year. The Shoah may also be addressed in classes on literature and philosophy. A small percentage of students visit memorials in France such as the Memorial to the Martyrs of the Deportation (dedicated by Charles De Gaulle in 1962) or the Mémorial de la Shoah (originally the Tomb of the Unknown Jewish Martyr). Even fewer participate in school trips to places related to the Shoah in France (such as the Drancy transit camp and the Izieu orphanage) or in Germany or Poland. Teachers may receive optional training in teaching the Shoah from non-governmental institutes in France and a small number participate in training in Israel. There are optional programs through which students undertake a journey to the museum at the Izieu orphanage, the Anne Frank house in Amsterdam and finally the site of the Bergen-Belsen concentration camp in Germany. This program emphasizes a biographical approach to Shoah study, and students do individual and group work based on photographs and witness testimonies.[99]

It is important to note that France was the only ITF member country which listed student opposition as a barrier to Shoah education. Particularly in certain regions of France, Shoah denial and opposition to learning about the Shoah, voiced mainly by Muslim students, has

97 Aron, 1969; Birnbaum, 1994; Cohen, 2011a; Szajkowsky, 1970; Wolf, 1999.

98 Greene, 1999. Professor Annie Kriegel asserts that Lanzmann's movie will be the most enduring document relating the Shoah (personal communication, 1988).

99 Doerry, 2011

become widespread enough to disrupt the classes. This is particularly disturbing in the context of physical and verbal attacks against Jews, especially Jewish students, in the past decade, also mostly perpetrated by Muslim youth. An Inspector General of the French Ministry of Education found, "It is in effect, under our eyes, a stupefying and cruel reality: in France, Jewish children—and they are alone in this case—can no longer be educated in just any school... [because of anti-Semitic acts]."[100] French-Jewish writer and scholar Alain Finkielkraut lamented the situation, saying "Every day, another intellectual denounces Zionism as a crime, and teaching the Holocaust has become impossible at the very moment when it has become imperative...."[101]

Ongoing controversy over what terminology to use in the teaching of World War II is another indication of the difficulty of addressing the issue in French public schools. The title of a history curriculum for 11th graders in French public schools uses the French term for annihilation *(anéantissement)* instead of Shoah. At the same time, the Arabic term *Nakhba* (meaning "catastrophe," refering to the displacement that followed the creation of Israel in 1948) began to appear in French Ministry of Education publications. Claude Lanzmann, director of the film which introduced the term *Shoah* to French society (and much of the world) criticized this term as masking the differences between historical events, allowing, for example, perceived equivalence between the planned mass murder of millions of Jews to the "annihilation" of German citizens in Allied bombing runs to or the Palestinians' displacement and losses during their conflict with Israel.

A proposal for an innovative project to personalize Shoah education in French schools suggested by President Nicolas Sarkozy in 2008, namely that each French student "adopt" a French-Jewish child who was killed in the Shoah, learn about that child's background and fate caused considerable controversy and was eventually dropped. Interestingly, projects that documented the fate of individual French-Jewish children who were deported have been awarded prizes for Shoah education in a program co-sponsored by French-Jewish institutions and the French Ministry of Education.[102]

---

100 http://www.nytimes.com/2006/03/26/international/26antisemitism.html; ITF country report France, 2006a; Observatoire du monde juif, 2001; UJSF, 2002.

101 Finkielkraut, 2003, 9.

102 http://www.fsju.org/info/culture/prix-annie-et-charles-corrin.html.

The case of the Jews has long served as a sort of barometer of the state of French Republican society; it seems that Shoah education offers another indicator regarding issues related to anti-Semitism, cultural distinctiveness and equality of citizens in contemporary France.[103] In light of the ongoing controversies, the government convened a committee to improve Shoah education in French schools.

e. Former Soviet Union and satellite Communist regimes. State schools in the Communist countries taught about the German's invasion of Eastern European countries and the Soviet Union, the local population's suffering under Nazi occupation, and the pivotal role of the Soviet Union in defeating the Axis Powers and liberating the death camps. The mass murder of Jews by *Einsatzgruppen* (SS task forces) and by local supporters in the German-occupied areas was unacknowledged, minimized, rationalized, or denied. For example, in Romanian schools there is almost no mention of the role of Ion Antonescu and his government's role in the murder over 250,000 Romanian Jews and thousands of Roma (Gypsy) people during World War II. For many people in the USSR's satellite states, the violence of the Nazi regime has been overshadowed by that of the Soviet regime.

Since the fall of the Soviet Union and the other Communist regimes and the integration of some of the former Soviet satellite states into the European Union, there have been major changes in the educational systems and curricula, including new approaches to teaching the history of World War II and the Shoah. Lessons regarding the Shoah are integrated into a program of education for citizenship in a democracy.

Some innovative projects for teaching about the Shoah have been initiated. Lithuanian schools sponsor an annual student essay contest on the topic: "My Grandparents' and Great-Grandparents' Jewish Neighbors." In other countries such as Croatia students learn about Judaism in religion classes and discuss the history of anti-Semitism and the Shoah. A recent project in the Czech Republic, "Lost Neighbors" encourages students to research and write about Jewish history in their own communities. In Poland, in addition to the learning about the Shoah in school, hundreds of thousands of students in Polish high schools participate in educational and commemorate activities at the former death camps in their country. Recently, Polish youth groups have begun

103 AFP-EJP, 2008; Konopniki, 2011; Lanzmann, 2011.

to take part in the March of the Living and to meet with delegations of Israeli students. The educational centers which have been developed at several of the sites of former death camps, most notably the Memorial Museum at Auschwitz-Birkenau, also provide training for teachers.

However, today's teachers were educated in the Communist era, limiting their level of knowledge and impacting their perspective on the subject. Informal educational activities and open discussions, fundamental to Shoah education in many other parts of the world, have not yet been widely adopted in most educational systems in post-Communist countries and teachers have little training in these methods. Further, university faculties tend to perpetuate "old school" attitudes about both history and pedagogy. Training seminars, historical documents, and educational materials offered through international institutes such as Yad Vashem and the Simon Wiesenthal Center provide a counter-narrative to what was taught during the Communist era.[104]

f. United Kingdom. Since the UK fought on the side of Allies and no British Jews were deported to concentration camps, teaching the Shoah is less problematic in terms of national identity than it is in most of Europe. At the same time, since most UK citizens do not identify with either the victims or the perpetrators, there is some ambivalence as to why the Shoah should be given more emphasis than other examples of genocide. In England, the Shoah is included in the national curriculum in junior high school. It is most often taught in history classes as part of a unit on World War II. There are no standards for how much emphasis must be given to the Shoah within units on World War II. Study of the Shoah is recommended but not mandatory in Northern Ireland, Scotland, and Wales. The Shoah is also addressed in religious education, literature, and citizenship classes, and students of all ages may participate in activities marking the International Holocaust Remembrance Day (which the UK began observing in 2001). Documentaries, films and literature are often used in study of the Shoah in classrooms in England. Several museums in the UK have exhibits pertaining to the Shoah which are visited by student groups, and survivors are invited to visit schools. Students may take part in journeys to sites such as Auschwitz; in recent years there have been more students interested in participating than

104 Reports of Auschwitz-Birkenau memorial museum: http://en.auschwitz.org.pl; Cioflanca, 2004; Ioanid, 2000; ITF 2006c, 2006d (country reports Croatia, Lithuania); Misco, 2008; Shafir, 2004.

available places in these programs. Alumni of the journeys make presentations to their classes or publish writings in student publications, expanding the impact of the program.

Surveys of UK students and teachers found that the Shoah is taught as a means to address values of tolerance, anti-racism and participatory democracy. Teaching about Judaism, Jewish culture and the history of anti-Semitism and particularly the role of the Church are minimal. Further, the actions of the perpetrators, rather than the experiences of the victims, tend to be emphasized, thus presenting the Jews as objects rather than subjects.[105]

In 2009, the Holocaust Educational Trust launched a nation-wide program in high schools in the UK called Lessons from Auschwitz. The program includes an orientation seminar which includes testimony by a survivor, a one day visit to Auschwitz-Birkenau, a follow-up seminar and a project in order to share what they learned with their peers and communities, such as organizing assemblies or creating educational displays for their schools or writing in the school newspaper. The program is voluntary, and participating students are a self-selected population with strong prior interest in the subject. Universal values such as respect for diversity, dangers of prejudice, individual responsibility and the importance of memory are stressed, and students reported positive impacts on their attitudes in these areas. The follow-up projects had secondary skill-building benefits, but it was found students needed more guidance to be successful in this undertaking.[106]

2.3. Muslim countries and communities. Denial of the Shoah has become a feature of the political landscape in the Muslim world over the past decade. This denial is generally linked to rejection of the Shoah as a rationale for the need for the existence of the State of Israel. Most infamously, in 2006 Iranian President Ahmadinejad sponsored a conference following his own statements that the Shoah was a myth. None of the Muslim or Arab countries are members of the ITF and none has a Shoah memorial of any kind. Hitler's *Mein Kampf* and the fabricated *Protocols of the Elders of Zion* have become popular in many Muslim-Arab countries and communities. Turkey, alone among the Muslim countries

---

105 Brown and Davies, 1998; Burtonwood, 2002; Carrington and Short, 1997; ITF country reports on UK, 2006e, 2010; Pettigrew and Foster, 2009; Short, 1994, 1995, 2000a; Short, Supple, and Klinger, 1998.

106 Holocaust Educational Trust, 2009.

(and despite political tensions with its longtime ally Israel) marked International Holocaust Remembrance Day in 2012 for the first time by broadcasting Lanzmann's documentary Shoah (with subtitles) on national television.[107]

In the Palestinian Authority territories of the West Bank and Gaza, popular media simultaneously deny the Shoah occurred and use images and symbols from the Nazi era to demonize Israelis. Textbooks used in schools in the Palestinian areas of the West Bank and Gaza strip make no mention of the Shoah. While the United Nations Relief and Works Agency for Palestine Refugees in the Near East (UNRWA) established a general unit on human rights, it does not directly address the Shoah. In 2011, UNRWA declared its intention to include a short unit on the Shoah in the human rights curriculum in its schools in the Palestinian Authority areas. The Palestinian Authority, the PLO and Hamas' Education Minister, Mohammed Asqoul, attacked the plan and insisted that the history of the Shoah would never be taught in schools in Gaza.

The Palestinians' and Arabs' refusal to recognize the persecution of the Jews in Europe—mirrored by Israeli minimization of Palestinian suffering—has been put forth as one of many obstacles to productive talks between the sides. In Israeli universities, where Jewish and Arab students learn together (with few exceptions they learn separately through high school), discussions of the Shoah can be confrontational and acrimonious, revealing the extent to which perceptions of history are intertwined with current political events in the students' minds.

To counter this disturbing trend, some important initiatives have been launched to promote dialogue between Muslims and Jews, including education about the Shoah. Yad Vashem created a website in Arabic and offers special tours, panels and workshops aimed at increasing awareness of the Shoah and combating denial among Muslim and Arab populations in Israel and surrounding countries. In 2009, the United Nations Educational, Scientific and Cultural Organization (UNESCO) started the Aladdin Project, which makes historical information on the Shoah available in Persian, Arabic, and Turkish. To make the subject more acceptable to the Muslim public, the project highlights cases of Muslim and Arab leaders or individuals helping Jews during World War II and positive historical ties between Muslims and Jews. In Morocco,

107 Associated Press, 2012.

King Mohammed VI proclaimed that the era—including their country's opposition to the Vichy regime—should be remembered and not denied. Following this, Al Akhawayn University has co-sponsored with Kivunim[108] a conference devoted to study of the Shoah (organized by local Muslim students) and a Museum of Moroccan Judaism. In Australia, specific Shoah education programs are being developed for use in schools with high Muslim populations. A Muslim man opened the Arab Institute for Holocaust Research and Education in the Arab-Israeli city of Nazareth, on the principle that Palestinians and Israelis must know each other's history if the conflict is to be resolved. Tellingly, this initiative has been criticized from both sides: by Arabs angered at the diversion of attention from Palestinian suffering and the generation of sympathy for Israelis; and by Jews (including the ADL) offended by comparisons between the Shoah and the Palestinian *Nakhba* and a message that the Palestinians are being punished for the crimes of Europeans through the creation of the State of Israel.[109]

The Arab-language state schools in Israel present a distinct and interesting case, which has only begun to be investigated. The schools are expected to follow the state curriculum, including the history unit on the Shoah. Nevertheless, denial of the Shoah is rising among Israeli Arabs and there is resentment at what they perceive as a mandate to study the Jews' history rather than their own. Independent institutes such as the Givat Haviva Center for Peace, with the cooperation of the Israel Ministry of Education, organizes teacher training session for teachers in the Arab school sector. A survey of Israeli Arab citizens found conflicting universalistic-moral views of the Shoah as a crime against humanity and particularistic-political views in which the Shoah is seen as a justification for Israeli oppression of Palestinians.[110]

In summary, a few key points may be reiterated. Education and public discussion about the Shoah were largely forestalled for decades follow-

108 Kivunim is a program in international Jewish education founded by Peter Geffen.

109 Elbaz-Luwisch, 2004; Freedman, 2011; Gur-Ze'ev, 2001; Fathi, 2006; Hadid and Barzak, 2011; Jahanbegloo, 2006; Litvak-Hirsch, Chaitin and Zaher, 2010; Michael, 2007; Pappé and Hilāl, 2010; Picheny, 2003; Radin, 2005; Rudge, 2005; Rutland, 2010; Said, 2001; Wicken, 2006; Wistrich, 1997; see www.projetaladin.org/en/the-aladdin-project.html; www.unrwa.org/etemplate.php?id=434; www.YadVashem.org/yv/en/pressroom/pressreleases/pr_details.asp?cid=203.

110 Litvak-Hirsch, Chaitin and Zaher, 2010; Shoham, Shiloah, and Kalisman, 2003; www.givathaviva.org.il/english/peace/peace-001.htm; on a Haifa University study regarding Israeli Arabs' denial of the Shoah see http://newmedia-eng.haifa.ac.il/?p=434.

ing World War II. In the late 1960s, following the Eichmann trial and the Six Day War, public interest in and acknowledgement of the Shoah emerged, in Israel, in the Jewish Diaspora world and in European and North American public schools. This interest and attention in the Shoah increased significantly over the next several decades. Today, schools through most of the Western world dedicate at least some classroom time to study of the Nazi era. Informal educational activities such as memorial ceremonies, hearing testimonies of survivors or viewing films are increasingly widespread as pedagogic tools. In non-Jewish educational settings, emphasis is usually given to the Shoah's implications for humanity, universal values, and citizenship. In Israel, interpretation has shifted from seeing the Shoah as proof of the futility of life in Diaspora to a more complex discourse on Jewish continuity and universal themes.

III. THE NATIONAL SURVEY OF SHOAH EDUCATION IN ISRAEL: DATA COLLECTION METHODS AND ANALYSIS TECHNIQUES

• Both qualitative and quantitative methods were used: questionnaires, focus groups, observations, interviews.

• Interviews with experts in the field, including academics and educators at universities and research centers, provided a theoretical basis for the study.

• The empirical survey reached three main populations: principals, teachers, and students.

• Two main school streams were included: general and religious state schools.

• To explore differences at various age levels, the study was conducted at the junior high and high school level

• Data were interpreted using Facet Theory methods such as Smallest Space Analysis, which uncovers structural relations among data.

* * * * * *

The main part of this book is based on a nation-wide survey on Shoah education in Israeli state schools, which I conducted between 2007 and 2009.[1] While there have been previous studies on specific Shoah education programs among small targeted populations, this was the first national study of the issue in the Israeli state school system. This survey was designed to give as broad, detailed, and complete a picture as possible by surveying a large and diverse population, employing both qualitative and quantitative research methods and applying sophisticated data analysis tools. The entire process was overseen and advised by a steering committee, which included experts and professionals from the Israel Ministry of Education, Yad Vashem, the Conference on Jewish Material Claims against Germany, Hebrew University, Bar Ilan University, and a

1 The survey was commissioned by Bar Ilan University's School of Education and the Conference on Jewish Material Claims against Germany.

representative principal and teacher working in the state school system (see list of members on acknowledgements page).

A. The Structure of the Israeli Education System

1. Language. The Israeli state school system consists of several streams according to religious and language preferences. Parents choose in which stream they wish to enroll their children. There are two streams according to the primary language of instruction: Hebrew and Arabic. In the Arabic language schools, Hebrew is taught as a second language and the majority of adult Israeli Arabs are at least functionally literate in Hebrew. In the Hebrew schools, students generally only take a few years of Arabic language classes. English is also taught in both school systems. There are a very small number of bi-lingual/cross-cultural schools.[2]

2. Religion and level of religiosity. The state schools taught in Hebrew are attended primarily, but not exclusively, by Jewish students. A small minority of Israeli-Arab students attend the Hebrew language schools, as do non-Jewish children of foreign workers and immigrants from the Soviet Union who came to Israel with Jewish family members. In some schools in the Hebrew sector, the non-Jewish population reaches 10%, but in most cases it is less. Hebrew language state schools are further divided into *general* and *religious* streams (as in the case of the bilingual schools, there are a small number of ideologically motivated secular-religious schools). Although the core curriculum for general and religious state schools is the same, there are several important differences.

The general schools are fully co-educational through high school. In most state religious schools, boys and girls learn separately after a certain age, which varies from school to school. In the general schools, Jewish studies are part of the curriculum: Jewish holidays, history and traditional texts are taught from a cultural/historical perspective with no requirements on students regarding belief or ritual practice. The religious schools strive to balance religious and modern educational concerns. In addition to the standard curriculum, more classes on Jewish

2 Bekerman, 2004; Bekerman and Horenczyk, 2004; Spolsky and Shohamy, 1999.

subjects are included and they are taught from a more religious perspective. Students are expected to abide by certain standards regarding modest dress and behavior. Prayer is part of the daily schedule.[3] There are also various independent schools, particularly for the ultra-Orthodox (*haredi*) or Hasidic religious population. Some of these use Yiddish as the primary language of instruction. The independent schools are not required to follow the Ministry of Education's core curriculum.

Most Israeli-Arab students (Muslim, Christian, Bedouin, Circassian, and Druze) attend state schools in which the teaching is conducted in Arabic. They have classes on Arab history, literature and culture.[4] Other basic curricular requirements are the same as for the Jewish schools, including the unit on the Shoah in 10th grade.

The Arabic-language state schools and the independent schools were not included in the present survey, though it is hoped that future research will complete the picture of Shoah education in these settings. A pilot survey on Shoah education in ultra-Orthodox community colleges was conducted in the 2010-2011 academic year;[5] some of the findings are cited where relevant.

B. The Surveyed Populations

The first people consulted were high-level professionals at the Israel Ministry of Education. With their help, a list of experts in the fields of Shoah research and teaching was compiled. In-depth interviews were conducted with 47 of these experts: educators, researchers, historians and professionals associated with universities in Israel and abroad, Shoah memorial institutes (especially Yad Vashem), local colleges, high schools, and seminaries in Israel (for a complete list of the experts interviewed see Appendix A). This step was essential in setting the parameters of the research and identifying the key issues to be explored.

The field research in the schools encompassed three survey populations: principals, teachers, and students. Each offered a distinctive and

---

3 Ayalon and Yogev, 1996; Gross, 2003; Iram and Shemida, 1998; www.moia.gov.il/NR/rdonlyres/9FBC4448-CB15-4309-BA82-96DC681E7A11/0/education_en.pdf.

4 http://www.mfa.gov.il/MFA/Facts+About+Israel/Education/EDUCATION+Primary+and +Secondary.htm.

5 Cohen and Cohen, 2012.

important perspective. It was ensured that the schools represented the full range of academic tracks (vocational, comprehensive, theoretical and special needs), socio-economic ranking,[6] urban/rural settings, size, and geographic regions across the country.

Junior high and high schools were included. At both levels, we surveyed the principals, teachers involved in Shoah education, and a representative sample of students in grades 9 (final year of junior high school) and 12 (final year of high school). The survey of Shoah education among junior high school students in Israel is almost unprecedented, and provides a look at a little-understood phase of Shoah education. The data collected on the 9th grade students documents the beliefs and attitudes of students *before* they have undergone the intensive Shoah education program of the high school. Comparing the attitudes and evaluations of the 9th and 12th graders allows for an assessment of the impact of the Shoah education curriculum.

Another important feature of the survey was the inclusion of both religious and general schools. There are about four times as many general as religious state schools in Israel and the survey populations reflect this distribution.[7] Conducting the research in both religious and general Hebrew state schools enables a comparison of the goals and impacts of Shoah education in these two parallel systems.

C. Survey Methods

A combination of quantitative and qualitative methods was used, as a multi-method approach yields richer results than either in isolation. In my own experience conducting national and international surveys, I have consistently found that the two types of research are both essential to understanding complex social phenomena. A large database compiled

---

6 The ranking reflects the predominant socio-economic status of the student body, not the resources of the school. The Ministry of Education Development Index is calculated according to the percentages of families with low resources, parents with low education, families with numerous children, and new immigrants. There was a slight over-representation in the sample of students in higher socio-economic brackets. To assess any possible impact of this over-representation, the data was weighted and some key data were compared with the un-weighted data. In both cases, the differences were very small (less than 1%). Accordingly, it was decided to use the un-weighted data.

7 Israel Central Bureau of Statistics, 2010: 393.

from questionnaires reveals large trends and patterns in responses and enables a comparison of results along many variables. This provides a strong, empirical basis to the study. Qualitative research—interviews, observations, focus groups—gives voices and faces to the numbers and provides subtlety, depth, and details not obtainable through multiple-choice questions.[8]

1. Quantitative survey. The main tool for collecting quantitative data was distribution of questionnaires to principals, teachers, and students. The questionnaires were developed with the input and advice of the interviewed experts. They included a range of questions pertaining directly to Shoah education as well as items designed to assess values and attitudes towards education and identity in general. In order to enable comparisons between sub-populations, some basic demographic data was collected. The full questionnaires may be seen in Appendix B. All student and teacher questionnaires were completed anonymously and coded by type of school.

1.1 Principals' questionnaire. Questionnaires were completed by 307 school principals. Two thirds (204) of the surveyed principals direct general schools and one third (103) direct religious schools: 184 were principals of high schools and 123 principals of junior high schools. The questionnaire given to the high school principals included an extra section on the journey to Poland. Junior high school principals were asked to what extent they think students understand the issue of the Shoah at the end of junior high school and how well-prepared they are to continue learning the subject in high school. Otherwise the principals' questionnaires were identical.

1.2 Teachers' questionnaire. Questionnaires were completed by 519 teachers. Of these, 408 (79%) teach at general state schools and 111 (21%) at religious state schools. Over half (56%) of the teachers work in high schools, 15% in junior high schools and 29% in both. All the surveyed teachers were involved in some type of educational activities related to the subject of the Shoah. Questionnaires were distributed to relevant teachers by the principals or school coordinators.

1.3 Students' questionnaire. The largest survey population was the students: 2540 students in grades 9 (1114 students) and grade 12 (1426 students) completed questionnaires. Of these, 82% attended general

8 Cohen, E.H, 2008; 2010; 2011a, 2011b; Newman and Benz, 1998.

schools and 18% religious schools. The student questionnaires were distributed towards the end of the school year. The questionnaires distributed to the 12th graders included a section on the journey to Poland. The 9th graders were asked whether or not they intended to travel to Poland in the future. The questionnaire for the older students also included a list of items (events, people, places, etc.) related to the Shoah, in order to draw out their self-assessed knowledge of the subject. This list was not included in the questionnaire for the 9th graders, who would not be expected to have yet learned about many of the items included. Aside from these two sections, the questionnaires were identical.

An integrated file including the responses of each student and the corresponding questionnaires of his/her principal and teacher was designed in order to allow for contextual analysis of the students.

2. Qualitative research. At the end of each questionnaire, respondents were invited to add their own remarks. All of these were read and an analysis was made of common themes expressed. Many of the quotes from students, teachers, and principals which are cited in this book come from the open comments section of the questionnaire.

Four focus groups were conducted: one each with students in general schools, students in religious state schools; teachers in general state schools and teachers in religious state schools. Numerous observations of school activities related to the Shoah, particularly the memorial ceremonies in the schools on *Yom HaShoah* and (in the religious schools) on the tenth of Tevet, which is a traditional day of fasting and general mourning. The in-depth interviews conducted with people in the Ministry of Education and other experts in the field contributed greatly to interpretation of the results.

D. Data Analysis

The data were analyzed using a variety of techniques. The frequencies of the responses to each question were calculated for the whole of each population (principals, teachers, students) and for a number of subpopulations (type of school, grade, subject taught, etc.).

To further explore certain issues we used factor analysis and a multidimensional data analysis technique known as Smallest Space Analysis.

1. Factor Analysis has been widely used in social science research for over a century. Factor Analysis begins with a correlation matrix between selected observed variables and identifies the minimum number of categories of derived independent variables (called "factors") necessary to describe the pattern of relationships among the variables. The strength of the relationship is expressed in the factor loading. Ideally each variable has a high loading on one factor ("primary loading"), although it may have a weaker but significant "secondary loading."[9]

2. Smallest Space Analysis (SSA) is a multidimensional data analysis technique based on Facet Theory. Pioneered by the late Louis Guttman, Facet Theory (FT) is a meta-theoretical framework and systematic approach to theory construction, research design, and data analysis. FT tools represent structural relationships of the data in an easily readable fashion, so they are particularly useful in dealing with data sets including numerous variables for a large survey population.

SSA creates a "cognitive map" for a set of variables according to their correlations. SSA also begins with the construction of a correlation matrix for the selected variables. The correlations range from -1 to +1, with 0 indicating no correlation between a pair of variables.[10] A computer program plots the variables as points such that closely correlated variables are close together and weakly or negatively correlated variables are far apart.[11] The entire correlation matrix for all the variables is taken into accounting simultaneously. In general, two or three axes are used, creating a two or three dimensional representation of the data.

Once the map is generated, the researcher looks for contiguous regions of related variables. Thus, while the placement of the points is objective, based on the correlation between the data, the interpretation of the map is subjective, reflecting the theoretical basis of the analysis.

There are a number of possible types of structures, such as a *sequen-*

---

9 Brown, 2006; Gorsuch 1983; Spearman, 1904, 1932; for a detailed mathematical explanations of Factor Analysis, see Loehlin, 2004.

10 I have found the monotonicity correlation (MONCO) to be particularly useful and strong. MONCO is a regression-free, non-linear coefficient of correlation. MONCO measures whether or not two items vary in the same direction (i.e. both increase) (Guttman, 1986). It recognizes a wider variety of correlations as "perfect," and therefore MONCO correlations are always higher in absolute value than linear correlations. An SSA may also be done successfully using the more common Pearson coefficient.

11 The original reference for this procedure is Guttman 1968. We used The Hebrew University Data Analysis Package (HUDAP) data analysis software package developed by Reuven Amar and Shlomo Toledano of the Hebrew University of Jerusalem. A manual on the use of HUDAP (Amar 2005) may be downloaded from: http://www.facet-theory.org/files/HUDAP%20Manual.pdf.

tial series of parallel slices (showing a progression from most to least), a *center-periphery* structure of concentric circles, or a *polar* structure consisting of pie-shaped wedges emanating from a common center and arranged in sets of oppositions.[12] More than one of these structures may be found in the same map according to the facet (set of conceptually related variables) considered. The designation of regions is analogous to that of geographic maps, whose fixed features may be divided into regions according to political boundaries, natural features, population density, etc. For example, the towns of Aqaba, Eilat, and Taba are situated close to each other at the northern tip of the Gulf of Aqaba, yet are in three different countries (Jordan, Israel, and Egypt, respectively). Therefore, they would be included in the same region of a map divided according to natural habitat types, but in different regions in maps divided according to political boundaries. The divisions are determined according to the purpose of the map.

Sub-groups of the survey population may be compared by introducing them as "external variables" in the SSA map. The correlations are calculated between each external variable and the set of primary variables. The external variables are then introduced into the map according to the same principal of the strength of the correlation determining the location. The map of the primary variables is "fixed" so that its structure is not affected by the introduction of the external variables. The external variables are placed in such a way that they are close to primary variables with which they are strongly correlated and far from those with which they are weakly or negatively correlated. In placing each external variable, the computer program considers its correlation with all the primary variables simultaneously.[13]

12 Levy, 1985.
13 Cohen and Amar 2002, 2005; Levy 2005.

IV. A PORTRAIT OF SHOAH EDUCATION IN ISRAELI STATE SCHOOLS

Some demographic traits of teachers and students impact perceptions of the Shoah:

- Teachers and students are almost all Jewish and mostly Israeli-born.
- There is a clear differentiation between those in the general and religious school systems in terms of religious beliefs and behaviors. However, both systems include a significant minority of teachers and students who define themselves as 'traditional'—between secular and religious.
- Personal connections to Shoah victims were common and strongly emphasized.
- The school is the primary setting for learning about the Shoah.
- History classes are the main but not the only forum for Shoah education. The Shoah is also addressed in other classes (literature, civics) and in a wide range of informal activities. Thus, history teachers are not the only ones involved in Shoah education.
- Enrichment courses on Shoah education are a distinctive feature of the educational landscape, attended by many teachers of history and other subjects.
- By the time they have reached junior high school, students have been exposed to a wide range of Shoah-related educational activities including memorial ceremonies, visits to museums and survivors' testimonies.
- Shoah education encompasses a range of issues including history, resistance against the Nazis and Jewish community life in Europe.
- Both cognitive knowledge and affective/experiential connection to the subject are strongly emphasized.

* * * * * *

To understand Shoah education in Israeli schools, it is necessary to know who is doing the teaching and who is being taught. A basic demographic portrait of the teachers and students helps set the context for interpretation of their attitudes regarding the Shoah and its presentation in the schools.

A. Teachers

1. Personal characteristics. The vast majority (82%) of the teachers were born in Israel. Those aged 50 or older represented 40% of the population; 30% were in their 40s, a quarter were in their 30s and about 5% were in their 20s. The teachers in the religious schools were, on average, a bit younger than those in the general school system. Almost 40% of the teachers in the religious schools were in their 30s, compared to 22% of those in the general schools.

Three quarters of the teachers were women, reflecting the general predominance of women as teachers in the state schools. There was a slightly higher representation of male teachers in the religious schools (28%). There is some evidence that female teachers tend to have a more informal style and are more open to, sensitive to, and inclusive of students' views as compared to their male colleagues. While this was not a central point of this study, the fact that most students at this age are learning about the Shoah (as well as other subjects) mainly from women may have underlying impacts on how the material is presented.[1]

Teachers were asked to define themselves as secular, traditional or religious. These categories are widely used and familiar in Israeli society. "Religious" in this context indicates not only belief in God, but a fairly high degree of observance of Jewish religious laws concerning diet, Sabbath and holidays, prayer, dress, etc. "Secular" designates little or no observance of ritual; it may indicate atheist or agnostic views, although those defining themselves as secular may believe in God, and observe some basic traditions (many "secular" Israelis, for example, fast on *Yom Kippur* and have the Passover *seder* meal).[2] "Traditional" is an intermediate category, encompassing a wide range of practice and beliefs, though it may be assumed to indicate belief in God and observance of the basic Jewish ritual laws.

Overall, 27% of the teachers defined themselves as religious, another 16% called themselves traditional and 56% defined themselves as secular (only 2% didn't identify with any of these categories). The breakdown in the two school streams is starkly different. The teachers in the religious

---

1 Lacey, Saleh, and Gorman, 1998; Laird, Garver, and Niskodé, 2007; Statham, Richardson, and Cook, 1991.

2 See the Guttman Institute various surveys on religiosity in Israel; see also Cohen, 2008.

school system are almost universally (92%) religious themselves. The general school system is somewhat more diverse: although the majority (73%) called themselves secular, almost a fifth is traditional. Only 6% of those teaching in the general schools called themselves religious. Thus, students in religious schools are exposed almost exclusively to religious teachers, students in general schools mainly to secular teachers with some traditional teachers. Since the Shoah almost inevitably touches on deep theological and ethical questions, the teachers' religious views have implications for how they present the Shoah and how they react to students' questions. This will be discussed in more detail in the chapter comparing the two streams of schools.

2. Connection to the Shoah. The teachers' interest in teaching about the Shoah reflects a personal connection to the subject. First, all the teachers surveyed are Jewish. (With the exception of Arabic language teachers, there are few non-Jewish teachers in the Hebrew state school system). Thus, regardless of any other trait—religiosity, family history, ethnicity—the teachers are linked to the subject. Further, almost three quarters come from an Ashkenazi (European) background: 63% defined their ethnic background as only Ashkenazi, another 10% said their background is a mixture of Ashkenazi and Sephardi-Mizrahi (see page 24 for explanations of these terms). Although, as discussed, Jews in North Africa and the Middle East were not shielded from the war, the likelihood of having a personal, familial connection to the Shoah is clearly stronger among Jews from Europe. 59% of the teachers lost family members in the Shoah and 56% have Shoah survivors in their families. Among the Ashkenazi teachers, the percentages are even higher: 79% lost family members and 74% have Shoah survivors in their family. Although none of the teachers indicated that they were Shoah survivors themselves, and few were old enough to have been in the war, even as children, several of the teachers and principals specified in the open section that they were children or grandchildren of survivors or victims. One (a literature teacher) described herself as "...a second-generation daughter of Shoah survivors and an educator who developed in the shadow of the Shoah and its consequences..." Others noted that they cite their own family histories when teaching the Shoah.

> I try to transform Shoah teaching with personal stories, usually connected to my own family members who were

> survivors. This gives the students a connection to historical knowledge and makes it a more personal experience.—*Male history and citizenship teacher*

> I became interested in teaching the Shoah because I believe it is an inseparable part of our identity as Jews in Israel, and also because I didn't have the privilege of knowing my grandfather and grandmother; my father's whole family was killed in the Shoah.—*Female English teacher*

The strong personal link to the subject among so many teachers is clearly significant. In teaching about the Shoah, Israeli teachers may—and are encouraged to—express their own feelings, experiences of family members or their memories related to learning about it.[3] It may be noted, however, several of the teachers (particularly history teachers) explicitly opposed any insinuation that teachers must have a personal, familial link to the Shoah in order to teach about it in an effective and moving way.

Since most of the teachers were raised in Israel, they received at least some Shoah education in school, through the media, and in social settings such as youth organizations. Since, as discussed above, attitudes towards the Shoah changed over the years and education on the subject developed gradually, the age of the teachers is relevant in terms of what they learned about the subject during their own school years. The oldest cohort of teachers would have been exposed to the major shift in attitude towards the Shoah and Israeli identity which took place following the Six Day War. While their schools were likely to have marked *Yom HaShoah* with ceremonies and may have visited Yad Vashem or other memorial museums, the number of class hours they spent learning about the history of the Shoah is likely to have been limited, as it was not yet part of the mandatory curriculum. Teachers who were in their 40s at the time of this research would have been in high school in the 1980s, when the Shoah was being incorporated into the standard curriculum and informal activities were becoming more extensive. The younger teachers would have learned extensively about the Shoah when

3 Goodman and Mizrachi, 2008.

they were students, and were exposed to similar curricula as the ones currently being taught. Some may even have participated in the early trips to Poland.

3. In the classroom. Representing the nationwide proportion of the two streams within the state school system, 79% of the surveyed teachers worked in general schools and 21% in religious schools.

The majority of teachers worked with students at several grade levels, and almost a third taught in both junior high schools and high schools. They must try to adapt their lessons to students of different ages; difficult enough for any subject and particularly challenging in teaching such an emotionally sensitive subject.

The survey included teachers who address the topic of the Shoah via a wide range of disciplines and informal activities. In the early stage of designing the survey, some members of the Ministry of Education requested that only the teachers of history be contacted. However, this was discussed at length by the members of the steering committee, who eventually concluded that it was important to locate teachers involved in other aspects of Shoah education, in order to explore the full exposure of the students to the subject and the realities of how the topic is addressed in practice, beyond the official curricular units.

Approximately three quarters of those involved in Shoah education at their schools were history teachers. Half taught *only* history, and a quarter taught both history and another subject. Most frequently they were homeroom teachers. The remaining quarter of the surveyed teachers, those who do not teach history but are involved in Shoah education, address the subject in a variety of other classes such as citizenship, Jewish studies, English, literature, or art. Both history teachers and others may be involved in organizing and leading informal activities such as ceremonies and field trips.

Virtually all of the teachers (97%) said they draw connections between the Shoah and current events, and almost as many (90%) try to integrate Shoah studies with other subjects. The principals support this practice: 90% said there is an effort to integrate Shoah studies with other subjects at their schools. This is more prevalent in the general schools; just under half (47%) of the principals of general schools said there is a definite (not just "partial") attempt at integration, compared to 26% of principals of religious schools.

Related to this is the prevalence of a coordinator for Shoah studies at the school; 41% of the general school principals said their school has a coordinator, compared to 24% of the principals of the religious schools. A coordinator links teachers teaching the mandatory history units with other teachers who may assign reading material and projects or organize informal activities related to the Shoah. Without a person overseeing this type of cooperation, other teachers may touch on the subject of the Shoah, but their lessons are less likely to be coordinated with the main Shoah lessons and activities. Indeed, the principals of the general schools were significantly more likely to say that there was cooperation between history and other teachers involved in Shoah education at their schools (84% compared to 65% of religious school principals). The designation of an educational coordinator with the explicit task of integrating Shoah studies into other subject areas is a special feature of Shoah education in Israeli schools.

4. Training. The people teaching the Shoah in Israeli schools are highly educated and experienced. Virtually all the teachers hold at least a bachelor's degree and almost half earned a master's degree. Well over half have been teaching for 15 years or longer, and only a small minority has been teaching for five years or less.

Further, most have received at least some specialized training in teaching the Shoah. This is in stark contrast to the lack of training noted as one of the weaknesses of Shoah education in many other countries (repeatedly noted in the ITF country reports). Of the teachers in both the religious and general schools, 80% took university or college courses on the history of the Shoah or pedagogy of teaching it. There was a graphic difference in training among the history teachers and the teachers involved in other aspects of Shoah education. While 95% of the history teachers studied the Shoah in university or college, only a quarter of the non-history teachers did.

The teachers' education about the Shoah did not end when they earned their degrees. Well over half (58%) of the teachers have taken enrichment courses in the subject and 61% do independent reading, showing their strong interest and motivation in continuing to learn about the subject and to improve their methods of teaching it. Interestingly, the highest level of attendance at the enrichment courses was among those who teach both history and another subject; their interest in creating interdisciplinary activities or expanding Shoah education beyond the mandatory history curriculum may prompt them to enroll in such courses. As a result of their more extensive training, the history teachers were more likely to say they felt highly proficient in the historical background of the Shoah and the Nazi era. A large percentage of all the teachers, including the history teachers, said they felt they should learn more about Jewish community life before and during the Shoah.

The wide availability of enrichment courses specifically geared towards teaching the Shoah is another distinguishing feature of the Israeli educational landscape. Yad Vashem, in Jerusalem, is the most widely attended venue; 41% of the teachers had taken one of their courses on Shoah teaching. 22% took courses offered through the Ministry of Education. Smaller numbers of teachers had taken Shoah education courses at other sites such as the Ghetto Fighters' Museum (in the north), the Massuah Institute for Holocaust Studies (between Tel Aviv and Haifa) and some of the major universities. These workshops cover issues such as developing an inter-curricular approach, multi-media tools for teaching the Shoah, and how to address personal, collective and universal identity and values. Some settings, such as the Israel Center for the Treatment of Psychotrauma, are now beginning to offer courses addressing the emotional impact of being a Shoah educator, to build teachers' personal resilience and enable them to transmit this difficult subject in a psychologically sound way.[4]

B. Students

1. Personal characteristics. The sample of students surveyed represents the demographic makeup of the Hebrew-language Israeli state school system. The vast majority (89%) were born in Israel. Over 95% were Jewish.

The 9th graders were mostly either 14 or 15 years old. The 12th graders were between 16 and 18 years old.

A third of the students said they were of Ashkenazi origin, a third of Sephardi-Mizrahi origin, a fifth said they were "both" and 12% "other" (Ethiopian, Indian, etc.). The proportion of students from Ashkenazi backgrounds among the 9th graders was lower than among the 12th graders, particularly in the religious schools. Interestingly, in both school

4 Dr. Danielle Erez, personal communication, 2011.

systems there were a notably higher percentage of younger students who placed themselves in the "other" category (not Ashkenazi, Sephardi-Mizrahi or "both"). It may be that the younger students are less aware of their families' ethnic background or less likely to classify themselves according to these categories.

Following a similar pattern, the 12th grade students were more likely to say there were Shoah survivors or victims in their families. Overall, slightly more than a third of the students said they had family members who were killed in the Shoah or who were Shoah survivors. The older students in both school systems were more likely by about 10% to say they had Shoah victims or survivors in their families. This reflects the relatively higher percentage of students from Ashkenazi students in the 12th grade. Again, the younger students were more likely to say they did not know this part of their family history.

2. School stream. In many ways, the Israeli students in the religious and general schools were similar. The differences between were mainly—but not exclusively—in the realm of specifically religious beliefs and values. In the general school system, about 60% of the students said they and their families were secular Jews, 30% said they were "traditional" and only 5% said they were "religious." The other 5% did not classify themselves according to these categories (some of these may have been not Jewish). There was no difference between the level of religiosity among the 9th and 12th graders in the general schools. In the religious schools, less than 5% said they were secular Jews and only 1% classified their families as secular. Just under a fifth said they and their families were traditional. About 80% said they and their families were religious. In the religious school stream, there was a notable difference in religiosity between the grade levels. The 12th graders were more likely to say they were religious (84% of the 12th graders compared to 72% of the 9th graders). It may be that in high school some of the "traditional" students move over to the general school system, and that those who stay in the religious schools are those who define themselves as religious.

It follows that the students in the religious schools reported a much higher level of observance of Jewish traditions. Almost all of those in the religious schools said they mainly observe traditions, and over a third do so scrupulously.

For example, all the students in the religious schools said they eat only kosher food at home, while just under half of those in the general schools said they observe the traditional dietary restrictions.

In the religious schools, the percentage of Sephardi-Mizrahi students was relatively higher: almost half the student body, as compared to less than a third in the general schools. The religious schools also had a larger percentage of students from lower and lower-middle class families. Further, there was a gender gap in the religious school system, which has a significantly higher percentage of girls. Religious families are more likely to send their girls to religious public schools and their boys to independent *yeshivot*. In the general school system, boys and girls were equally represented.

Within both school streams there are classes and schools which cater to populations of students with special needs such as new immigrants just learning Hebrew, or students with learning difficulties. These students make up a small minority of the survey population.

C. A Multidimensional Pedagogy

How to teach about such an emotionally difficult and intellectually challenging subject is controversial. Throughout the research, from the first interviews with the experts in the field, through the surveys in the classrooms a number of pedagogic concerns were raised regarding the issues such as what aspects of the Shoah to teach at various age levels, which methods and materials are most appropriate and effective, and the appropriate balance between cognitive, emotional and experiential approaches.

We found that Shoah education in Israeli schools is rich and multidimensional, with a wide range of methods, materials and approaches used.

1. Exposure to the issue of the Shoah in and out of school. There are numerous ways in which young Israelis may be exposed to the issue of the Shoah: through popular media, by talking to relatives, with their youth movements and of course at school. It may be expected, given that over a third of the students have Shoah survivors or victims in their families and that Israel is home to hundreds of thousands of survivors and their descendants, that Israeli youth would have received much of their information about the Shoah at home and in their community. This turned out to not be the case. While there may be informal discussions about the Shoah among family members (this was not asked in the questionnaire), even activities such as viewing films and visiting museums were uncommon in the home and community framework.

The surveyed students were asked to indicate activities in which they have participated at school, with their family, or through a youth movement. School was overwhelmingly the main framework for not only formal but also informal education about the Shoah. Virtually all students (95%) had taken part in a memorial ceremony at school, while a quarter or less did so with family or youth movement. Well over three quarters heard the testimonies of Shoah survivors, visited institutes for commemorating the Shoah, and watched performances on the subject with their schools; only a small minority (a third or less) undertook any of these activities with their youth movement and even fewer with their families. Learning about the Shoah through the internet was the only activity undertaken more often with youth movements than at school. It may be noted that unguided use of the internet to learn about the Shoah could be counter-productive due to the amount of inaccurate information posted online, including sites by groups denying the Shoah.[5] Youth movements sometimes showed films on the topic, but other forms of Shoah education outside school were minimal. A very small percentage of students visited Shoah sites in Poland with their youth movement (7%) or families (3%).[6]

To further emphasize the importance of the school as a venue of Shoah education, the following table summarizes the level of exposure to the issue of the Shoah in each framework. Over two thirds of the students participated in none of the listed activities with their families. This category of "no exposure" does not mean the subject is never discussed, but that no educational activities—even watching movies or reading books about it—were undertaken with their families. Less than 10% had even moderate exposure (participation in at least of the listed activities) to the subject at home. This finding is quite striking, given the importance attached to preserving memory of the Shoah in Israeli society even more so since Israeli youth are known to spend a large proportion of their leisure time with their families.[7] Youth movements

5 Nickerson, 2010.

6 For students' participation in Shoah-related educational activities according to framework (family, school, youth movement), see Appendix C, Table a.

7 Cohen, 2008.

play a somewhat stronger role in Shoah education: the large majority of students (86%) said they had participated in at least one activity related to Shoah education through their youth movement and almost half (46%) had a moderate or high level of exposure to the subject in this framework. Schools offer the widest range of Shoah-related educational activities. Less than one percent of the students had never been exposed to the subject at their schools. The vast majority (89%) had taken part in at least four of the various types of activities through their schools, and 44% had a high level of exposure to the subject, taking part in most if not all of the listed activities sometime during their school career.

Table 1: Summary of exposure to the issue of Shoah in various frameworks

	Family	**Youth movement**	**School**		
			By 9th grade	**By 12th grade**	**Total**
No exposure to issue of Shoah	68%	14%	1%	0%	<1%
Minimal exposure (1-3 activities)	23%	40%	14%	7%	10%
Moderate level of exposure (4-7 activities)	8%	40%	47%	42%	45%
High level of exposure (8-10 activities)	1%	6%	38%	51%	44%

There was little difference between junior high school and high school students in terms of their exposure to the subject at home or in youth movements. The 12th graders, not surprisingly, were more likely to have a higher degree of cumulative exposure to the subject at school: 51% had taken part in eight or more of the activities, compared to 38% of the 9th graders. Interestingly, students in the religious schools were more likely to have taken part in many of these activities with their families. In particular, a far greater percentage of the students in the religious schools attended Shoah commemoration ceremonies with their families (40% as compared to 22% of those in the general schools). The students in the religious schools were also somewhat more likely to have seen documentary and feature films on the Shoah and to have heard testimonies of survivors with their families. Supplementary education received at home may affect students' overall approach to the issue.

There were almost no differences between the older and younger students' participation in Shoah-related activities outside the school. The older students were very slightly more likely to have taken part in each of the various activities with their families or youth movements, which is logical given that the question was phrased to ask if they had ever taken part in the activities in each framework, not just during the year of the survey.

Though apparently marginal in terms of Shoah education, Israeli youth movements represent a distinct setting in which Jewish and Israeli identity in general may be formulated and manifest, and the impact of membership on students' understanding of and attitudes towards the Shoah is interesting, even if not predominant. Of the surveyed students, 62% were or previously had been involved in a youth movement; 13% held positions as counselors in their movements. There was a sharp difference in participation in the general and religious school systems, as well between the 9th and 12th graders. 83% of the religious school students were or had been members of a youth movement, compared to 57% of the students in the general schools.[8] The 12th graders in the religious schools were more than twice as likely to still be involved as youth movement counselors. A very small percentage of 12th graders who did not become counselors had continued as members; only 2% or

---

8 This figure confirms the research of Shapira, Adler, and Fire (1999), which uncovered a strengthening of the religious youth movements.

3% in both streams. The greater involvement among religious students is interesting given that in previous generations youth movements were largely the domain of secular Zionism, often socialist in ideology. These movements have gradually declined in popularity, while nationalist-religious youth movements such as Bnei Akiva have grown.[9] Though they are not main topics of this research, trends in youth movement membership and the changing role of youth movements in Israeli society are interesting in their own right.[10]

A Smallest Space Analysis (SSA) was conducted using the data on activities in different educational frameworks. As seen in Figure 1, the activities are grouped by framework, not by type of activity. This shows that students who participated in a certain type of activity with the school—for example going to a museum—were not necessarily likely to have gone to a museum with their family. They were more likely to have done other activities with school. All the types of activities done at school were closely correlated and are thus located close together. The activities done with the family are portrayed as a particularly dense group. The strong inter-correlation of these items reflects that a student who went to a museum with his or her family was also likely to have attended a ceremony or watched a documentary with them. It seems that a small number of students come from families who take an active interest in learning about the Shoah, and most of the others learn little about it at home. The youth movement region is more diffuse. Those who watched films and documentaries or looked at websites related to the Shoah with their youth movement were not necessarily likely to have also attended ceremonies or gone to museums with them.

9 Shapira, Adler, and Fire, 1999.
10 See Cohen, 2012; Kahane, 1997.

Figure 1: SSA graphic representation of exposure of students to issue of Shoah, activities and frameworks

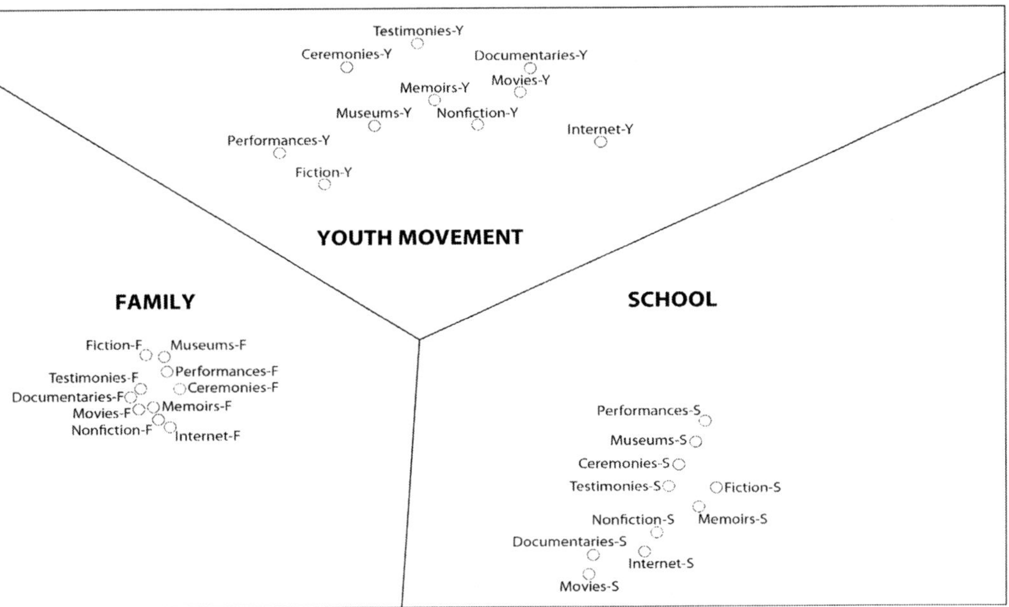

Legend

Items	**Definition**	**Classification**
Testimonies	Heard survivors' testimonies	F—with family
Ceremonies	Participated in Shoah memorial ceremonies	S—with school
		Y—with youth movement
Memoirs	Read memoirs by Shoah survivors/victims	
Museums	Visited Shoah memorial museum in Israel	
Nonfiction	Read nonfiction about the Shoah	
Performances	Saw Shoah-related performances or plays	
Fiction	Read fiction about the Shoah	
Internet	Learned about the Shoah via the internet	
Documentaries	Saw documentaries about the Shoah	
Movies	Saw feature movies about the Shoah	

2. Methods and materials used in schools. That the Israeli students learn about the Shoah primarily at school, rather than at home, corresponds to a larger trend in modern society affecting Jewish youth worldwide: that is, the task of teaching children about their heritage has become the domain of educational institutions, rather than families.[11] There are many implications of the shift towards heritage-history education outside the home. This next section looks at the educational tools used to teach about the subject of the Shoah in Israeli state schools.

As seen above, Shoah education is already firmly established at the junior high school level, and intensifies in high school. By 9th grade over 90% of the students had attended memorial ceremonies, over 80% had seen performances related to the Shoah, 70% had heard testimonies of survivors either in person or on videotape, three quarters had gone on a field trip to a Shoah museum, and more than half had seen documentaries or films and read fiction, non-fiction and memoirs on the Shoah with their classes. Since students were asked if they had ever participated in each activity with their school the 12th graders' responses show the cumulative experience and, logically, a significantly higher percentage of the older students had encountered each type of activity by the end of their schooling. In particular, the older students were more likely to have seen documentary and feature films, gone to memorial museums, and heard survivors' testimonies. Almost half the surveyed seniors had taken part in the journey to Poland, (discussed in-depth in chapter IX), which was not offered to the younger students.[12]

A few types of activities—namely reading fiction and seeing performances—seem to have gained popularity in recent years, as the 9th graders were more likely to indicate them as part of their educational experience than were the older students. Performances and presentations refer to plays or readings by students or outside groups, not to simulations, role-playing or reenactments. Simulation games, though they may be effective teaching tools for other subjects, are highly controversial when applied to Shoah studies and have been explicitly discouraged by the US Holocaust Memorial Museum and the Anti-Defamation League. A famous simulation game with unexpectedly problematic results was

11 Dashefsky and Lebson, 2002; Steinberg, 1984.

12 For a comparison of students' participation in Shoah related educational activities by school stream and grade level see Appendix C, Table b.

dramatized in the movie *The Wave* (1981); the movie, which shows how quickly students internalized the roles of persecutor and victim, has become a powerful teaching tool, but the role-playing itself is not repeated in classes. Simulations are not widely used in Israeli schools' Shoah education programs, although a new exhibit at the Yad Mordechai memorial museum in southern Israel, which hosts school groups, includes a simulated train ride past images of ghettos and death camps.[13]

A large majority of all groups said they had heard survivors' testimonies; this was somewhat more common in the religious stream. The students in the general schools were more likely to have seen performances, gone on field trips and read books of all types (fiction, non-fiction and memoirs) as part of their Shoah education. One principal of a general junior high school noted that students also heard testimony from and met with non-Jews who helped save Jews during the Shoah (commonly referred to as the "Righteous among the Nations").

Only 40% of the students said they had used the internet to learn about the Shoah in school. The students in the general schools, particularly the 12th graders, were more likely to have used the internet to learn about the Shoah. At the time of the study, the student-computer ratio in Israeli schools was low compared to other developed countries. In recent years, sophisticated online resources have been developed by institutions such as Yad Vashem and the USHMM; testimonies of survivors have been made available online.[14]

While informal activities were widespread and constituted an important part of Shoah education, classic formal techniques were still predominant. According to both the principals and the teachers, lecturing was by far the most common method, used by almost 90% of those teaching about the Shoah. Close to half of the teachers assigned individual work such as reports. Group projects and creative works were far less common, used by a third or less of the teachers. The most widely used materials were historical sources, films and testimonies of survivors. Less than half the teachers said they used literature to teach about the Shoah. Teachers in the general schools used a wider range of materials and teaching styles. They were more likely than those in the

---

13 Anti-Defamation League, 2006; Fallace, 2007; Lindquist, 2006; Saar, 2011; Totten, 2000; 2004; USHMM, 2001.

14 Kashti, 2010; Manfra and Stoddard, 2008.

religious schools to assign individual and group work, to use the internet in teaching the Shoah, and to take their students to see performances on the subject.

Despite the range of experiential and informal activities included, it was obvious that there was a striking emphasis on teaching towards exams. Between 7th and 10th grade the average number of hours varies slightly from about 15-20 hours per year. In the 11th grade—the year students prepare for matriculation exams in history, including an exam on the era of the Shoah—the number spikes dramatically to over 45. It then drops again in the 12th grade to about 25 hours per year.

Table 2: Yearly number of hours of Shoah education by grade level

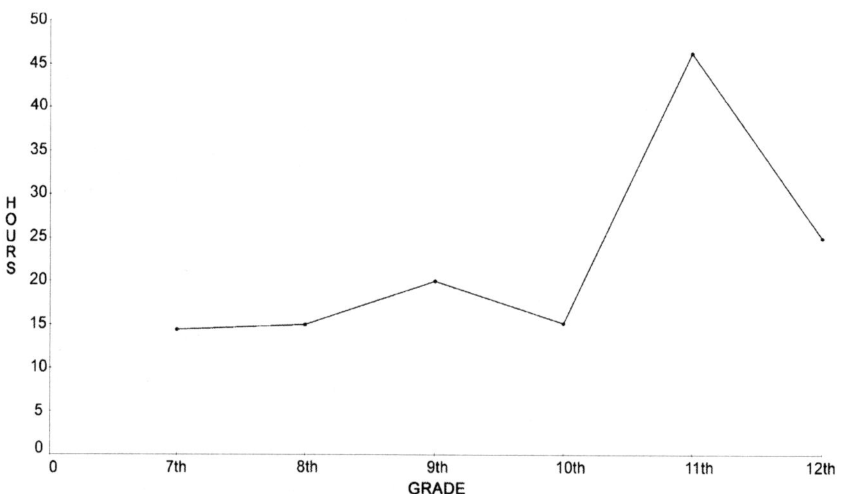

> This subject is fascinating, to the students, and we don't address it enough in junior high school. When students begin their matriculation studies in 10th grade they don't stop asking, "When do we learn about the Shoah?" and are disappointed to hear that it is only included in the curriculum for 11th grade. —*Female coordinator of junior high school history program*

> The Ministry of Education doesn't include the subject of the Shoah in the study curriculum for junior high school.

> Teaching the Shoah in our school was the initiative of the school's administration, because we think it is important.—*Female junior high school principal*

> I think Shoah education should be taught as its own discipline for one hour a week in grades 7th through 12th.—*Female junior high school principal*

The textbooks and literature used to teach the Shoah have a significant impact on how students perceive the subject, depending on how they present (or don't) issues such as Jewish culture, history of anti-Semitism, perspectives of victims, perpetrators, bystanders and resistors, and links to other issues such as democracy or other genocides.[15]

Most of the Israeli teachers used the same few textbooks. *Shoah and Memory* by Yisrael Gutmann[16] was the most widely used text in the general schools: three quarters of the teachers use this text, which has official recognition by the Ministry of Education. The author is a history professor at Hebrew University and one of the head historians at Yad Vashem. Born in Poland in 1923, Gutmann was involved in the Warsaw Ghetto Uprising and survived imprisonment in several Nazi concentration camps before immigrating to British Palestine and joining a kibbutz. The book is based on broad and current research. It begins with a section on Jewish life in Europe prior to World War II, showing that many European Jews were highly integrated into the modern societies in which they lived. It presents the history of Jewish settlement in British Palestine and the founding of the State of Israel in the context of the Shoah. It also addresses issues such as the experience of Shoah survivors in Israel and—as indicated by the title—Shoah memory. Gutmann's book is often taught in conjunction with a book on post-war Jewish history around the world.

In stark contrast, less than 10% of the teachers in the religious school stream said they use the Gutmann text. In the religious schools, 60% of

---

15 Crawford and Foster, 2007; Schweber, 2011.

16 Yisrael Gutman is a history professor at Hebrew University and one of the head historians at Yad Vashem. Born in Poland in 1923, he was involved in the Warsaw Ghetto Uprising and survived imprisonment in several Nazi concentration camps before immigrating to British Palestine and joining a kibbutz. http://www1.Yad Vashem.org/yv/en/exhibitions/survivors/gutman.asp?WT.mc_id=wiki.

the teachers used *The Shoah of the Jewish People during the Second World War* by Abraham Hadad although this book is not officially recognized by the Ministry of Education. It is a simple summary of historical facts, geared towards memorization for exams with little interpretation, analysis or directives for either teachers or students.[17]

Only a minority of the teachers in either stream used books or educational materials aside from those provided through their school. However, over a quarter said they wrote some of their own material, a relatively high percentage for such a time-consuming and entirely voluntary undertaking.

Aside from textbooks, memoirs and novels about the Shoah are used in many classrooms. The poetry of Hannah Senesh (a member of the Haganah who parachuted into Nazi-occupied Europe in an attempt to save Jews about to be deported to Auschwitz; she was caught and executed) is widely read in Israel. Yad Vashem offers lessons plans for teaching the Shoah using poetry and literature at various grade levels, highlighting the works of authors such as Primo Levi, Ida Fink, Uri Orlev, and Mordechai Gebirtig.[18]

> ...the curriculum that I developed gives a central role to reading books (especially about children), creative writing, research, watching films, presentations and listening to music...—*Female English teacher in religious school of low socio-economic level*

> At the school where I teach, Shoah studies have a central place in the academic curriculum and in educational and cultural activities. There is a project for 11th grade students... [which includes]... production of a book with names and stories of Shoah victims and with a ceremony for students and their families. The trip to Poland is a continuation of the commemoration activities. We make a connection between the commemorative work and the sites which the students visit during the trip. It is impor-

17 Personal communication, Dr. Yael Klein of Bar Ilan University.

18 Yad Vashem, Teaching the Holocaust through Literature: www1.Yad Vashem.org/yv/en/education/newsletter/04/main_article.asp.

> tant to note that there are parallel activities, films, and trips to museums ...—*Male teacher of history and citizenship in general high school of very high socio-economic level*

> It is good that we learn about the Shoah in class and it is interesting, but there also need to be other things such as museums, films and trips to Poland. —*Male 12th grade student in a religious high school of median socio-economic level*

> The Shoah should be taught through literature and modern poetry that deepen our world and give us more perspective on the subject of the Shoah.—*Female student*

The emphasis on formal learning was stronger among the teachers who exclusively taught history classes.[19] Delivering lectures was the most common teaching style among all three groups, and it was ubiquitous among the history teachers. Less than half of the non-history teachers gave classroom lessons on the Shoah, compared to well over 90% of history teachers. Both groups of history teachers, not surprisingly, relied heavily on historical sources.

Those who taught the Shoah in multiple frameworks, such as those who were simultaneously history and homeroom teachers, were more likely to present the subject through survivors' testimonies and memoirs, the internet, literature, and performances. They were also relatively more likely to chaperone visits to Shoah memorial institutes in Israel, journeys to Poland, and lead other enrichment activities than were those who exclusively taught history or those who did not teach history classes at all.

The greatest area of activity for non-history teachers was informal activities such as organizing ceremonies and chaperoning field trips. The non-history teachers were relatively more likely than the history teachers to assign group work and creative projects (for example a play or art display) and to use performances and literature to teach about the Shoah.

---

19 For a comparison of those who teach only history, history and another subject, and non-history teachers, see Appendix C, Table c.

It is worth noting that in Israel special needs educators are also expected to address the issue of the Shoah, at least on *Yom HaShoah*, and that addressing such a demanding subject presents particular difficulties for teachers of students with learning, emotional, and/or behavioral challenges. The Ministry of Education's branch for special education has developed a teacher's guide and educational kit including photographs, artwork, short biographies and audio-visual materials. Yad Vashem offers seminars for educators at special needs schools.[20] There is no scholarly literature addressing Shoah studies in the framework of special needs schools in other countries, and it seems that the Israeli school system is pioneering this aspect of the field.

> This school is for youth who have dropped out of the formal educational system. Most of the students have learning difficulties and the majority isn't used to studying at all. The students do not connect to the subject of the Shoah and many of them hold racist ideas....there is a need at this school to find alternative ways of teaching the subject of the Shoah.—*Female coordinator at a special needs high school*

3. Memorial ceremonies. Memorial ceremonies on the national Day of Remembrance of the Shoah and Heroism in April (*Yom HaShoah*) have become a virtually universal part of Shoah education in Israeli state schools, both general and religious. They are a distinctive part of Jewish-Israeli educational culture. As part of the survey, the research team conducted observations in some fifteen schools, revealing some common themes. The ceremonies are almost all are timed to coincide with the siren which sounds throughout the country in mid-morning on *Yom HaShoah*. In the political culture of Jewish-Israeli society, carrying on a normal school day without in some way acknowledging the Shoah would be an explicit and somewhat defiant statement. The religious state schools do not wish to make such a statement and almost all hold ceremonies on *Yom HaShoah*. However, some underlying discomfort regarding the civic holiday in April became apparent as the "issue" of the date was mentioned in the course of several ceremonies we observed

20 Israel Ministry of Education Special Needs Branch, 2011 (in Hebrew); Yad Vashem, 2006, 9.

in religious schools. Some of these schools also hold ceremonies on the 10th of Tevet, a religious fast day in December. "Two days to remember the Shoah victims is not too many" a speaker at one school declared.

The moment of silence during the siren is a unifying feature of all the ceremonies, as is the lighting of memorial candles (usually six, symbolizing the six million Jews killed during the Shoah). Beyond that, the schools are free to design their ceremonies to their own style, though there are some common features. In the high schools, the students who went to Poland often take an active role in organizing the ceremonies, during which they talk about their experiences, read texts, sing songs, put on dramatic performances, or show slides of their journey. Survivors or children of survivors may be invited to speak; if this is not possible, survivors' testimonies are read or shown in films. Both religious and national symbols are prevalent in general and religious schools, particularly Israeli flags and Yellow Stars of David, often imprinted with the word *Jude*, recalling those the Jews of Europe were forced to wear by the Nazi regime. The speeches and theme of the ceremonies often invoke the necessity of the State of Israel, the responsibility of remembering the Shoah and—in the religious schools—the responsibility of carrying on the Jewish tradition. Some ceremonies include quite graphic and disturbing readings and images, while others, especially the junior high schools, downplay the horrors of the Shoah and focus on themes of hope for the future and pride in national survival. The religious schools' rabbis give speeches interpreting memory of the Shoah through the lens of traditional texts and prayers. The students in all the schools take the ceremonies seriously, with little disruption and an atmosphere of respect.[21]

> Shoah memory is being limited, focused mainly on Yom HaShoah and the 10th of Tevet. The subject should be learned throughout the year, in the appropriate dosage, so that it doesn't become just another "ceremony." —
> *Junior high school teacher*

---

21 Of the numerous schools in which observations were conducted, the only one in which students were inattentive during the ceremony was a school for students with academic and emotional difficulties.

4. Academic emphases in Shoah education

Teachers. The teachers' points of view have a strong impact on how each subject is taught. One of the ways the teachers' attitudes towards Shoah education may be seen is in the relative emphasis they give to various aspects and issues within the larger subject. Teachers were given a list of specific content issues which may be covered in Shoah education and asked to what extent they emphasize each. These were: 1) Nazi ideology (political fascism, anti-Semitism, racial superiority of Aryans etc.); 2) the destruction process (the Final Solution, the work and death camps); 3) the influence of the Shoah on the Jewish world and Israel (may include political, theological, cultural, demographic and other impacts); 4) the struggle of the Jews against the Nazis (may include armed resistence, rescue missions, retaining personal dignity, maintaining Jewish tradition and more); 5) historical background (including issues such as WWI and the rise of fascism); 6) the place of the individual during the Shoah (individual responsibility under a totalitarian regime, may cover Jewish resistance, non-Jewish resisters and "righteous among the nations," perpetrators and bystanders etc.); Jewish life before the Shoah (religious, cultural, degree of assimilation, anti-Semitism, the Zionist movement) and Jewish life during the Shoah (in hiding, in the work and death camps).

The teachers as a whole gave the most emphasis to Nazi ideology and the destruction process; well over half (58%) said they emphasize each of these 'to a very great extent'. Half said they highlight the historical background of the Shoah. Just under half (46%) said they put a great deal of emphasis on the place of the individual during the Shoah. Smaller percentages of teachers said they give emphasis to Jewish community life before (23%) and during the Shoah (33%).[22]

The teachers in the religious schools were less likely to teach about Nazi ideology and the historical background of the Shoah and more likely to stress Jewish community life in Europe before and during the Shoah, the role of the individual and the process by which the Jews of Europe were destroyed.

History teachers (including those who also teach additional sub-

---

22 See Appendix C, Table d, for the percentage of teachers who said they emphasize each content issue "to a very great extent" among the whole population of teachers; sub-populations of teachers in religious and general schools.

jects) were much more likely than the non-history teachers to say they emphasized teaching about Nazi ideology and the mass killings. Non-history teachers were more likely to give emphasis to Jewish life before and during the Shoah and the impact of the Shoah on the Jewish world and Israel. Each of these areas touches on deep cognitive and emotional issues in terms of how they are presented to the students. For example, teaching about Jewish life during the Shoah may focus on resistance efforts, stories of survival and hiding, efforts to maintain the Jewish religion and culture under Nazi occupation, or even controversial subjects such as the role of the *Judenräte* councils. In lessons about Jewish life before the Shoah, teachers may present the religious communities of Eastern Europe, the modernized Jews in Western Europe, the emergence of the Zionist movement, and more. Teaching about pre-war European Jewish life as part of Shoah education in Israeli schools is particularly interesting from a pedagogic standpoint. In other cases of teaching the history of people who have been persecuted (such as Native Americans or Australian aboriginal people), there has been criticism of either stereotyping or romanticizing the victims, since only a tiny minority of the teachers or students are linked to the culture being studied.[23] In Israeli schools, teaching about how Jews in Europe, for example, observed holidays which the students themselves celebrate reinforces the sense of identification with the victims. The intrinsic connection, however, does not negate the danger of misrepresentation or romanticization. Teachers may over-simplify or exaggerate certain elements (religiosity of European Jews, active participation in the Zionist movement, *shtetl* life, etc.) in accordance with their own ideologies. Nevertheless, the decision to teach about the people and communities who were destroyed—and not just the destruction itself—is an intriguing and important aspect of Shoah education in Israel.

Principals. The principals had a somewhat different prioritization of the issues to be taught. The struggle of the Jews against the Nazis was the issue which the majority of principals (80%) said should be emphasized in the classroom. In comparison, 52% of teachers said this issue should be emphasized. This may reflect what they learned as students some decades ago, when physical resistance was a core theme. Nazi ideology, the greatest priority for the teachers, was of less concern

23 Ward, 2011.

to the principals; less than half (46%) said this should be give great emphasis. Training teachers to discuss the causes of the Shoah has only been included as part of teacher training courses since the 1980s.

Like the teachers in the religious schools, the principals of the religious schools were more likely than their counterparts in the general schools to say that attention should be given to Jewish life before and during the Shoah. The principals of the general schools were more likely to say their teachers should spend time on Nazi ideology (55% compared to 27% in religious schools).

There were no significant differences between the junior high school and the high school principals except that the former were somewhat less likely to say teachers should emphasize the destruction process, likely reflecting a concern that this gruesome topic may not be appropriate for the younger students. Even here, the difference was not dramatic and only a tiny minority said the topic should be avoided.

> The subject of the Shoah is important regarding Jewish tradition and Zionism and in particular the crystallization[24] of the student's personal identity regarding homeland and Judaism. —*Male junior high school principal*

> The subject Shoah should be addressed in different ways, raising national and universal questions connected to the essence and nature of humankind, the meaning of memory, the testimonies of the survivors and the implications of the Shoah on the generations to come. —*Female high school principal*

24 The concept of "crystalization" (*gibush* in Hebrew) is a strong value in Jewish-Israeli society and the term is commonly used (Katriel, 1988; Katriel and Nesher, 1986).

Table 3: Principals' emphases in Shoah education—percentage of principals answering "to a very great extent"

"To what extent do you think the teachers in your school should emphasize each of the following?"	Principals of general schools	Principals of religious schools	Total
Nazi ideology	55%	27%	46%
The destruction process	65%	54%	62%
Struggle of the Jews against the Nazis	83%	72%	80%
Historical background	67%	48%	61%
Jewish life during the Shoah	56%	68%	60%
Jewish community life before the Shoah	58%	68%	61%

It is hard to summarize the long and rich interviews conducted with experts. Nevertheless, a common theme among the experts interviewed was that the Shoah needs to be taught within a comprehensive context of European history and Jewish history in Europe, to help the students understand the complexity of what happened and how the Shoah occurred.[25] At the same time, some emphasized the need to make the subject personal by including testimonies and personal stories; that is, that the historical context not be comprised only of dry facts.[26] The culture of European Jewry must be taught in order for students to understand what was lost.[27] It was suggested that attention be given to the different ways various groups of the Jewish People have dealt with

25 These experts were: Ephrat Balberg-Rotenstreich; Dr. Goldberg, Dr. Blatman, Dr. Orvieto, Dr. Dreyfus, Dr. Mankowitz, Dr. Feldman, Dr. Consonni, Dr. Auron, Dr. Barzel, Dr. Porat, Gross, Dr. Schweid, Dr. Bachrach.

26 Dr. Auron, Dr. Barzel, Dr. Gertner, Dr. Gutman, Dr. Mankowitz, personal communication, 2009.

27 Dr. Yablonka, personal communication, 2009.

the legacy of trauma from the Shoah.[28] Graphic details of the genocide should be minimized, as they might either be too disturbing or may become voyeuristic, focusing on emotional "thrills" at the expensive of deep understanding.[29]

In an SSA of the goals and messages of Shoah education from the perspective of the principals, there is a clear division between subjects to be covered (at the top) and messages to be imparted (at the bottom). Along the horizontal axis, there is a differentiation between universal aspects at the left side of the map and Jewish aspects at the right (it is important to note that this orientation is in no way related to political concepts of Left and Right; the mirror image of the map would have the same meaning). Teaching about Jewish community life before and during the Shoah appears in the right-hand side of the map, as do the educational messages pertaining to Jewish continuity and Israeli identity. This reflects the tendency for principals who think their schools' Shoah education programs should emphasize Jewish or Zionist messages to also say it is important for teachers to include lessons about Jewish community life. In contrast, the goals of upholding democracy, instilling universal values, fighting racism and promoting individual courage are on the left side of the map with the subjects of Shoah history and Nazi ideology. Principals who support more universal goals also were more likely to advocate teaching these broad historical aspects of the Shoah.

---

28 Dr. Rosenson, personal communication, 2009.

29 Dr. Consonni, Dr. Dreyfus, Dr. Yablonka, personal communication, 2009.

Figure 2: Contents and messages of Shoah education from the perspective of the principals

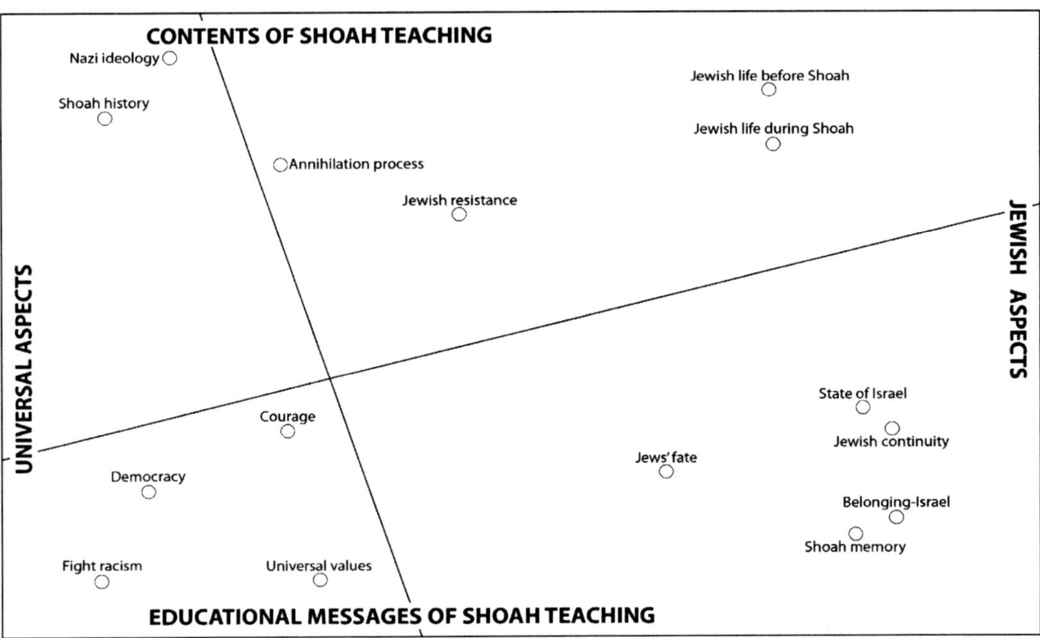

Legend

How important is it that the teachers emphasize each of the following subjects when teaching about the Shoah?

Content

Nazi ideology
History (historical background of Shoah)
Annihilation process
Jewish resistance (against the Nazis)
Jewish life before Shoah (spiritual and cultural community life)
Jewish life during Shoah (community life)

Educational messages

Heroism
State of Israel
Jewish continuity
Jews' fate
Belonging
Memory
Universal values
Fight racism
Commitment to democracy

D. Pedagogic Approaches to Shoah Education

Taken together, the activities, methods, and materials employed by the teachers represent their overarching pedagogic approaches to Shoah education. Over the course of their education, students encounter many teachers with different approaches, each impacting their knowledge of and attitudes towards the subject. As we have seen, Shoah education encompasses many types of learning: formal and informal; cognitive and affective; classroom learning and experiential activities.

While "informal education" often refers to educational activities outside the school framework, school-sponsored activities which are not part of a formal classroom setting are also a type of informal education. In fact, formal and informal education are not opposed or mutually exclusive types, but rather endpoints on a spectrum that covers differences in context, aim, content, and methodology. Israeli sociologist Reuven Kahane developed a typology of "informality" pertaining to interpersonal relations, activities and goals that may be applied to *any* educational act. He posits that informal education is becoming increasingly important in the post-modern age, particularly in imparting values related to democracy and personal responsibility, which are clearly applicable to Shoah education.[30]

Classic educational theory differentiates between cognitive, affective and instrumental or behavioral domains. To some extent, educational experiences encompass all three, and education itself has been described as a process of developing "...habits of mind, hand, and heart."[31] In looking at Shoah education in Israel, it is significant that Jewish learning at its very roots links knowledge, emotion, and behavior through an inter-related system of texts, ritual actions, and strong emotional and social bonds.

Cognitive learning is one of the three basic domains of education in Bloom's classic taxonomy (alongside affective and psychomotor/instrumental).[32] The cognitive domain spans a spectrum of categories, from simple and concrete through complex and abstract: knowledge, comprehension, application, analysis, synthesis and evaluation.

---

30 Kahane, 1997.

31 Shulman, 2004.

32 Bloom et al., 1956; Krathwohl, Bloom and Masia, 1964.

Cognitive learning indicates "knowing about" a subject. It is the accumulation and processing of information, primarily through classic classroom types of lessons (lectures, books, documentaries, etc.). Formal education tends to emphasize the cognitive domain. Standard history classes based on texts and lectures form a large part of Shoah education.

The affective domain refers to education designed to impact students' feelings, values, and attitudes. This domain spans a spectrum of awareness, response, valuation, prioritization, synthesis, and internalization. Hearing testimonies of witnesses and participating in memorial ceremonies, for example, invoke affective responses in students. Discussions in class may also explore students' emotional reactions to the subject.

The instrumental domain may be invoked in such activities as putting on performances for *Yom HaShoah*, creating displays for the school, rituals and marches at memorials, and especially during the journey to Poland.

Another approach is "experiential" learning, in which knowledge and abstract concepts are developed through overlapping processes of observing, reflecting, and experimenting. Learners apprehend the subject through direct experience. Of course in Shoah education the subject can never be "experienced" directly (as can, for example, a subject such as practicing medicine). As mentioned earlier, even simulation activities are not widely practiced in Israel and are considered inappropriate by many experts in the field. Visiting Shoah sites in Europe, meeting Shoah survivors, taking part in ceremonies, and putting on performances are examples of experiential learning about the Shoah.[33]

1. Teachers' didactic approach. Teachers were asked to what extent they emphasized cognitive learning and experiential learning in planning and conducting lessons and activities about the Shoah. The first striking observation is that there is no dichotomy. Virtually all the teachers said they emphasize both: 94% said they emphasize cognitive knowledge and 90% said they emphasize experiential aspects. This was equally true in both school streams and both grade levels, although in high school the balance shifts somewhat more towards cognitive learning, as the teachers prepare their students for matriculation exams.[34]

---

33 Chazan, 1981; Cohen, 1997; Coombs et al., 1973; Friedman, 1995; Harrow, 1972; Heilman, 1992; Helmreich, 1986; Kolb, 1984; Simkins, 1977.

34 For a comparison of didactic approach of the full population of teachers and sub-populations of teachers in religious schools, general schools, high schools, and junior high schools see Appendix C, Table e.

> There is a need to find the correct balance between increasing knowledge and putting emphasis on an emotional and national experience.—*Male principal of general junior high school of low socio-economic level*

> Shoah teaching is lagging behind Shoah "experience."—*Dr. Nili Keren*

> The conflict between knowledge and experience isn't a conflict in my eyes —*Female history and Bible studies teacher*

A difference in approach was found between history and non-history teachers, though, again, a large majority said they invoke both approaches to at least some extent. Those who teach *only* history were twice as likely as the non-history teachers to say they emphasize cognitive knowledge about the Shoah "to a great extent." However, the reverse is not true; that is, the history teachers were only slightly less likely to say they emphasize the experiential. In other words, history teachers balance the two approaches while non-history teachers tend more towards the experiential. As noted earlier, there was a distinct difference in activities the history teachers and teachers of other subjects, the history teachers being more likely to be involved in classroom teaching of the Shoah, and non-history teachers more involved with ceremonies and field trips. Several of the experts we interviewed expressed concern that the experiential was being overemphasized, to the detriment of a deep cognitive understanding of the issue. The teachers were less likely to see this as a problem, and saw a need for experiential activities to balance out history lessons taught to prepare students for exams.

Table 4: Didactic approach of teachers by subject taught—percentage indicating they emphasize each to a "great" or "very great" extent combined (in parenethses—percentage indicating to a "very great extent")

	Teachers of only history	Teachers of history and another subject	Non-history teachers
Emphasize cognitive knowledge	98% (50%)	98% (46%)	82% (24%)
Emphasize experiential aspects	88% (40%)	91% (43%)	95% (45%)

> We at the school, and I as the coordinator of the history department, try to exert our influence to add hours for non-formal activities ...—*Female teacher of history and mathematics at religious school of low socio-economic level*

Based on these results, a typology of teachers according to didactic approach was developed, with four categories representing teachers according to whether they said they place a great deal of emphasis on: 1) cognitive knowledge; 2) experiential aspects; 3) both; 4) neither. The types were fairly evenly distributed. A fifth of the teachers said they emphasize the cognitive (but not experiential) to a very great extent. Another fifth said the opposite, that they emphasize the experiential to a great extent, but not the cognitive. Slightly more than a fifth (22%) emphasized both to an equally great extent. The remainder did not emphasize either to a very great extent.

There are some interesting links between pedagogic approach and other aspects of Shoah education, as seen in Table 5. The teachers who emphasize both types of learning were also the most likely to say they feel highly competent in the subject. Those who emphasize the experiential over the cognitive tended to feel less confident. As noted earlier, the teachers whose main involvement is organizing ceremonies and similar non-academic activities are often not history teachers and may have received less training. The teachers who emphasize both types of learning were also the most likely to make a strong effort to integrate Shoah studies into other parts of the curriculum.

Table 5: Typology of teachers according to pedagogic approach with selected variables

	Emphasize **cognitive** 'to a great extent'	Emphasize **experiential** 'to a great extent'	Emphasize **both** 'to a great extent'	Emphasize **neither** 'to a great extent'
Teachers who feel highly competent in the subject of the Shoah	38%	25%	48%	14%
Teachers who 'absolutely' integrate Shoah studies with other subjects	46%	51%	63%	42%

The students, teachers and principals have an inherent *a priori* attachment to the subject. A large percentage has a direct family connection to people who suffered at the hands of the Nazis, and all are fundamentally linked through their common Jewish heritage. Interestingly, despite these family connections, Israeli youth are mainly learning about the Shoah at school, not at home.

The teachers display a high level of motivation and interest in teaching this subject. Many have taken advantage of the available options for extra training. They have the training, the resources and—crucially—the intention and desire to offer a varied program of both formal and informal activities. History classes are the primary, though not the only, time dedicated to Shoah education. The subject of the Shoah is also addressed in other classes such as literature or citizenship and through informal activities. In part due to time limits and curricular requirements lecturing towards exams predominates (a situation lamented by many educators and students alike, as will be discussed later). The same few books are used; one being dominant in the general schools another in the religious schools. Literature and memoirs supplement the textbooks. The internet is still a relatively marginal tool for teaching the Shoah in Israeli classrooms, though it may be expected to increase.

Teachers and principals expect the classes to make students familiar with a range of aspects about the Shoah, starting with (chronologically, not in terms of emphasis) the Jewish communities that existed beforehand—giving students at least some knowledge of what was lost, who was killed. Although this was far from the most emphasized aspect, it is notable that it represents a distinctive approach towards Shoah education, in which the teaching is personalized and the narrative comes from a Jewish perspective. Another aspect of this approach is teaching about the ways Jews from those communities resisted the concentrated effort to destroy them, and more broadly how individuals reacted to a situation which stripped them of their individuality. While the concept of resistance once predominated in Israeli Shoah education, this is gradually becoming balanced with other aspects, as evidenced by the difference between the principals and the teachers. The ideology that demanded the destruction of those communities and the historical background which gave rise to it, and of course the genocide itself, are other basic components of the curriculum.

The majority of teachers favor an approach that combines cognitive and experiential learning when addressing the Shoah, and this is manifest in the range of activities. Outside the class, virtually all students take part in memorial ceremonies, usually held on *Yom HaShoah*. Many visit at least one of the numerous Shoah memorial museums in Israel. Students watch films and presentations (also often on or around *Yom HaShoah*). Another example of the personalized approach is the prevalence of inviting survivors to tell their stories.

This "portrait of Shoah education" is in reality a work in progress. The research gives a snapshot at one point in a long and ongoing process of developing materials, writing and adapting curricula, training teachers, and so forth. The effort which has been invested in this process attests to the importance attached to it. The motivations behind this effort, the goals of Shoah education, are examined in the next chapter.

V. GOALS AND MESSAGES OF SHOAH EDUCATION

> Despite the supreme difficulty in interpreting the Holocaust, the attempt to do so must be made.—*Professor Terry Evens*[1]

> In teaching the Shoah there is both a lot of potential for educational work and change in values. At the same time, there is also the danger of nationalist education, justification of unethical behavior of the victim, and so on. Therefore it is exceedingly important to focus Shoah teaching and the teachers' enrichment courses on universal values and messages. —*Female junior high school principal*

> I want it emphasized with five exclamation points that the most important message is the essentiality of the State of Israel!!!!! —*Yisrael Rosenson, Hebrew University*

• Despite some discomfort with drawing "lessons" from such an atrocity, today there is widespread agreement that the Shoah cannot be taught without imparting values.

• The issue of what values should be taught is among the most complex and controversial aspects of Shoah education in Israel. Positions advocated in the media and in academia tend to be more polarized than those in the school system.

• Israeli teachers and principals advocate a blend of messages encompassing national (Zionist), Jewish, and universal.

• Principals and teachers in the general school system give relatively more emphasis to universal values than do their colleagues in the religious schools.

• Teachers encourage their students to ask questions regarding ethical and theological questions regarding the Shoah.

---

1 2008: 84.

* * * * * *

The pedagogic approach, activities undertaken and materials used are tools to achieve the underlying educational goals and to transmit its messages, the core of the educational act. Everyone in the Israeli educational system: students, teachers, principals, experts in the field, and government officials up to the highest level agree that the Shoah should be taught. As described in the last chapter, there is general agreement that a broad range of activities and materials should be used, with a balance between cognitive and emotional approaches. There is less agreement on the goals of Shoah education and the messages to be transmitted. These ideological questions are more sensitive than those related to pedagogy.

It should be noted that there is an opinion that no message can or should be drawn from the Nazis' extermination campaign. The Shoah touches on the most fundamental questions about human nature and evil; questions which are difficult if not impossible to answer. Some feel that any attempt at explanation diminishes the horror of the reality, that any lesson is exploitive. In 1958, Primo Levi, a Jewish scientist and writer who survived Auschwitz wrote, "Perhaps one cannot, what is more one must not, understand what happened, because to understand is almost to justify."[2] A religious tractate published in 1947 asserted, "...two years after the end of World War II, we have not ceased asking these difficult questions [as to how God could have allowed the killing of six million Jews] but everyone goes in silence ... there is no answer, there is no response, we can't open our mouths ..."[3] Similarly, according to Claude Lanzmann, director of the documentary film *Shoah*, "...there is indeed an absolute obscenity in the project of understanding the Shoah ... there is no why."[4] The imperative according to this view is to remember the Shoah and its victims but not to try to explain their deaths.

Similarly, several of the interviewees in the current research were uncomfortable with the premise of learning "lessons" from the Shoah, preferring that teachers try to help students gain some understanding of the events or clarify questions without offering ready-made or simplistic conclusions.[5]

---

2 Levi, 1958, 395.

3 Tzimerman, 1947: 5. Following this disclaimer, the tractate then goes on to offer a number of responses based on religious precepts.

4 Lanzmann, 1990, 279.

5 Dr. Daniel Blatman, Dr. Amos Goldberg, Dr. Yael Orveito, personal communication, 2009.

> The first lesson is there are no lessons ... I don't think we need to find unequivocal answers, but we need to keep asking questions, as this is the basis of education.—*Dr. Yael Orveito, Hebrew University*

> I prefer to stay at the level of clarifying questions rather than making decisive conclusions, but it's clear that you can't leave such a tragic historical event without asking what we can learn from it.—*Dr. Daniel Blatman, Hebrew University*

A. Are There "Lessons" from the Shoah?

The feeling that no meaning can or should be taken from what happened during the Shoah, which was predominant in its immediate aftermath, may be seen as akin to the shock and denial experienced in the first period of grief following a death, as described in Kübler-Ross' psychological model of the stages of mourning.[6] Recognizing that the magnitude of initial grief permits no response, according to rabbinic law, for the first three days following a death one should not even ask mourners in the deceased's close family about their wellbeing.[7] In the Book of Job, the three comforters first sit with Job in silence for seven days (chapter 2, verse 13), and only later did they begin to try to suggest reasons behind or lessons from what happened.

Also when students learn about the Shoah, an initial stage of silence may be a common and legitimate first response, prior to questioning or attempts at explanation and interpretation. Schweber[8] describes students who sat silently for several minutes after hearing Shoah survivors' testimonies; only after some prompting did the students begin to ask questions, which then came in a flood, showing their first silence was

---

6 Kübler-Ross, 1969; Worden, 2009. It is interesting to note that early in her career Elisabeth Kübler-Ross volunteered in clinics in Poland that served Shoah survivors during the immediate aftermath of World War II and in 1945 she visited the recently liberated Majdanek concentration camp (Worth, 2005).

7 Kraemer, 2000. This is discussed in the Babylonian Talmud *MoedKatan* 21.

8 Schweber, 2006.

not due to indifference. A teacher of Shoah literature wrote, "Sometimes my students seemed stilled by the material—not hostile, not bored, not apathetic—just silent."[9]

However, there is an increasing perception that the Shoah must not be taught only as any other history lesson, and that in teaching the subject its meanings for students today must be addressed. Trying to make meaning of a tragedy corresponds to a later stage of mourning in Kübler-Ross's model. The goals of major Shoah education foundations and institutions express this search for meaning explicitly.

The Holocaust Educational Foundation, a non-profit organization established by survivors and their children, aims "...to give students an understanding of the place of the Holocaust in history and of the current and universal implications of this event. Making our young people conscious of the enormity of this tragedy will, we hope, contribute in some measure to preventing another human calamity of this magnitude." The Holocaust Educational Trust, a UK-based organization works to "...educate young people from every background about the Holocaust and the important lessons to be learned for today." The Contemporary Holocaust Education Foundation, a US organization, "...attempts to make the history of the Holocaust relevant to contemporary society and to young people today." The United States Holocaust Memorial Museum "...inspires citizens and leaders worldwide to confront hatred, prevent genocide, and promote human dignity ... cultivating a sense of moral responsibility among our citizens so that they will respond to the monumental challenges that confront our world." Yad Vashem's International School for Holocaust Studies promotes "... an attempt to understand human beings and the manner in which they contended with extreme situations and with profound ethical dilemmas.... The program inculcates universal values of preservation of human rights, and promotes individual responsibility in fighting racism and xenophobia." Contemporary Jewish philosopher Emil Fackenheim, a survivor of the Sachsenhausen concentration camp, insists that while the Shoah presents a "challenge to philosophy and theology" Jews in the post-Shoah age have a responsibility not only to remember, but through that memory to "mend the world," thus imbuing Shoah education with a deep purpose.[10]

---

9 Baum, 1996.

10 Fackenheim, 1982; Hayes, 1991, ix (Holocaust Educational Foundation); www.het.org.uk;

While critics agree that such goals are laudatory, they question the extent to which classes about the Shoah in schools can hope to achieve them. Preventing future genocide through Shoah education has been criticized as unrealistic, as "...knowledge of past brutality and violence has never prevented their repetition...We hear a great deal about the supposed 'lessons' of the Holocaust, but the precedent of the 'lessons' of war offers no encouragement at all."[11] Several of the interviewees noted that despite the oft-quoted motto "Never Again," genocide continues to plague the world.

Of course, the necessity or effectiveness of an educational program cannot be judged based on criteria such as the abolition of war or racism. The objectives of Shoah education programs, more realistically, are to teach students about what happened and to positively impact their views on related issues.

B. Universal and Particularistic Messages

One fundamental question regarding Shoah education at large is whether it should be taught with a universal view, as one particularly extreme example of racism and tyranny, or from a particular perspective, as the culmination of centuries of persecution of the Jews of Europe. In most public settings outside Israel, the goals of Shoah education are mainly universal. The Shoah illustrates broadly applicable lessons related to human rights, tolerance of minorities, attitudes towards the Other, the dangers of prejudice and abuse of power, etc.

In Israel, there is a complex debate and discussion surrounding the question of the messages to be imparted through Shoah education. Four main approaches can be distinguished: 1) the Shoah should be used to teach universal values about human rights; 2) Shoah education should emphasize Zionism and the value of the State of Israel in protecting Jews from violent anti-Semitism; 3) Shoah education should reinforce Jewish values and the importance of preserving Jewish tradition; and 4) rather than drawing "lessons" from the Shoah, students should be taught the history and encouraged to ask questions and derive their own meanings.

---

http://www.ushmm.org/museum/about/.

11 Kochan, 1989: 25.

The extent to which each of these approaches should be emphasized and in what combinations were core issues explored throughout this research and in a pilot survey of Shoah education in ultra-Orthodox settings in Israel, which I directed in 2011.

As discussed in the chapter on the history of Shoah education, the messages which the Israeli educational system has undertaken to impart through teaching about the Shoah have become much broader and more sophisticated over time. Classic Zionist ideology has come under critique from within Israel and without, and some such critiques have dealt directly with Shoah memory and education. The most strident of these say Shoah memory is exploited to justify a nationalist Israeli position in its conflict with the Palestinians. Adi Ophir writes, "The Holocaust is used and abused as a means in the construction of Jewish identity, and identity...A whole nation is now prepared for the losses of a new war soon to come [with the Palestinians], which it is willing to justify in advance on the basis of the call emanating from the remainders—reminiscences and reminders—of the old loss."[12] Similarly, Uri Ram critiques Zionist-based educational approaches in which "the memory of the Holocaust has been nationalized in Israel and used for political purposes, while universal lessons have been ignored."[13] Israeli philosopher and social critic Yehuda Elkana, himself a Shoah survivor, went even farther in criticizing the ways in which Shoah memory is constructed in Israeli schools and published an essay entitled "The need to forget," in which he wrote "For our part, we must learn to forget! Today I see no more important political and educational task for the leaders of this nation than to take their stand on the side of life, to dedicate themselves to creating our future, and not to be preoccupied from morning to night with symbols, ceremonies, and lessons of the Holocaust. They must uproot the domination of that historical 'remember!' over our lives."[14]

In the school system, the views overall were less polarized. The predominant view among the interviewed experts, principals and teachers was that universal, Jewish and Zionist messages were all vital parts of Shoah education in Israel. The question was not so much a matter of choosing between mutually exclusive approaches as finding the most

12 Ophir, 2000, 179-180.
13 Ram, 2007, 211.
14 Elkana, 1988.

appropriate balance between them. Most felt that the universal and the particular (Jewish) aspects should be included and balanced and that these approaches can be seen as mutually reinforcing, not contradictory. Nevertheless, as Professor Dan Michman noted, "The universal interpretation versus the particular interpretation is implicitly very political and related to identity," and thus the question of finding a balance between the approaches is far from simple in practice. The interviewees acknowledged both the impossibility of ignoring the Jewish narrative when teaching about the Shoah in Israeli schools as well as the danger that an overly narrow perspective could be exploited to justify nationalist ends.[15]

Dr. Amos Goldberg advocated an approach which did not convert all particular perspectives to a universal one, but rather reciprocal recognition and respect for a variety of unique and distinctive perspectives. "There is undoubtedly a Jewish and Zionist aspect to the Shoah," said Professor Yuval Dror, "But this doesn't contradict that there are universal lessons; it's not either/or, it's both." Some would prefer to see more emphasis put on the universal: Dr. Daniel Blatman said, "The particular is the offspring of the universal, not the other way around." Blatman cautioned that Shoah education in Israel tends to put too much emphasis on the particularly Jewish narrative, marginalizing the universal as well as specific narratives of other people's experiences of genocide.[16] Others felt the Jewish and Zionist messages were essential: Yisrael Rosenson said, "I want it emphasized with five exclamation points that the most important message is the essentiality of the State of Israel!!!!!" Henya Weintraub, a teacher at a religious girls' school, said she teaches a broad historical background, "...but when we dive into the Shoah from my viewpoint it is a chapter of Jewish history and that is how I think it should remain." Aryeh Barnea poignantly expressed the synthesis of the different approaches: "I think we need to find an interpretation of the Shoah which will make us better Jews, better Zionists, better citizens and better human beings."

Based in part on the input of the interviewed experts, several items in the questionnaires were designed to explore the goals of Shoah education

---

15 Dr. Manuela Consonni, Dr. Jackie Feldman, Dr. Yisrael Rosenson, Heniya Weintraub, Professor Yair Auron, Ephrat Balberg-Rotenstreich, Dr. Yair Orvieto, Dr. Tova Pearlmuter, personal communication, 2009.

16 Dr. Yair Auron, Prof. Neima Barzel, Dr. Manuela Consonni, Jackie Feldman, Dr. Uri Fargo, personal communication, 2009.

in the state school system. Further, many respondents elaborated on this subject in the open comments section at the end of the questionnaire and in focus groups. The subtle and individualized opinions expressed indicate the complexity of this issue and the depth to which the teachers, principals and students think about the issue of the Shoah and how it should be addressed in the school. A recurrent theme was the extent to which Shoah education should emphasize universal, Jewish and Zionist messages.

C. Goals of Principals

> From the administration's point of view the subject of the Shoah is important regarding Jewish tradition and Zionism and in particular the crystallization of the student's personal identity regarding his heritage and Judaism. —*Female principal of junior high school*

> The subject should be addressed in different ways while raising national and universal questions connected to the essence and nature of humankind, the meaning of memory. —*Female high school principal*

> I try to educate the girls to see that "heroism" was not only resistance to the Nazis but also sanctification of God's name by preserving one's humanity, helping the weak, and making sacrifices to uphold the religious commandments in impossible circumstances.—*Female principal of religious girls' school*

To understand the context in which the Shoah is being taught, the principals were first asked about overall goals for their schools The vast majority of principals said it was "very important" that their schools educate students in concepts such as human dignity (94%), social equality (78%), and democracy (77%). Principals of general schools were somewhat more emphatic about the importance of instilling values of social equality and dignity, and far more ardent about teaching about democracy, though the differences were between responses of "very important" and "important" as virtually none in either stream responded that these values were minimally or unimportant. The principals strongly felt their schools should teach Judaism and Zionism. Zionism was equally emphasized in the two streams. Judaism and religious values, unsurprisingly, were more likely to be stressed by the principals of religious schools.

Teaching students "adherence to the law" was considered very important by 92% of the principals. This finding has interesting implications in the context of Shoah education, given Nazi ideology regarding obedience to law and orders, and that examples of "righteous gentiles" introduced in Shoah education were almost individuals who not only risked personal safety, but broke the law for a higher ideal. Also relevant is the ongoing debate in contemporary Israeli society regarding the place of civil law among other overlapping and competing value structures, such as religion and national security.[17]

Next, the principals were asked to indicate the extent to which they think teachers at their school should emphasize various goals, specifically in the realm of Shoah education. The list was designed to represent a wide range of possible goals, reflecting the various approaches described and debated by the experts: Zionist, Jewish, and universal. A first important observation is that *all* the messages were considered important by 90% or more of the principals in both school streams. The principals do not propose that their school give a uni-dimensional portrayal of the Shoah, or push one ideological line to the exclusion of other perspectives. Nevertheless, by drawing comparisons between those who said each was "very important," differences in emphasis emerge.

These reflect a similar pattern as was seen in the goals for the school at large. For principals from both streams strengthening commitment to the existence of an independent Jewish state emerged as the most important goal followed closely by strengthening identification with the fate of the Jewish people. These responses clearly express a significant difference in perspective regarding the purpose of Shoah education in Israeli schools as compared to the way the subject is taught in public school systems in other countries.

All the principals thought that bravery and heroism should be among the educational messages of Shoah studies, reflecting the type of messages they almost certainly received during their own education.

The most graphic differences between school streams occurred in

---

17 Arendt, 1963; Goldhagen, 1997; Yagil and Rattner, 2002.

response to the goals of Shoah education strengthening the democratic regime and fighting racism: the principals of the general schools were twice as likely rate these as "very important." Strengthening Jewish identity was more important for the principals of the religious schools. At the same time, strengthening universal-humanist values, the democratic regime, and commitment to fighting racism were also goals supported by almost all the principals in both streams. They propose, in other words, a balance between nationalist and universal messages.

Table 6: Principals' assessment of importance of goals of Shoah education—percentage answering "to a very great extent"

	Principals of general schools	Principals of religious schools	Total
Strengthening commitment to the existence of an independent Jewish state	88%	95%	90%
Bravery, heroism	97%	88%	94%
Strengthening identification with the destiny of the Jewish People	83%	90%	85%
Strengthening commitment to remembering the Shoah	75%	91%	81%
Strengthening the democratic regime	83%	41%	69%
Strengthening humanistic-universal values	86%	70%	81%
Strengthening commitment to fighting racism	83%	37%	67%
Strengthening Jewish identity (continuation of Jewish legacy)	75%	91%	80%
Strengthening Israeli identity (belonging to Israeli nation)	70%	74%	71%

A Smallest Space Analysis was conducted using the principals' responses to the lists of general and Shoah-related educational goals, as shown in Figure 3. Four main regions arranged in two sets of opposed concepts can be recognized. At the top are goals that pertain to directly to Shoah education. All six of the specific topics to be covered are in this region (historical background, Jewish life before and during the Shoah, the destruction process, Nazi ideology and Jewish resistance). Two educational messages are in this region: identification with the fate of the Jewish People and commitment to preserving the memory of the Shoah. This region may be divided into two sub-regions. The four items in the right-hand part of this region are academic goals related to teaching the history of the Shoah. Those on the left are educational, more related to Jewish identity as it relates to the Shoah; commitment to preserving its memory, instilling a sense of common Jewish destiny, and teaching about Jewish community life before and during the Shoah. Opposite this, at the bottom, is a region of goals pertaining to personal development (achievement, social skills, self-knowledge, etc.).

Along the horizontal axis, there is a polarization between particular-Jewish messages and goals on the left and universal messages and goals on the right. The particular-Jewish region includes goals for the whole school of teaching Torah, Judaism, Zionism, Jewish culture, and instilling religious values as well as two messages for Shoah education in particular: instilling a sense of commitment to continuity of Jewish people and belonging to the Israeli nation. The universal region includes subjects such as law, science and art, and goals related to universal values and democracy.

Into this map were placed five sub-groups of principals according to their school's stream (general and religious) and the socio-economic level (high, medium, low). The principals of the religious schools and those of schools in the lowest economic bracket (a category which includes many of the religious schools) were placed at the top, in the region of goals related to Shoah education. The principals of the religious schools were towards the right of the map, close to the region of particular-Jewish goals. The principals of the schools of lower socio-economic status were closer to the center of the map, near goals and messages related to Jewish communal life.

The principals of the general schools and schools of the highest economic bracket were placed in the region of goals related to universal values and messages. Principals of schools of median economic status were at the bottom of the map with goals related to personal development.

Figure 3: Smallest Space Analysis of Principals' Goals

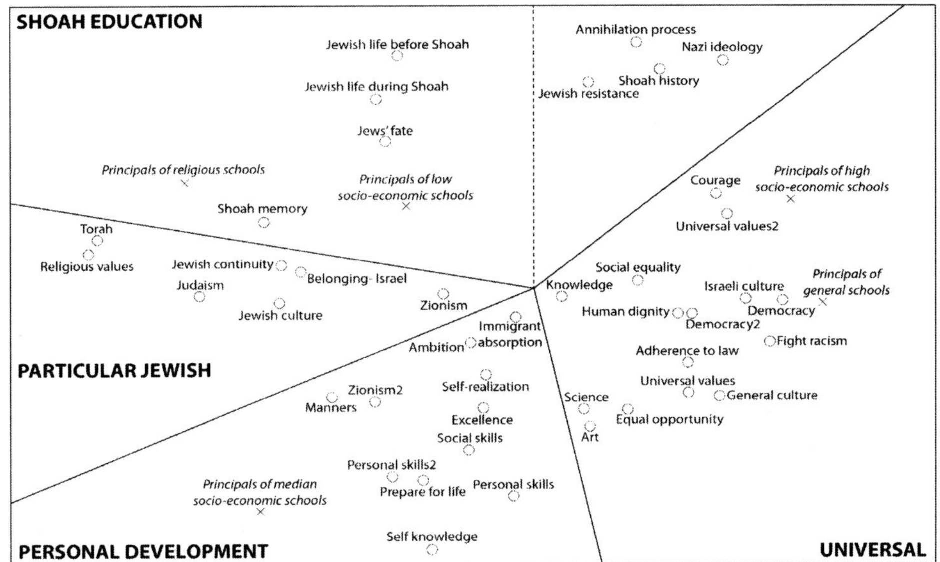

Legend

Note: Most of the questionnaire items in the map may be understood by their shortened labels. Those which have similar labels are defined below. For complete wording of the questionnaire items see Appendix B.

Personal skills—important that school teaches personal skills
Personal skills 2—goal of school
Zionism—important that school teaches Zionism
Zionism 2—goal of school to instill Zionism
Democracy—important that school educates towards democracy
Democracy 2—educational message of Shoah education
Universal values—goal of school to instill universal values
Universal values 2—educational message of Shoah education

D. Goals of Teachers

Teachers were asked to rank the importance of a similar list of goals. As with the principals, the vast majority of teachers indicated that each of the goals was important. The principals' aspirations that Shoah education should cover various perspectives related to Israeli identity, Jewish identity and universal values are reflected in the teachers' goals for presentation of the issue in the classroom. However, in comparison to the principals they were more cautious; a smaller percentage rated each as "very important." Further, their prioritization differed from that of the principals. For the teachers, strengthening commitment to remembering the Shoah was the most important goal, followed by increasing historical knowledge about the Shoah. Politically-oriented goals of strengthing the democratic regime and commitment to an independent Jewish state were less stressed by the teachers than the principals.

The teachers in the religious schools, like the principals of their schools, were much less likely to think that fighting racism, strengthening democracy, or imparting universal values are "very important" goals of Shoah education. They gave relatively more emphasis to strengthening Jewish identity. There was an interesting interaction between pedagogic approach and the goals. The teachers who were most concerned with strengthening Jewish and Israeli identity through Shoah education stressed using a combination of cognitive and experiential methods. Universal values were equally emphasized by teachers with different didactic approaches, cognitive, experiential, or a combination of the two. Weaker emphasis on didactic approach was linked to a weaker emphasis on ideological goals. Such teachers, it seems, express a lower level of enthusiasm overall.[18]

> It seems to me that it we are required to educate youth to be tolerant and also to teach them where they came from and to what an amazing nation they are connected.... I am very involved with developing a variety of educational materials ...with the goal of contributing to the education of a whole generation of Jews who are proud of Israel and

---

18 For a comparison of the goals of Shoah education among sub-groups of teachers according to their didactic approach, see Appendix C, Table f.

their people, and are also tolerant towards all human beings.—*Female English teacher in religious school of low socio-economic level*

Table 7: Teachers' assessment of importance of goals of Shoah education—percentage answering to a "very great" extent

	Teachers in general schools	Teachers in religious schools	Total
Strengthening commitment to remembering the Shoah	76%	81%	77%
Increasing knowledge of Shoah history	63%	77%	66%
Strengthening identification with the destiny of the Jewish People	63%	78%	66%
Strengthening commitment to the existence of an independent Jewish state	68%	72%	69%
Strengthening commitment to fighting racism	63%	30%	56%
Strengthening humanistic-universal values	57%	28%	51%
Strengthening Israeli identity	47%	54%	49%
Strengthening the democratic regime	52%	29%	47%

> In Shoah education there is a lot of potential for learning and for changing values, but there is also a danger of teaching nationalism or justifying immoral behavior of the victim. Therefore it is important to stress the universal values and lessons of the Shoah in the classroom and teachers' training courses.—*Female junior high school principal*

The goals of the principals and teachers reflect a deep and fundamental issue in the Israeli socio-political landscape, namely the nature of a democratic Jewish State. There are a number of challenges to popular understanding and acceptance of democratic values in Israel, such as non-democratic traditions in the countries from which many Israeli families migrated, political attitudes developed in reaction to the ongoing conflict with the Palestinians and the surrounding Muslim and Arab nations, and value systems that put religious concerns before democratic ones. Further, the history of the Shoah itself gives rise to some cynicism regarding the culpability of democracy. The National Socialist Party (Nazis) initially rose to power through democratic elections, though Hitler quickly dismantled Germany's democratic structures and assumed absolute authority. Additionally, popular anti-Semitic and anti-immigration sentiments affected the positions adopted by the United States to strictly limit the number of Jewish refugees it would accept during World War II.

Citizenship education itself has undergone a complex evolution during the decades of Israel's political and military conflicts. Since 2001, the Ministry of Education has required a course in civics education for all public high schools, based on the principle of Israel as a democratic and Jewish state. A survey of civics education in sixteen countries found that Israeli 11th graders' knowledge of basic democratic principles was comparable with the international average, although mandatory civics education begins later in Israeli schools than in many countries.[19] In 2011, this issue rose to the forefront of a political and pedagogical debate within the Ministry of Education and among different groups of teachers, regarding the extent to which civics education should emphasize democracy studies versus Jewish-Zionist studies. This, in turn,

---

19 Amadeo, et al., 2002.

relates to the changing and diverse ways in which core cultural concepts of individualism and collectivism are understood and manifest in Israeli society.[20]

E. Ethics and Theology in Shoah Education

Fundamental theological questions about the Shoah have been asked by numerous prominent Jewish writers and thinkers. In his book "To be Jewish" French-Jewish philosopher Benny Lévy writes that the post-Shoah world, "...requires a critique of the theology of the modern Jew, the theology of the silence of God after Auschwitz ... and finally a return to the notion of absolute Evil ..." a challenge he then expands the Jewish collective to "...any man insofar as he is still sensible to the question of the origin of Evil."[21]

As the Shoah has become part of Jewish-Israeli civil religion, the obligation to preserve its memory and carry on the spiritual heritage (in the various ways that may be understood) of the Jews who were killed has taken on religious overtones: Shoah survivor and contemporary Jewish philosopher Emil Fackenheim refers to remembering the Shoah as the "614th *mitzvah*," adding it (in theory) to the 613 religious commandments in Jewish traditional law.[22]

It is far beyond the scope of this study to do justice to the depth, complexity and diversity of thought which has gone into this subject, but a few major trends in theological approaches to understanding (or not) the Shoah can be indicated. A strict Orthodox worldview includes an assumption that God's hand is behind every event. Some Orthodox rabbis have contended that the Jewish People had to pay for collective sins accumulated over time or that the Shoah was punishment for modern sins of secularism and Zionism. Others see the Shoah as part of the perennial cycle of persecution of the Jews and therefore not requiring any unique theological response. Some Jewish writers have taken

---

20 Ichilov, Salomon, and Inbar, 2005; Fischer, 2002; Kashti, 2011; Mann, 2005; Neuberger, 2007; Rosenfeld, 1995, 1997; Sagy, Orr, and Bar-On, 1999; Shtull-Trauring, 2011; Velmer, 2011; Wyman, 1984.

21 Lévy, 2003.

22 Fackenheim (1982). According to the Talmud and Maimonedes' Mishneh Torah, there are 613 positive and negative commandments.

an atheistic stance; for them Auschwitz proved the impossibility of the existence of an all-powerful, benevolent God.[23]

Almost all of the teachers (90%) said they encourage their students to discuss values and ethics in classes about the Shoah, and just under half (46%) said they "absolutely" encourage such discussions. There was little difference between the religious and general schools. Two thirds of the teachers said their students raise theological questions pertaining to the Shoah. Not surprisingly, such questions were much more frequent in the religious schools: almost half (46%) of the teachers in the religious stream said their students raise theological questions very often, compared to 14% of those in the general stream. But even in the general schools, over half (58%) of the teachers said theological questions came up regularly.

Addressing students' theological questions regarding the Shoah presents a number of dangers and challenges. A study of Shoah education in the US found theological interpretations of the Shoah could lead students to blame the victims, and that, particularly in schools where students and teachers came from a Christian background, a religious interpretation of the Shoah could reinforce anti-Semitic beliefs which were themselves part of classic Christian European theology.[24] Ironically, in a parallel phenomenon in Jewish schools in France, some Shoah survivors who came to speak to classes felt students' questions regarding their level of belief and religious practice before the war cast guilt on them, as if the students saw them as guilty for their own deportation from France and suffering in the Shoah. Some felt so disturbed and offended that they ceased giving talks at these schools.[25]

In Israeli schools, teachers are faced with students' questions on difficult theological questions such as how a merciful God could allow the Shoah to happen, or what the Jews did to "deserve" such a fate. These are questions which have been posed (and remain largely unanswerable) by some of the most important Jewish writers, thinkers and philosophers of our time. Almost all of the teachers said they encourage discussions of values and ethics when teaching about the Shoah. Not surpris-

23 For authors advocating such a stance see: Berkovits, 1973; Rubenstein, 1966; Tzimerman, 1974; For academic reviews of studies discussing such an opinion see: Braiterman, 1998; Caplan, 2001; Friedman, 1991; Katz, 1983; Porat, 1992; Yablonka, 2009.

24 Spector, 2007.

25 Hazan, 2005.

ingly, theological discussions are much more prevalent in the religious schools; whereas just over half of the teachers in general schools say that their students ask theological questions regarding the Shoah, 88% of the teachers in religious schools are asked theological questions during Shoah education. Overall, the teachers felt comfortable responding to these questions. The teachers in the religious schools feel somewhat more comfortable responding to such questions. The teachers in the religious schools were more likely to say they felt 'absolutely' comfortable responding to such questions. A tenth of the teachers in the general schools felt distinctly uncomfortable addressing theological questions regarding the Shoah.[26]

The students themselves said that they are largely interested in religious and moral questions pertaining to the Shoah. While, predictably, a higher percentage of students in religious schools said they are interested in specifically religious questions (76%), over half (57%) of those in the general schools are also. Interest in more general "moral questions" was even stronger, and was similar in the two streams (86% of students in religious schools and 84% of those in general schools). A small (but adamant) minority was not interested "at all" in addressing such issues. One student wrote, "Enough with the stupidities of *Tanakh* (Bible) and faith ... it's a waste of breath."

> Students aren't encouraged enough to ask questions, to think for themselves, to be curious, to ethical questions that relate to our lives today as humans and not just as Jews.—*Female student*

> The emphasis doesn't always have to be on the horrors, which we already have seen in enough awful pictures. We need to explore the ramifications of the Shoah on the world today...and to pay attention that today there are similar horrors and the State of Israel isn't doing anything...it's something to think about. —*Female student*

Shoah education in Israel has multiple goals, variously emphasized by

26 For data on teachers' responses to questionnaire items regarding theological and ethical discussions of the Shoah in their classes, see Appendix C, Table g.

different individuals in the system. Universal messages about tolerance, support for democracy, Jewish religious values, and Zionist-national ideology all have their proponents and critics. Most educators advocate some balance between the three, along with encouraging students to question and draw their own conclusions based on what they learn about the subject.

In both streams, instilling in students a commitment to remembering the Shoah strong and strengthening their identities as proud Jews and Israelis were considered of primary importance. The teachers and principals of the general schools attributed relatively more importance to messages related to universal values and democracy than did those in the religious schools.

The pilot survey among students in ultra-Orthodox teaching colleges found a third approach, which placed religious considerations above all else. In this segment of Israeli society, Shoah education is taught through the lens of the schools' religious worldview, with the goals of strengthening students' faith and commitment to religious tradition. Universal goals are marginalized and there is a somewhat antagonistic view of the classic Zionist approach. In comparison to the independent religious school system, the two state school systems are more similar than different from each other.

Teachers make an effort to integrate Shoah studies with other subjects such as citizenship and Jewish studies. They encourage their students to raise questions and discuss the meaning the Shoah has for their world today. The next chapter looks at the ways in which these goals of Shoah education are reflected in the beliefs and attitudes expressed by the students.

VI. BELIEFS, VALUES AND ATTITUDES TOWARDS THE SHOAH

A connection to Israel and Zionism has to be built around strong values of the Israeli nation and moral social ethics, not on the basis of the Shoah.—*Female junior high school principal*

You can't form identity on tragedy. People naturally want to flee from tragedy.—*Prof. Eliezer Schweid, personal communication, 2009.*

Questions about the Shoah bothered me enough that I had to investigate my system of values, the things I do and don't do in order to be a better person who has a positive impact and makes a contribution to my environment.—*Female student*

Shoah education in Israel occurs in a context of strongly developed Israeli-Jewish identity combined with values related to democracy and universalism.

- Students are proud to be Jewish and Israeli.
- They also espouse commitment to universal values, democracy and the need to fight racism.
- The Shoah affects the worldview of most Israeli students and particularly the teachers. They are committed to preserving and perpetuating its memory.
- At the same time, memory of the Shoah is *not* among the most compelling aspects of their Jewish identity—family, Israel, culture, language and religion are all more important components of identity.
- The majority of students said they feel a sense of identification with Shoah survivors; this highlights a shift from previous generations which wanted to distance themselves from an identity of victimization associated with the Shoah.

• The Shoah is perceived as a tragedy for all humankind, not only the Jews, by students and teachers alike.

• Teachers and students see the creation of the State of Israel as a necessary response to the Shoah, and feel it is less likely that another genocidal attempt against Jews could happen in Israel.

* * * * * *

French historian and philosopher Pierre Nora differentiates between the social science of history, which is concerned with chronicling events of the past, and the social phenomenon of memory, which links an affective understanding of past events with identity and sense of belonging in the present.[1] As seen in the previous chapter, the goals for Shoah education simultaneously concern history, memory, and identity, past and present. Such ambitious and diverse goals as promoting tolerance, upholding democracy, commemoration of victims, instilling Jewish identity (in Jewish schools), and collective atonement (in countries where the Shoah was perpetrated) cannot be achieved if the subject is approached in a purely academic manner. The values, attitudes and beliefs of educators—principals, curriculum designers, museum curators, tour guides, and especially school teachers—impact how it is taught. The values, attitudes, and beliefs brought by the students are no less significant in how the lessons are received and understood.[2] Thus even when the same historical facts are taught using similar materials and methods, the nature and tone of Shoah education differs dramatically in various school environments.

Adolescence is a critical time in moral development, when individuals begin to move beyond childhood's egotistical concepts of obedience, punishment, and reward. Adolescents' consideration expands beyond the self towards that of the larger group, and they strive to be perceived positively by others. Many people remain at this stage of "conventional" morality into adulthood.[3]

In recent years, some researchers have critiqued this classic cognitive approach to moral development, arguing that there is a parallel social

---

1 Nora, 1989, 1998.

2 Schuitema, Dam, and Veugelers, 2008; Evans, 2008 and personal communication, 2008.

3 Kohlberg, 1981.

process by which children and youth absorb the moral code of conduct they are expected to follow from interactions in their home, community, and school environments.[4] Another limitation of the cognitive approach is that someone may profess a high level of moral development, yet act immorally.[5]

"Moral education" has become part of the educational landscape, although it raises numerous challenges and controversies in multicultural societies.[6] Shoah education inherently challenges people to consider issues pertaining to the higher levels of moral development of post-conventional and principled morality. Eichmann's oft-quoted defense during his trial was that he was "following orders" and the passivity of the countless bystanders typify a 'law and order' morality gone awry. In contrast, those who resisted the Nazis or non-Jews who sheltered Jews during the Shoah displayed a high level of morality only a minority of people ever achieve. The stated goals of Shoah education challenge teachers to probe the deeper questions surrounding the Shoah, to try to make such complex moral issues understandable to high school and even junior high school students.

Education programs and curricula used in other countries that include the Shoah as part of studies of racism and genocide have been found to reduce stereotyping and prejudice in general and anti-Semitism in particular among students, at least in the short term. An analysis of a teacher-training program in connection with an anti-segregation campaign in Boston found half the participating Caucasian teachers subsequently took action to implement changes in their classroom based on the ideas taught in the course. Several studies in Europe found that students reported positive, if modest, changes in their attitudes regarding tolerance in general and the Jews in particular following Shoah education programs. One of the few studies tracking longitudinal impacts of Shoah education on students' attitudes found among their sample in Scotland that differences in attitude between students who took part in a Shoah education program and those who did not faded over time. While much has been written advocating or critiquing Shoah education as a part of multicultural, anti-racist or

---

4 Alexander, 2003, 2004; Strike, 1996.

5 Mordecai Nisan, personal communication, 2010. See his works on Kohlberg and moral judgment in general (Nisan 1992, 1993).

6 Schuitema, Dam, and Veugelers, 2008; Wardekker, 2001.

tolerance education, there have been few empirical assessments of the short- and long-term impacts of such programs on attitudes. This research makes a contribution to filling this gap.[7]

Part of the current research looked at the values and beliefs held by the students and teachers in order to understand how these affect and are affected by Shoah education in Israeli state schools. In particular, the value system of the students was explored in depth. This included not only beliefs pertaining directly to the Shoah, but also regarding Israel, the Jewish religion and the Jewish People, and attitudes about education in general.

A. Students' Basic Values

The questionnaire distributed to the students included several items designed to assess their underlying value system, not limited to attitudes about the Shoah itself. In terms of their school lives, they were asked to rank the importance of various aspects of their school lives (i.e. friends, grades, learning environment) and specific academic subjects (math, Jewish studies, history, etc.). They were also asked to rank the importance of general values.

In many ways, the students in the religious and general schools were similar to each other and their peers in other countries.[8] Their main concerns in school were being with friends, having fun, and getting good grades. They also placed strong emphasis on personal development. They want to learn things which are practical for their future and interesting in a pleasant school environment. Only a small percentage of students in either stream said it was very important for them to be the best in their class. Most described themselves as "good" or "very good" students; only a small minority saw themselves as either excellent or below average. The stark difference in the degree of importance attached to getting good grades (65%) versus being at the top of the class (12%) indicates that students did not value competition with one's

7 Carrington and Short, 1997; Hill and Augoustinos, 2001; Ijaz and Ijaz, 1981; Lawrence and Tatum, 1997; Maitles, 2008; Maitles and Cowan, 2008; Short and Reed, 2004; Turner and Brown, 2008.

8 The students' responses in this survey mirror those given to a parallel set of questions in a general survey of Israeli high school students done in 2000 (Cohen, 2005), so their basic outlook can be said to be fairly consistent among this generation of Israeli youth.

classmates. They were more concerned with being part of the *hevre* (group of friends). Social cohesion and crystallization (called *gibush,* in Hebrew) is a core value in contemporary Jewish-Israeli society.[9] Over 90% of the students said they are happy, and 30% said they are "very happy," indicating that social alienation is not a large problem among these students.

The students placed a lot of value on enjoying life and being at peace with oneself. The students in the general schools gave stronger emphasis to the former, those in the religious schools to the latter. Respecting parents was a value for all students (99%) though the students in the religious schools were more likely to say it was "very important" to them. Students in the religious schools, predictably, gave significantly more emphasis to believing in God and being a religious person. The differences in values extended beyond the narrow realm of religion: students in the general schools were more likely to say that working hard and making money were important to them, while those in the religious schools gave relatively more emphasis to helping the needy and doing volunteer work. These last two values were manifest in action: students in the religious schools were more likely to do volunteer work through their schools and to participate in youth movements, which are also often involved in community work.

Learning English was considered more important by the students than any other subject (math, science, history), indicating the extent to which Israeli youth culture has been Americanized and linked to global media and entertainment networks conducted in English. Bible and Jewish studies were given less emphasis than most of the secular subjects, though the students in the religious schools, logically, were about twice as likely as their peers in the general schools to say these subjects were very important to them. Particularly telling for the discussion of Shoah education is that in the general schools a larger percentage of students said history was more important to them than Bible or Jewish studies, whereas in the religious schools the three subjects were equally important.

---

9 Katriel and Nesher, 1986; Lemish, 2002.

B. Jewish and Israeli Identity

Study of the Shoah among Jewish populations anywhere in the world and particularly in Israel touches on fundamental and complex issues of group identity. The concepts of "Jewish identity" in all its manifold manifestations, including the relatively recent "Jewish-Israeli identity" are notoriously difficult to define, and have been the subject of much research and academic discussion.[10] It is far beyond the scope of this study to offer an overview of this theoretical debate.[11] In the context of the study on Shoah education, respondents were asked various questions regarding their identities as Jews and Israelis, and how they saw study of the Shoah as related to these identities. The questionnaire items regarding Jewish and Israeli identity were designed to address all the various parameters such as religion, culture, family connections, education and so forth. See the students' questionnaire in Appendix B and resultant data on these issues in Tables 8 and 9 and Figure 5.

While some Israeli and international critics have said that Shoah education is being exploited to fortify ethnic-religious-nationalist identity,[12] it seems more accurate to say that in Israel the Shoah is being taught to students with an already strongly developed sense of identity. In the open questions and interviews, students expressed a wide range of opinions, from strongly national ("We have no other country!") to religious ("It is important to remember the Shoah and to make an effort to pass Jewish heritage to future generations") to universal ("I think we should all live together without divisions by race, religion or origin.").

Overwhelmingly, the students said they were proud to be Jewish and Israeli. They identified strongly with the Jewish People and said it was important to them to feel like part of that collective. They would not choose to be members of a different religion or nationality even if, hypothetically, they could; that is, over three quarters said that they would elect to be Jewish Israelis again if they were "born again." The Jewish elements of their identity were slightly stronger than the nationalist ones, a finding in line with other studies documenting a shift in Israeli society from a predominance of national aspects of identity among previous

---

10 Auerbach, 2001; Cohen and Horenczyk, 1999; Goldberg and Krausz, 1993; Graham, 2004; Herman, 1977; Horowitz, 2000; Rebhun, 2004; Wettstein, 2002, among many others

11 See in particular, Cohen 2010 for a state of the art of Jewish identity study.

12 Gur-Ze'ev, 2000, 2001; Ram, 2007; Zertal, 2005; Zuckermann, 2010, among others.

generations to a relatively greater emphasis on Jewish aspects among younger generations.[13] Even so, almost all expressed a commitment to the existence of the State of Israel, further manifest in their stated intentions to continue living there and to serve in the army. Almost all the males (97%) and a large majority of the females (84%) said they intend to serve in the army. In the religious schools, 18% said they do not intend to go into the army, compared to 7% of those in the general stream: this is likely attributable to the fact that many girls in the religious stream chose to do alternative national service such as in schools or hospitals, which is a common and well-accepted option for them.

The students' strong Jewish and Israeli identities do not preclude a commitment to universal values, democracy, and the need to fight racism. The vast majority (83%) said they felt committed to democratic values, though this was somewhat less strongly expressed than their commitment to the national and religious collectives.

The feeling of connection between Israeli-Jewish youth and their peers in other countries was not as strong as the professed identification with the abstract concept of the Jewish People would imply. Only 60% said they feel connected to Jews in the Diaspora, raising questions about their perception of the Jewish People as a global entity. Mutual alienation between Israeli and Diaspora Jews has been an issue of great concern in the Jewish world for decades.[14] Projects such as sending emissaries from Israel to work in Jewish educational settings and organizing meetings between visiting Diaspora youth and Israelis have been launched to try to make the connection more real and personal.[15]

1. Differences by school stream. Since the majority of students answered affirmatively to each of the values, differences between the sub-groups can better be seen by looking at the percentage that chose the strongest possible response. Students in the religious schools were significantly more likely (20% or more) to say they were "absolutely" proud to be Jewish and that being part of the Jewish people was important to them. They were also more likely to say they were "absolutely" proud to be Israeli, though the gap was smaller. It has been repeatedly

---

13 Auron, 1993a, 2008; Liebman and Yadgar, 2004.

14 For students' degree of agreement with statements expressing Jewish, Israeli, and universal values, see Appendix C, Table h.

15 Beilin, 2000; Cohen, 2000, 2011b; Della Pergola and Rebhun, 1994; Elazar, 1977; Kopelowitz, 2003; Levy, 2002; Marans and Bell, 2006.

found that religious youth in Israel have a stronger sense of loyalty to the collective, whether defined as the family or the Jewish People or Israel as a whole, while secular youth are more concerned with individual freedom.[16] The students in the religious schools also identified more strongly with universal values. These values were not specified in the questionnaire, but may be assumed to include values such as honesty, generosity, and respect for others.

Table 8: Jewish, Israeli and universal values of students by grade and type of school—percentage answering "absolutely"

	Students in 9th grade, both streams	**Students in 12th grade, both streams**	**Students in general schools, both grade levels**	**Students in religious schools, both grade levels**
Proud to be Jewish	73%	74%	70%	90%
Important to feel part of Jewish people	66%	70%	64%	87%
Proud to be Israeli	63%	64%	61%	73%
Committed to fighting racism	53%	52%	53%	50%
Identify with democratic values	38%	47%	43%	36%
Identify with universal values	26%	35%	31%	36%

16 Levy and Guttman, 1976; Levy, Levinson, and Katz, 1993; Sagy, Orr, and Bar-On, 1999.

2. Differences by age. In comparing the 9th and 12th graders, we found that both universal values and religious-national pride were well-established by junior high school and gradually strengthened over the course of their school careers. The older students were more strongly committed to universal and democratic values. As civics education is not a mandatory part of the curriculum in Israel until high school, the younger students were likely to be less familiar with what is meant by "democratic values." Additionally, the more mature students may have a greater understanding of the higher moral concepts related to democracy and universal values. The older students' stronger identification with universal values, democracy and the commitment to fight racism may be understood in the context of theory regarding cognitive and emotional development of young people. Among older students there tends to be increased emphasis on cognitive understanding compared to emotional feelings, and one-dimensional dichotomies are replaced with multi-dimensional, complex comprehension of issues.[17]

C. Shoah Memory in the Israeli Worldview

Against this background, it is now possible to better understand the role the memory of the Shoah plays within the worldview of the students and the culture of the school. The importance attached to the subject was expressed again and again by the surveyed experts, principals, teachers, and students.

1. Perceived impact of the Shoah on worldview. Three quarters of the students and virtually all of the teachers (96%) said that the Shoah influences their worldview.

Respondents were not asked to specify what that worldview was or in what way the Shoah influenced it, although this was explored by some in the open questions, interviews and focus groups. The ways in which the Shoah may impact one's worldview are varied indeed. Even among those who went through the Shoah themselves, the impact of the trauma was far from homogenous, as can be seen in the wide range of political, religious and social attitudes which have been expressed and attributed to

17 Aboud 1988; Godsi, 1998; Kohlberg, 1981; Phillips-Berenstein, 2001; Piaget, 1932.

their experience.[18]

The key result of the responses to this questionnaire item was the widespread perception among the students and teachers in both school streams that knowledge of the Shoah impacts the way they see the world.

The role of Shoah memory in Israeli national identity is highlighted by the comments of several principals regarding new immigrants, and the importance of educating them to be able to share in this aspect of the common culture.

> Most of our students are new immigrants from the CIS and Ethiopia, or they were born in Israel but haven't been sufficiently integrated into "Israeliness" with all its implications. This is the Ethiopian students' first encounter with the subject of the Shoah.... I integrate [Shoah education] activities at the school with activities at the dormitory.—*Male high school vice principal*

> Many immigrants who came from the former Soviet Union have no roots or awareness of national affiliation, therefore our emphasis is to strengthen the feeling of affiliation and the backbone of Zionist values.—*Female junior high school principal*

2. Commitment to memory preservation. Remembering pivotal events, particularly those in which the Jews' national survival was threatened, is a fundamental religious imperative in Judaism, and these students, religious and secular alike, have fully integrated this concept. The Shoah is not simply something to be studied; they feel an obligation to carry on the memory. 94% of the students said they were committed to preserving the memory of the Shoah. Two thirds said they are "absolutely" committed to it, with a higher percentage of students in religious schools—particularly the 12th graders—asserting this more emphatic response.

---

18 In addition to the diverse views expressed in the writings of Shoah survivors, psychological studies on the impact of trauma on worldview have found a range of attitudes among Shoah survivors, see for example: Carmil and Breznitz, 1991; Isserman, 2009; Palgi, Shrira, and Ben-Ezra, 2011; Young, 1990.

We may ask, what does it mean to preserve the memory of something which occurred before the students and even their teachers were born, and far from the country in which they live? How collective memories are formulated and transmitted is a fascinating subject itself. Maurice Halbwachs pioneered the concept of collective memory, based on the sociological theories of Durkheim, his mentor. Collective memory is carried by a social group whose identity is connected to an event (often a traumatic event). Halbwachs differentiated between *autobiographical memory* of events one personally experienced, *historical memory* learned from historical sources, and *collective memory*, the formation of which is an active relationship between the past event and a group's present sense of identity. Thus different groups will have different collective memories of the same event, even if they have access to the same historical sources.[19]

Collective memories of the Shoah held by Jews and non-Jews, Israelis and Europeans, will inevitably differ. In the countries where the Shoah occurred (as described in a case study of Shoah memory in Poland) there is a multi-layered process of "remembering to remember" (mourning, commemorating, coming to terms with the past), "remembering to benefit" (rectification and reconciliation) and "remembering to forget" (backlash, historical revisionism).[20] In Germany, Shoah memory is based primarily on official documentation and the narrative is from the perspective of the perpetrator, even if the tone is one of regret and apology.[21] In each case, the Jews are the object of the remembering.

In Israel (and Jewish Diaspora communities), the Jews are the rememberers as well as the remembered. The testimonies and memoirs of survivors are of the utmost importance. Yad Vashem, the largest of Israel's Shoah memorial museums, presents itself as, "...the Jewish people's living memorial to the Holocaust." The interpretation is not meant to be impartial; the narrative is from the Jewish perspective. The phrase "living memorial" indicates an ongoing interaction between the present and past. Even within the Israeli-Jewish collective, memory of the Shoah

19 Halbwachs, 1950. Maurice Halbwachs (1877-1945) was a French philosopher and sociologist who died at the hands of the Nazis. His family was Catholic, but he was a prominent socialist and as such was deported to Buchenwald, where he died of dysentery (Friedman, 1946). His seminal work *La mémoire collective (On Collective Memory)* was published posthumously in 1950.

20 Michlic, 2012.

21 Schlant, 1999, among many others.

is not homogenous among different segments of society: religious, secular, Ashkenazi, Sephardi-Mizrahi, etc. Different perspectives within the Jewish narrative are expressed in some of the other Shoah educational sites in Israel. For example, the archives aimed towards the ultra-Orthodox population emphasizes presenting examples of how Jews preserved their humanity, values, faith, and religious practice even in the extreme conditions of the Shoah and the death camps. The common denominator is the conviction that the Jewish People should not forget the attempt at their annihilation in the twentieth century. The burden of carrying the memory of Shoah, first bequeathed to the children of survivors, is now seen as the task of the Jewish People as a whole.[22]

3. Identification with survivors. Almost three quarters of the students (73%) said they feel a sense of identification with Shoah survivors. This is an important finding for several reasons. First, it shows the extent to which the collective memory of the Shoah has been internalized. It illustrates the active relationship between the historical event of the Shoah and the present sense of identity among Jewish Israeli youth. Though they do not see their Jewish identity as being founded upon the memory of the Shoah, they see themselves as linked to the victims and survivors through their common identity as Jews. Second, this shows a radical shift in attitude since the early days of the State, when Israeli veteran pioneers saw a rift between themselves, representing the New Jews, and the refugees they saw as representing the Diaspora mentality they wanted to shed. Over time, the sense of common identity has strengthened, not faded. This is the product of education and socialization which now encourages Israeli youth to feel a sense of connection with the victims of the Nazis.

Identification with the survivors may be hypothetical, or concretely manifest as concern with their current well-being. In Israel, there has been considerable media attention given to the plight of elderly Shoah survivors and difficulties they had in receiving benefits,[23] and the students were inevitably aware of this issue. Barely a quarter (27%) said they think the State of Israel is treating Shoah survivors well. The sense of identification with the survivors translated into the opinion that the State has a high level of responsibility towards them.

---

22 Epstein and Lefkovitz, 2001.

23 Eglash, 2011; Zarchin, 2008.

> The treatment of Shoah survivors is disgraceful. Awareness of this has to be raised urgently in order to change how they are treated as quickly as possible.
>
> —*Female student*

Interestingly, while the students in the religious schools expressed stronger pride in being Israeli and especially in being Jewish, these differences did not translate into markedly different attitudes regarding the Shoah. The responses of students in the two school streams to these statements about the Shoah differed by only a few percentage points. For example, the students in the religious schools were more likely by 6% to say that that Israel is "absolutely" an answer to the Shoah. On other items their answers were even closer.

4. Scope of the tragedy. Students and teachers were asked if they saw the Shoah as a tragedy for all humankind or for the Jews alone. This question was included to explore one of the basic issues underlying Shoah education; namely, whether it should be portrayed as a crime against humanity, against the Jewish People, or a combination of the two.[24] Over 80% of the students and teachers said they see the Shoah as a tragedy for all humanity; this was consistent among all the groups. The younger students and students in religious schools were very slightly less likely to note the global dimension of the Shoah, but they differed by only a few percentage points. There was even less difference between the teachers in the religious and general schools. That is, they were essentially equally likely to think (and presumably to teach) that the Shoah was a tragedy for all people, not just the Jews. Interestingly, the junior high school teachers were more likely by 10% to say the Shoah was a tragedy for all, though their students were less likely to say so. This gap between the views of the teachers and their students deserves further study.[25]

Images from the Shoah have entered global collective memory as seminal symbols of evil, human brutality, and victimization.[26] As discussed earlier, in public forums outside Israel, discourse about the

---

24 Inclusion of this question in the survey was suggested by Dr. Mordechai (Morale) Bar-On during his interview.

25 For responses of students and teachers, with comparison by school stream and level, to the question regarding scope of the Shoah see Appendix C, Tables i and j.

26 Lévy and Sznaider, 2006; Olick, Vinitzky-Seroussi and Lévy, 2011.

Shoah has been increasingly universalized. This trend has been both advocated and criticized by many writers, Jewish and not. On the one hand, the Shoah serves as a powerful example for opening discussions about tolerance and racism, good and evil, minority rights, democracy, and other values applicable to all people and all times. It takes into account other victims of the Nazis (handicapped, homosexuals, political opponents) making possible broad empathy and identification with the victims.[27] On the other hand, such approaches have been criticized as de-contextualizing the events and minimizing or ignoring the history of anti-Semitism in Europe and the Nazis' concentrated effort to wipe out the Jewish People.[28] One teacher condemned the generalization of the Shoah as a universal rather than Jewish tragedy as a type of Shoah denial.

Another criticism is that sometimes the detachment of the Shoah from the Jewish experience leads to "reattachment" to other narratives: American, European, Palestinian, etc.[29] Extending this argument, if anyone can identify as a victim on the level of Shoah victims, their oppressors also become equal in evil to the Nazis.[30] Some writers have argued that although the Nazis killed millions of non-Jews as well, the targeting of the Jews as a race to be completely eliminated was unique, and therefore the tragedy suffered by the Jews was unparalleled.[31]

In a related issue, over half of the students said they strongly objected to use of images and words from the Shoah in relation to other political issues (including protests within Israel against various government policies, anti-Israeli rallies around the world, and a wide range of other issues such as abortion or animal slaughterhouses). A quarter felt it was marginally appropriate to use such images in certain circumstances. Opinion on this was similar in the two school streams.[32] One student

---

27 Lévy and Sznaider, 2006; Milchman and Rosenberg, 1997.

28 Cargas, 2003; Wyman, 1984.

29 Rothberg, 2009.

30 Alexander, 2009.

31 Alexander, 2009; Hancock, 1988.

32 Nazi images have been used both in Israel and in other countries, in relation to a range of political issues. Men and boys from an ultra-Orthodox community dressed as Shoah victims, in striped outfits with yellow stars, protesting what they called a "spiritual Holocaust" perpetrated against them by the Israeli authorities. In protests against the Israeli government's decision to dismantle the Gush Katif settlements in the Gaza strip, protesters wore orange stars similar to the yellow stars of the Shoah era. Outside Israel, it has become commonplace for anti-Israel protesters to use swastikas imposed on the Israeli flag and other Shoah images turned against Israel. An anti-

declared that people who curse others using words connected to the Shoah should be "severely punished."

The students' views reflect wider opposition to this political tactic. Politicization of the Shoah was listed as one of the obstacles to effective teaching of the subject noted by the Israeli representative to the Task Force for International Cooperation on Holocaust Education, Remembrance, and Research. In 2012 the Israeli government considered a ban on use of Shoah images in political protests.[33]

> There is too much talk about the Shoah. Instead of asking questions, the State should start to really help the survivors!—*Male student*

5. Israel as an "answer" to the Shoah. Another question posed to both the students and the teachers was whether they think the establishment of the State of Israel was an "answer" to the Shoah. Of the teachers, 83% answered affirmatively, as did 84% of the students. The students were somewhat more likely to say it was "absolutely" so. Among the teachers, the responses of those in the religious and general schools differed by only a few percent. The history teachers were somewhat less likely (by 8%) to say that Israel was an answer to the Shoah. Among the students, the older students in both school systems were more likely to agree with this sentiment, indicating it is a message they internalize over the course of their Shoah education, particularly in the religious schools; the 12th graders in the religious schools were more likely by 10% to "absolutely" agree that Israel was an answer to the Shoah.[34]

The older students were more likely to see the State of Israel as an "answer" to the Shoah. Some of the students had clearly internalized this message, as articulated in the open section of the questionnaire; one student, for example, cited the Shoah as a reason Israelis should not move to Diaspora countries. At the same time, others felt uncomfortable with linking the two too closely, as one wrote "It is a shame to emphasize the position that Israel was established because of the Shoah. In my

abortion film issued in the USA used images of concentration camps. (Anti-Defamation League, 2009; Associated Press, 2003, 2009; Barkat, 2004; Kershner, 2012; Neistat, 2011).

33 BBC, 2012; ITF country report on Israel, 2005: 7-8.

34 For students' responses to statements regarding the potential of another Shoah and protection offered by the State of Israel, with comparison by school stream and level, see Appendix C, Table k.

opinion the Shoah was a factor that expedited it, but not the only one."

Two related questions posed to the students asked whether they thought it was possible that another Shoah would happen somewhere in the world, and if they thought it would be possible for such an atrocity to happen in Israel. Just over two thirds of the students said they thought there could be another Shoah somewhere. Overall about a quarter said another Shoah could "absolutely" happen elsewhere in the world. As noted in the introduction, the term *Shoah* is understood to refer specifically to institutionalized mass murder targeting Jews (and not to other examples of genocide which have taken place). A quarter thought a Shoah could happen in Israel and about 10% said a Shoah could "absolutely" happen in Israel—this was consistent across the grades and the two school streams. Even this minority reflects some degree of decline in confidence that having an independent state offered ultimate protection to the Jews. As discussed earlier, Israelis' experiences in the numerous wars cast some doubt on this early Zionist tenet that Israel would offer a safe haven. Nevertheless, there is still a fair amount of confidence among the majority students that, at least, an atrocity of that magnitude could not happen in their country, while they fear it could happen elsewhere. There was more variation in the responses to this. The 12th graders were more likely to foresee the possibility of a Shoah in Israel, as were the students in the general schools. Despite the intensity of the political and military conflicts Israel faces, Israeli youth see their fate as more secure in Israel than in the Diaspora; nevertheless, some significant fears for the future in their home country persist.

6. Structural analysis of students' attitudes. The SSA in Figure 4 gives a holistic portrayal of the students' attitudes and beliefs. The statement that the Shoah affects one's worldview is at the center of the map. This is a core attitude, shared by students with differing attitudes regarding Judaism, Israel, and universal values.

There are three main vertical slices. At the left is a region containing the two statements regarding the potentiality of another Shoah. These statements are distinct in that they are attitudes about the Shoah that pertain to the future. In the middle is a region related to treatment of Shoah survivors. The third region, at the right, includes statements pertaining to students' personal values. Each of these vertical slices may be divided into two sub-regions: general at the top and specific (Jewish) at the bottom.

Beginning with the right side of the map, which contains the majority of the items, we see that the lower right-hand region contains the values which are related to Israel or Judaism, such as commitment to the State of Israel and proud to be Jewish. In the upper right-hand region are the general (not specifically Jewish) values. This may be divided into two sub-regions. The one towards the top of the map contains the universal values: commitment to fighting racism, identification with democratic and universal values, and interest in moral questions pertaining to the Shoah. The central sub-region contains two items which relate directly to the Shoah: commitment to preserving memory of the Shoah and identification with survivors.

The central region contains only a single item, the statement that the State of Israel is treating Shoah survivors well. The corresponding top half of this central region in the "general" side of the map is empty. The possibility of empty regions is one of the interesting features of SSA. Empty regions indicate unasked questions or unaddressed issues, guiding subsequent research. Students were not asked how they think Shoah survivors are being treated in other parts of the world, an area which would be interesting to explore in the future.

At the left side of the map are the two statements pertaining to the possibility of another Shoah somewhere in the world or in Israel. The belief that another Shoah could happen somewhere in the world is in the upper half of the map, which corresponds with general or universal concepts. The belief that a Shoah could happen in Israel is in the lower half of the map, which contains other attitudes specifically related to Judaism and Israel. The distance between these two items and all the other variables indicates that students' opinion on this question is not strongly impacted by their other views. The statements that a Shoah could happen in Israel and that the State of Israel is an "answer" to the Shoah are diametrically opposed.

Figure 4: SSA of students' beliefs, values and attitudes towards the Shoah

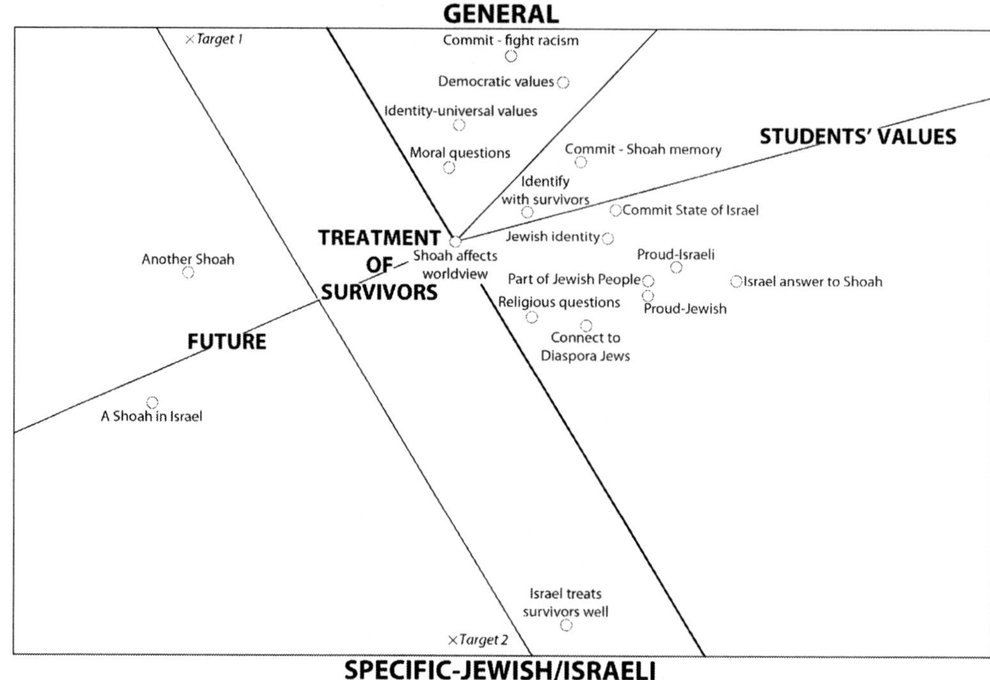

Legend

Target 1—Shoah was tragedy for all mankind

Target 2—Shoah was tragedy for the Jews alone

While the vast majority of both students and teachers agreed that the Shoah had implications beyond the specific experience of the Jews, it is difficult to ascertain precisely how they—and particularly the adolescent students—perceived the concept of universal versus specific dimensions of the tragedy. In order to better understand what the students meant when they said that the Shoah was a tragedy for all humankind, we introduced two sub-groups of students as external variables into the map of values: those who said the Shoah was a tragedy for all mankind and those who said it was a tragedy for the Jews alone. Those who said the Shoah was a tragedy for all mankind are at the top of the map, close to the items "commitment to fight racism," "identify with democratic values," and "identify with universal values." Those who said the Shoah was a tragedy for the Jews alone are at the bottom of the map. The placement of these groups is based on the correlation between responses to this question and responses to the other beliefs. Agreement with the statement that the Shoah was a tragedy for all humankind was more strongly linked with statements regarding universal and democratic values than with statements expressing Jewish and Israeli identity. The strongest links were with universal and democratic values. That is, someone who says the Shoah was a tragedy for all humankind was also likely to identify with universal values. In contrast, those who said the Shoah was a tragedy for the Jews alone had a negative correlation with these statements, "pushing" them to the opposite side of the map.

D. The Shoah and Anti-Semitism as Components of Jewish Identity

In another section of the questionnaire, students were given various "reasons to be Jewish" and asked to indicate all those they felt expressed a component of their Jewish identity. These were: birth, commitment, culture, family, loyalty, memory of the Shoah, choice, education, religion, Israel, hope, reaction to anti-Semitism, Hebrew language, connection to Jews around the world, and destiny.[35] This list of components of identity has been developed over the course of surveys of various populations of Jewish youth around the world. It draws on previous theories, scales, and typologies of ethnic-religious identity in general and Jewish identity in particular. The Jewish identity of the students in the two school systems were quite similar; the single item "religion" is the only one for which their responses differed by even 10%.

Kinship is the most widely recognized component of identification at large, and among this population "birth" and "family" were the most commonly chosen "reasons to be Jewish." Religion is also a strong component of Jewish identity among students in both school streams, though it was significantly more frequently chosen by those in the religious schools. Among the students in the religious schools, "religion" was chosen more frequently than "birth." Memory of the Shoah was *not* one of the more commonly chosen, selected by less than half the

---

35 For an in-depth explanation of the list of components of identity, see Cohen, 2009b.

students (44%). Even fewer—less than a fifth—saw "reaction to anti-Semitism" as a reason to be Jewish.[36] These two components, especially reaction to anti-Semitism, are reactionary elements of identity. Thus, while almost all students said that the Shoah affects their worldview, it is not a foundational element of their Jewish identity.

Also, tellingly, connection to Diaspora Jews was the weakest component for this population; while the vast majority of students said they identify with Shoah victims and survivors, they do not feel a strong sense of connection with their Jewish peers living in other countries.

A Smallest Space Analysis was conducted on the Israeli students' responses to the components of Jewish identity. Four main regions may be identified: Historical, Biological, Institutional, and Psychological. These surround a central item, "culture," which pertains to each of the regions. The two items "remembrance of the Shoah" and "reaction to anti-Semitism" are located in the Historical region, together with "relation to Israel." Within this region, Israel is closest to the center, while memory of the Shoah is further towards the periphery and anti-Semitism is at the edge of the map. The placement of these items reflects their degree of correlation with the other items. In other words, the students' relationship to Israel was more strongly correlated with other the components. A student who said, for example, that religion was a "reason to be Jewish" was relatively more likely to have also given Israel as a reason to be Jewish, as opposed to the reasons of memory of the Shoah or anti-Semitism.[37] Family and Israel—which form the basic context of their daily lives—are closer to the core of their identity than is the historical event of the Shoah.

36 These results were similar to those found among Diaspora youth. The primary difference was in relation to the two components "relationship to Israel" and "Hebrew language" which were selected by a far greater percentage of the Israelis (Cohen, 2008).

37 The same structure was found in a previous study which contained parallel sets of questions on components of Jewish identity; a longitudinal survey of Diaspora youth on tours to Israel (Cohen, 2008). This does not necessarily mean the Diaspora and Israeli youth gave the same degree of emphasis to each of the reasons, but rather that they cognitively organize the various aspects of Jewish identity in the same way. In other words, in each case the same items were strongly correlated with each other and were placed in corresponding regions. The only exception was that for the Israeli students, the Hebrew language was linked with primordial items such as family and birth, whereas for the Diaspora youth, Hebrew was linked with situational-historical items such as relationship to Israel and remembrance of the Shoah. The SSA of Diaspora participants in Israel Experience tours is given in Appendix D.

Table 9: Components of students' Jewish identity

There are many different reasons for being Jewish. Out of the following list choose all the reasons that you are Jewish:			
	Students in general schools	**Students in religious schools**	**Total**
Family	88%	86%	87%
Birth	81%	80%	80%
Relationship to Israel	79%	80%	79%
Religion	66%	86%	72%
Culture	70%	68%	69%
Hebrew language	67%	67%	67%
Education	56%	63%	58%
Fidelity	54%	60%	55%
Hope	48%	61%	52%
Memory of Shoah	45%	43%	44%
Fate	42%	39%	41%
Choice	39%	41%	40%
Commitment	37%	42%	39%
Reaction to anti-Semitism	19%	16%	18%
Connection to other Jews	13%	15%	14%

Figure 5: Structural analysis of components of Jewish identity (reasons to be Jewish), as assessed by Israeli 9th and 12th graders surveyed in current study

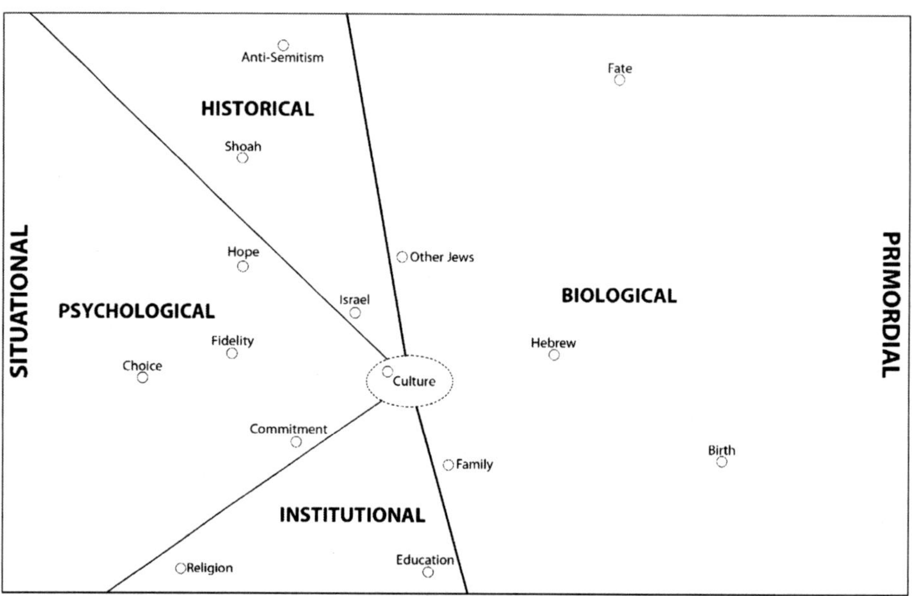

Taken together, these findings on students' beliefs and attitudes give some interesting insight into Jewish-Israeli identity and perception of the world and their place in it. The Shoah continues to affect their perception of the world, but their Jewish and Israeli identities are not formulated primarily in reaction to anti-Semitism and the history of attempted genocide. Neither has awareness of perennial persecution of the Jews led to a sense of cultural inferiority, as it sometimes can among victimized groups.

It is notable that the differences between the attitudes of the students in the two school systems are much smaller than would be implied by the stated goals of the teachers and principals. It seems that the great differences in the goals of the teachers and—especially—the principals, do not translate into equally great differences between the students. As mentioned, the student populations are diverse. They learn, over the years, with many different teachers. Further, while the school is the main venue for learning about the Shoah, young Israelis are exposed to a range of opinions on the subject outside of school as well. Two thirds of the teachers said that Shoah education in the classroom is affected by public discussion and debate of the subject in the public realm.

At the beginning of this chapter, it was posited that the basic beliefs and views teachers and students bring with them affect Shoah education in the classroom. In the next chapter on the survey populations' evaluations of Shoah education, it will be possible to see whether differences by level of religiosity or age translate into different perceptions of Shoah studies.

VII. EVALUATION OF SHOAH EDUCATION

• Shoah education was highly evaluated by principals, students and teachers.

• Principals see Shoah education at their schools as successfully imparting Jewish, Israeli and universal values.

• Teachers are satisfied with the training they receive.

• Students find the lessons thought-provoking and want to learn more about the Shoah.

• The program in religious junior high schools was weak in comparison to both general junior high schools and religious high schools.

• Students rated the journey to Poland and testimonies of survivors as the most effective means of learning about the Shoah, showing the importance of first-hand sources.

• Students' familiarity with Shoah-related concepts revealed that the academic core is the same in religious and general schools, but some aspects, particularly the individuals presented as heroes, differ in the two streams.

• Students who lost a family member in the Shoah were more likely to find the subject relevant to their lives, but other demographic traits (religiosity, ethnicity, socio-economics) had little impact, highlighting the universal importance of the Shoah in Israeli society.

* * * * * *

Evaluating educational programs is a complex task. There are a number of established paradigms for data collection and analysis, each with advantages and limitations. Particularly for a program dealing with a subject as sensitive as the Shoah, myriad political and sociological factors impact its evaluation. The current evaluation used a combination of methods. Students gave a *retrospective self-assessment*; that is, they were asked at the end of the school year to assess the program of Shoah studies and its impact on them, based on their own internal criteria. This is an explicit type of evaluation; respondents consciously reflect upon and intentionally state their attitudes. Self-assessment is a cumulative assessment in which students are asked to recall their level of understanding, state of mind or beliefs at the outset of the program, assess their understanding, state of mind or beliefs at the end of the program, and compare the two. Retrospective self-assessment has been found to be an effective evaluative tool, particularly appropriate when the program being evaluated is meant to be transformative, impacting participants' emotions, values and sense of identity. In addition, the principals and teachers were asked to assess the program, offering adults' external impressions of the impact on students. Finally, the interviews and open questions fleshed out the statistical data. The questionnaires were designed to enable students to assess various cognitive and affective impacts of Shoah education. This research did not assess a particular curricular unit, but rather the cumulative experience of Shoah education.

While there have been a number of evaluations of Shoah education curricula, and analyses by educators of their experiences in teaching the subject, few previous studies have looked empirically at the students' perceptions of learning about the Shoah in school.[1]

A. Principals' Evaluation

The opinion of the principal is a little explored aspect of Shoah education. While the main duties of principals are generally considered to be administrative and managerial, principals are also involved in guiding the school curriculum through selecting programs, helping to develop the school atmosphere, and promoting community-building among teachers, parents, and the extended community. For example, in Israel a group of principals involved in a Ministry of Education program to strengthen local school systems formed a public interest group with the goal of addressing underlying political and social issues affecting their schools, taking on an even broader role than was anticipated.[2]

The surveyed principals expressed general satisfaction with Shoah education at their schools. The high school principals gave slightly more

---

1 Dror, 2001; Holocaust Educational Trust, 2009; Short, 1995; Short, Supple, and Klinger, 1998; Totten, 1998; Wegner, 1995.

2 Eden and Hertz-Lazarowitz, 2001; Glatthorn and Jailall, 2008; Matthews and Crow, 2009.

positive evaluations than did the principals of the junior high schools. The principals of general schools were more satisfied than the principals of the religious schools. Virtually none of the principals thought too much time was spent on Shoah education, and a sizeable percentage—particularly among the junior high school principals—thought there was not enough time dedicated to it.[3]

Of the principals, 71% think the activities related to the subject of the Shoah offered in their junior high schools prepared the students for learning the subject in high school. However, the principals were not fully confident in the students' preparation: 21% think the students are prepared "to a very great extent." The feeling that students were less than fully prepared may be related to a lack of hours dedicated to the subject in junior high school. Just over half (55%) said that by the end of junior high school, prior to the intensive studies offered in high school, the students already have a fairly high level of familiarity with the subject.

Essentially all of the principals said they think Shoah education strengthened students' Jewish identity and Israeli identity. The vast majority also said Shoah education strengthens students' identification with universal values. The principals of the religious schools were somewhat more likely than the principals of the general schools to say that Shoah studies "absolutely" strengthens students' Jewish identity, while the principals of the general schools were slightly more emphatic about the impact of Shoah studies on students' Israeli identities.

The difference was greater regarding the perceived impact on universal values; the principals of the general schools were significantly more likely to say that Shoah studies strengthen students' identification with universal values. These results are an indication of the emphasis given to different types of values in the Shoah education programs of the two school systems, as was seen in the principals' goals for Shoah education (Table 6).

A greater percentage of junior high school principals said Shoah studies "absolutely" strengthens all three—Jewish identity, Israeli identity, and universal values. This may be because the younger students are more impressionable and their identities and values are less fixed.

---

3 For principals' evaluations of Shoah education, with comparison by school stream and level, see Appendix C, Table 1.

Table 10: Shoah studies impact on students' identity and values according to the principals—percentage answering affirmatively (percentage answering "to a very great extent" in parentheses)

Shoah education strengthens students'...	**Principals of general schools**	**Principals of religious schools**	**Principals of high schools**	**Principals of junior high schools**	**Total**
Jewish identity	99% (57%)	100% (62%)	99% (55%)	99% (65%)	100% (59%)
Israeli identity	97% (62%)	100% (58%)	97% (57%)	99% (66%)	98% (61%)
Identification with universal values	95% (44%)	73% (23%)	88% (33%)	90% (42%)	88% (37%)

B. Teachers' Evaluation

Teachers were asked to what extent they felt satisfied with the quality of Shoah education in Israel as a whole, not only in their own school. Two thirds said they were generally satisfied, though only a small minority (4%) was "absolutely" satisfied. The teachers in the general schools and in the junior high schools gave slightly more positive evaluations to the state of Shoah education in Israel. A more significant difference is seen when history teachers are compared with non-history teachers: the history teachers were more satisfied. The percentage that said they were *not* satisfied was relatively high, particularly among teachers in religious schools and the non-history teachers. This question pertained to Shoah education in Israel as a whole, not the specific program taught in their school. In the case of the religious school teachers, the negative reaction may have been in response to their perceptions of how the subject is taught in general schools as well as in their own stream.[4]

4 For teachers' evaluations of Shoah education, with comparison by school stream, level, and subject taught (history or other) see Appendix C, Table m.

Table 11: Teachers' satisfaction with training in Shoah education by subject taught—percentage answering affirmatively (percentage answering "to a very great extent" in parentheses)

	History teachers	**Other teachers**	**Total**
Satisfied with overall training in Shoah studies	87% (31%)	71% (28%)	84% (28%)
Feel proficient in teaching:			
The Shoah in general	92% (33%)	72% (14%)	86% (28%)
The annihilation process	97% (66%)	81% (36%)	93% (59%)
Historical background of Shoah	95% (61%)	81% (22%)	92% (53%)
Nazi ideology	95% (64%)	76% (26%)	91% (56%)
Jewish opposition to the Nazis	90% (45%)	76% (22%)	86% (42%)
Influence of the Shoah on the Jewish world and Israel	81% (37%)	81% (32%)	83% (37%)
Jewish life during the Shoah	71% (23%)	65% (19%)	71% (23%)
Jewish life before the Shoah	54% (18%)	63% (17%)	58% (19%)

Professional training is a critical piece in the picture of Shoah education. The vast majority of the teachers said they were satisfied with the training they have received on the subject of the Shoah. The teachers said they feel proficient in the subject, although most indicated they felt there was still room for them to become more knowledgeable about the Shoah—that is, they do not feel proficient "to a very great extent." Among the specific sub-topics listed, the teachers felt most confident in their ability to teach about the annihilation process, the historical background, and Nazi ideology. A smaller percentage (though still over half) felt proficient in teaching about Jewish life before the Shoah. Overall the teachers in the religious schools felt somewhat less proficient in teaching the subject. Again, a more graphic difference was seen between the history teachers and others involved in Shoah education. A greater percentage of history teachers said they felt well-qualified to teach the Shoah in general and each of the sub-topics with only one exception: more of the non-history teachers felt qualified to teach about Jewish life before the Shoah.

C. *Students' Evaluation*

1. Satisfaction, interest and perceived relevance. The vast majority of the students said they were satisfied with the Shoah education at their schools (87%) and that the lessons were thought-provoking (85%).[5] Over half said the material related to their personal questions. About a third said the material learned in class was relevant to their family lives. This last item was one of the few for which there was a large difference between students of Ashkenazi and Sephardi-Mizrahi backgrounds: 48% of the Ashkenazi students said the material is relevant to their family lives, compared to only 18% of the Sephardi-Mizrahi students. As noted earlier, some Shoah education curricula have been expanded to include the experiences of Jews in North African countries, so as to broaden the relevance to students' family histories, reflecting the goal expressed by the Ministry of Education as well as many of the principals and teachers that Shoah education should create a sense of

5 For students' satisfaction with Shoah studies with comparison by school stream and grade level, see Appendix C, Table n.

"shared fate" among the Jewish People and Israelis, regardless of their family connection to the Shoah. The ethnic background of the teachers and the makeup of the student body may affect the extent to which such a perspective is presented.[6]

When only the most emphatic answers ("absolutely") are considered, as shown in Table 12, the data reveal some interesting differences between the school streams and grade levels. The high school students in the religious schools were more strongly satisfied with their Shoah education than were their peers in the general high schools. However, the same does not hold true in the junior high schools. The 9th graders in the religious schools expressed less satisfaction with Shoah education than their peers in the general schools. In the religious schools, there was a large gap in the evaluation of Shoah education, with the older students giving consistently more positive responses. This gap was not seen in the general school system. While the experts expressed hesitation in drawing "lessons" from the Shoah, preferring that classes focus more on teaching the historical background, the students themselves are interested in discussing the meaning the Shoah hold for their lives, as was seen in many of their open comments.

> The problem is not always the time dedicated to Shoah studies, but the problem is that the subjects they chose to transmit in this subject, to my taste, don't hit the target. They are not directed to let the students think for themselves, express curiosity, questions of humanity and ethics that impact our lives today as people and not just as Jews. The intention and the depth is not enough for my taste.—*Female student*

> The subject needs to be learned in a comprehensive and deep way and not for matriculation exams.... we need to remember and to identify with the Shoah.—*Female student*

---

6 Heinman, 1999; Yablonka, 2008.

Table 12: Comparison of evaluations by students in general and religious schools—percentage answering "absolutely"

The subjects learned in class are *absolutely*....	General schools 9th graders	General schools 12th graders	Religious schools 9th graders	Religious schools 12th graders	TOTAL
Relevant to my family life	10%	11%	7%	15%	11%
Thought provoking	35%	32%	31%	50%	35%
Relevant to my life	26%	23%	23%	38%	25%
Related to personal questions I have	13%	14%	14%	22%	14%

The program in the religious junior high schools was weak in comparison to those in the general junior high schools as well as in the religious high schools. As seen earlier, the 9th graders in the general schools had more exposure to fiction, non-fiction and memoirs, performances, and field trips to memorial museums. The only activity which was significantly more common in the religious junior high schools was hearing the testimonies of survivors; an educational experience which—though rated the most effective method among both age groups—was less popular among the younger than older students.[7]

> It is very important that the young generation hears from the Shoah survivors while they can still tell their stories ... they can teach us, the young, from where we came and where we are going, and turn us into witnesses for future generations.—*Female student*

7 For students' evaluation of effectiveness of Shoah education activities, with comparison by grade level, see Appendix C, Table o.

In the religious high schools, there was an especially notable increase—by more than 20%—in the feeling that Shoah studies addresses personal questions. Shoah studies in the religious high schools were more successful, particularly in making the material relevant to the students. It seems there is room for improvement in the Shoah studies program in the religious junior high schools. [8]

Among the 12th graders, the journey to Poland was considered the most effective educational activity. The students' perception of the strength of the journey to Poland as a way to learn about the Shoah was also found by the Ministry of Education in a separate survey on the journey to Poland.[9] Testimonies were rated the most effective way of learning about the Shoah for the 9th graders and the second-most effective among the 12th graders. This shows the value the students attribute to learning about the Shoah through first-hand sources. In most cases, survivors are invited to schools to give a one-time presentation, but some schools have more in-depth programs, in which students meet with a survivor several times over the course of the year (Shoah education coordinator for high school, personal communication). In a less common practice, one school invited representatives of "Righteous among the Nations" (non-Jews who made efforts to save Jews during the Shoah) to speak at their school.

The importance of survivors' testimonies raises important questions regarding the future of Shoah education. The role of institutions such as Yad Vashem in recording the testimonies of survivors is critical.[10] Several of the interviewed teachers and principals stressed that as this is the last generation with the opportunity to hear survivors' testimonies in person, this opportunity most not be squandered. Over half the students said that field trips and films were highly effective ways for them to learn about the Shoah.

For the 9th grade students, ceremonies and performances (which, as seen earlier, are among the most common types of activities) were considered more effective than classroom lessons. For the 12th graders, however, classroom lessons were considered more effective than cer-

---

8 For comparison of the evaluations of Shoah studies given by 9th graders in general and religious schools, see Appendix C, Table p.

9 Israel Ministry of Education, 2011: 101.

10 On the ontology and institutional trustworthiness of testimony as it relates to Holocaust education, see Beim and Fine, 2007.

emonies and performances. In both cases, history lessons were more highly rated than other lessons.

Table 13: Students' evaluations according to their teachers' pedagogic approach—percentage answering affirmatively (percentage answering "absolutely true" in parentheses)

	Students of teachers who emphasize mainly cognitive aspects	Students of teachers who emphasize mainly experiential aspects	Students of teachers who emphasize both	Students of teachers who emphasize neither
Number	*583*	*359*	*358*	*1166*
Shoah studies are relevant to my family life	35% (11%)	35% (7%)	35% (13%)	33% (11%)
Shoah studies are thought provoking	85% (33%)	88% (36%)	82% (35%)	84% (34%)
Shoah studies are relevant to my life	78% (24%)	82% (25%)	83% (28%)	80% (25%)
Shoah studies are related to personal questions I have	54% (14%)	62% (13%)	64% (15%)	56% (15%)

2. Impact of teaching style on students' evaluation. To explore the impact of teachers' didactic approach on the educational experience of their students, we compared the evaluations of students according to the typology of teachers' didactic approach.[11] There was very little difference, once again highlighting that Shoah education is the product of many teachers and activities across the years. The impact of the current teacher does not determine the students' perception of the subject.

3. Students' interests. A large majority of the students (83%) said they wanted to learn more about the Shoah. Almost a third thought more time should be dedicated to Shoah studies while only 4% thought the amount of time should be reduced.

Slightly more than half the students (53%) said there were fewer disciplinary problems during classes related to the Shoah than in other classes, indicating a level of respect for the subject. This was less pronounced in the religious schools, and 14% said there were *more* disciplinary problems during classes on the Shoah. This may indicate some disruption due to the emotional content of discussions of the subject.[12]

Students were asked which specific aspects of Shoah studies interest them the most. As seen in Table 14 the atrocity of the annihilation of the Jews of Europe and the subsequent life of survivors were the subjects about which they were most interested in learning. Students in religious schools were more interested in theological questions, those in general schools in historical knowledge. Other than that, their interests were similar.

---

11 The questionnaires were coded in such a way that it was possible to link students and their homeroom teacher.

12 For students' perception of discipline in Shoah studies classes, with comparison by school stream, see Appendix C, Table q.

Table 14: Students' interests in Shoah studies—percentage answering "to a very great extent"

	General schools 9th graders	General schools 12th graders	Religious schools 9th graders	Religious schools 12th graders	TOTAL
The atrocity of the annihilation of the Jews	68%	70%	58%	71%	68%
The life of the survivors	62%	63%	60%	66%	63%
The power and brutality of the Nazi regime	59%	61%	48%	57%	59%
Physical resistance to the Nazis	60%	62%	54%	59%	60%
How the individual copes with difficulties	49%	55%	45%	54%	52%
Impact of the Shoah on the Jewish world and State of Israel	49%	46%	44%	53%	47%
General historical knowledge	41%	40%	28%	42%	39%
Questions of religion and faith	28%	34%	42%	59%	35%

4. Students' familiarity with Shoah-related items. Another way to evaluate Shoah education is to look at the cognitive impacts in terms of students' knowledge on the subject. About two thirds of the students felt they were reasonably knowledgeable on the subject of the Shoah. The students in the general schools were more confident about their level of knowledge than those in the religious schools.

> We don't concentrate enough on studying the German nation, its history and leaders like Hitler and Eichmann. It would be good if general subjects on the world during World War II were learned and known in Israel.—*Male student*

To further explore the effectiveness of Shoah education, we designed a questionnaire item to assess how familiar the students are with places, names and events related to the Shoah which are included in most of the school curricula.[13] The 12th grade students were given a list of 32 items related to the Shoah and asked to indicate all of those with which they are familiar (for a brief description of the items included in the list, see Appendix E). This survey was not a test and students were not asked to define or explain the terms. The purpose was to assess what concepts had been presented to them during the course of their studies. In this way, it is possible to see what aspects of Shoah education were emphasized in the school system as a whole and whether there were differences in the two streams of religious and general schools.

Over half the 12th graders recognized at least 25 of the 32 items. Less than 2% recognized 10 or fewer. A dozen of the items were recognized by 90% or more of the students, seven of which are directly related to the persecution of the Jews: the *Kristallnacht* riots and Nuremberg Laws which marked the beginning of the Shoah; the ghettos in which the Jews were confined; the Final Solution and its manifestation in the concentration camps and specifically the death camp of Auschwitz; and Anne Frank as a personification of the victims. These indicate a general and broad knowledge of the history of the Shoah.

The other five of the dozen most recognized items have to do with various aspects of resistance against the Nazis. The Warsaw Ghetto

---

13 Ephrat Balberg-Rotenstreich contributed to the design of this question.

Revolt was the epitome of Jewish armed struggle and has been given much emphasis in the Israeli narrative of the Shoah. The Righteous among the Nations, non-Jews who risked their lives to save Jews, are held up as another role model of resistance. In Eichmann's trial a primary perpetrator of the Shoah was tried and executed by the Jewish nation (as opposed to the Nuremberg trials before an international tribunal). Janusz Korczak ran an orphanage in the Warsaw Ghetto; though he had the opportunity to escape, he chose to accompany the children to Treblinka, where all were killed. The *Judenräte* are one of the most controversial aspects of Shoah history, and especially difficult to incorporate into a curriculum for high school students. They raise thorny questions, such as "To what degree did Jews and Jewish organizations assist, however unintentionally, in the Final Solution and to what degree did they resist, however successfully or not, this Luciferian undertaking?"[14] While in the early days of the State, the councils were widely perceived and portrayed as traitors, over time, gradually responding to research on the subject Shoah education in Israeli schools began to address ways in which *Judenräte* members attempted to protect and help Jews.[15] The data from this survey shows that the students are familiar with this concept. While we cannot discern their opinions on the subject, their widespread knowledge about the *Judenräte* indicates the extent to which Shoah education is addressing the complexities of daily life and the dilemmas faced by Jews trying to survive under the Nazi regime. Two other examples of resistance, the Partisan fighters and Hannah Senesh, were recognized by 87% of the students.

There was little difference between the students in the religious and general schools regarding these most familiar items. Only for one item—the Nuremberg Laws—was the gap between the two school streams more than 10%, the students in religious schools being less familiar with the term. The core of the academic curriculum, it seems, is similar in the two school systems. Regarding some of the other items, the difference was dramatic, showing the particular emphases of various schools. The Rabbi of Piaseczno, a Hasidic leader in the Warsaw Ghetto, was recognized by two thirds of the students in the religious schools, compared to 13% of those in the general schools. More of the students

---

14 Katz, 1996: ix.

15 Arendt, 1963; Bauer, 1977; Hilberg, 1979; Trunk, 1972; Weiss, 1988.

in the general schools were more familiar with some of the historic events such as the Molotov-Ribbentrop pact between Germany and the USSR, the Nazi Anschluss, the Wannsee Conference at which the Final Solution was officially initiated, and the German invasion of the Soviet Union in Operation Barbarossa.

Table 15: 12th grade students' familiarity with items related to the Shoah—percentage that indicated they recognize each item

	General	Religious	Total
Ghetto	98%	98%	98%
Anne Frank	97%	96%	97%
Warsaw Ghetto Revolt	97%	98%	97%
Kristallnacht (Bedolah)	97%	98%	97%
Auschwitz-Birkenau	96%	93%	96%
Righteous among the Nations	96%	92%	95%
Eichmann	94%	98%	94%
Final Solution	95%	91%	94%
Janusz Korczak (Yanush)	97%	95%	94%
Judenräte (Jewish council)	93%	94%	93%
Concentration camp	94%	85%	93%
Nuremberg Laws	94%	81%	92%
Wannsee Conference	90%	77%	88%
Hannah Senesh	87%	90%	87%
Partisans	87%	87%	87%
Schnellbrief (Igeret)	85%	91%	86%
Heydrich	86%	79%	85%

Molotov-Ribbentrop pact	88%	59%	84%
“Sanctification of life”	84%	83%	84%
Operation Barbarossa	85%	54%	81%
General Gouvernement	70%	65%	69%
Munich agreement	69%	57%	68%
German Operation (*Aktzia*)	66%	73%	67%
Himmler	62%	46%	60%
Mordechai Anielewicz	57%	52%	56%
Anschluss	58%	23%	53%
Einsatzgruppen (task forces/ *Uzvot*)	43%	55%	45%
Raoul Wallenberg	42%	39%	42%
Babi Yar	41%	42%	41%
Goebbels	42%	34%	41%
Emmanuel Ringelblum	22%	21%	22%
Rabbi of Piaseczno	13%	67%	20%

In an SSA analysis conducted on the students’ recognition of these items, the most widely recognized items are at the center of the map. These correspond almost perfectly with a list of items which several experts in Shoah education suggested should be “easy” for students to know by 12th grade (personal communication). Around the periphery are the items which were recognized by fewer students or predominantly in certain sub-populations.

It is also possible to see a region containing items related to resistance. The concept of resistance is broad. The partisans and the Warsaw Ghetto Revolt represent armed resistance. Hannah Senesh is an individual who first joined the Yishuv in British Palestine, then sacrificed her life attempting to help European Jews; she is known in a personal way through the poetry she left. The concept of *Sanctification of Life*, any attempt to survive, save others, or preserve one's human dignity during the Shoah, constituted a form of resistance against the Nazis. Janusz Korczak and the Rabbi of Piaseczno embody this concept; both of them chose not to save themselves but to remain with those dependent on them (Korczak with the orphans and the rabbi with his community), offering comfort as long as they could and ultimately sharing their fate. The *Judenräte*, as discussed, are related to the complex topic of resistance versus complicity.

The structure of the map indicates a basic logical division between items related to persecution and resistance. A large region of the map contains only items corresponding to persecution, such as Auschwitz, Final Solution, Babi Yar, etc. The upper-right quadrant of the map contains mainly items related to Resistance, such as the Partisans, Righteous of the Nations, and individual heroes of the era. However, some items related to persecution (the *Einsatzgruppen* death squads, *Kristallnacht*, the Wannsee Conference) are mixed among the items related to resistance.

How can this "noise" in the division between Persecution and Resistance be explained? It may in part be a reflection of the students' level of knowledge regarding these items, which may be uneven or not be fully developed; some items may be fully understood, others only superficially. At the same time, it must be recognized that many of the items in fact do contain elements of both persecution and resistance. Even in concentration camps people exhibited acts of resistance through helping one another survive. The role of the *Judenräte* councils in collaborating with the persecutors or aiding resistance is notoriously difficult to interpret. The unclear division in the map may be reflecting a lack of clarity due to the very nature of the subject as it is perceived today.

As this was the first survey of the familiarity of high school seniors with specific items related to the Shoah, it must be considered a preliminary inquiry, to be further explored in the future.

Figure 6: Structural analysis (SSA) of students' familiarity with Shoah-related items

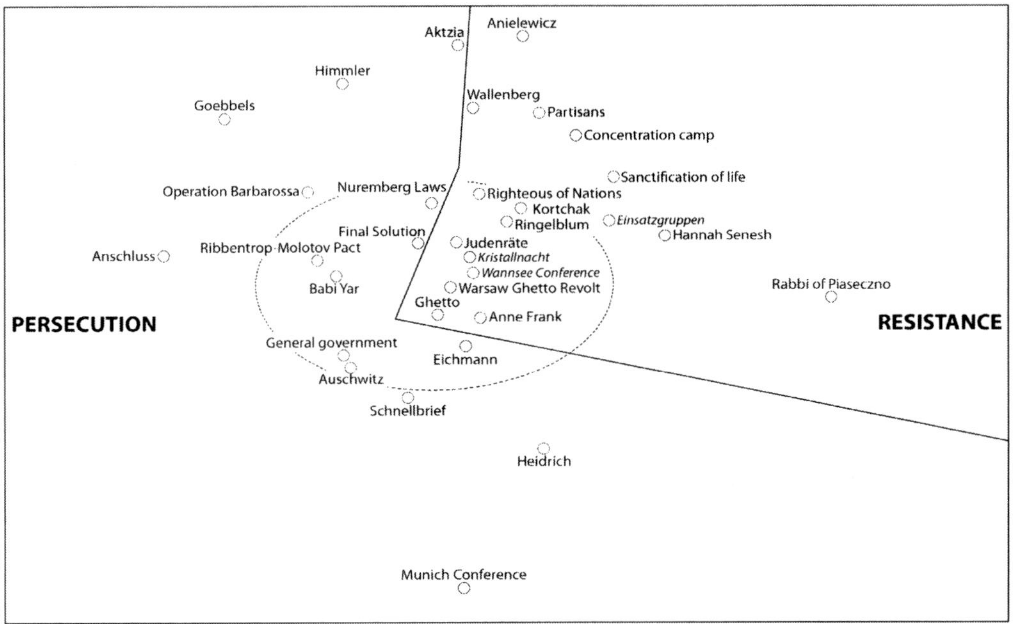

5. Socio-demographic impacts on Shoah education. Given the diversity of the student body, and the overarching hypothesis that the subject of the Shoah bridges gaps in Jewish-Israeli society, we explored whether Shoah education has a different impact on students with various socio-demographic characteristics.

The teachers were asked whether they think students from different sub-groups relate differently to the issue of the Shoah. Their responses give some insight into how Shoah education impacts various students, and how the teachers perceive their students' reaction to the subject. The majority of teachers thought students perceived the subject in more or less the same way, regardless of gender, ethnicity, socio-economic background or level of religiosity, attesting once again to the extent to which the subject of the Shoah bridges gaps in Israeli society.

Nevertheless, close to a quarter of the teachers thought Ashkenazi students and those from higher socio-economic brackets (there is some overlap between these categories) had a stronger connection to the subject. A small percentage (about 10%) thought girls indicated more interest in and identification with Shoah education, and virtually none thought this was true for boys, though the vast majority (over 80%) saw no difference among the genders.

A third of the teachers in religious schools thought religious students identified more strongly with the subject, though only 6% of the teachers in the general schools agreed; 12% of the general teachers thought secular students had the stronger identification with the Shoah, indicating how the teachers' perspective affects their perception of the impact of Shoah education on their students.

To ascertain whether and to what extent socio-economic characteristics of the students did in fact affect the pedagogic impact of Shoah education, a series of analyses were conducted ascertaining the strength of various traits in predicting different measures of students' perception of the subject. These measures were:

A) *familiarity* with the list of Shoah-items
B) degree to which students perceive Shoah studies as *relevant* to their life;
C) whether the students see the *scope* of the Shoah as a disaster for all humankind or only for the Jews;
D) participation in the *journey to Poland*

Together, these measures give a picture of cognitive, affective, axiological and instrumental aspects of Shoah education. The first two pertain to all the students, the second only to 12th graders. Although this section is somewhat technical, it is nevertheless important in providing details of the analysis.

The strength of the correlation between each of the socio-economic traits (the "predicting variables") and the four measures of pedagogic impact (the "predicted variable") was calculated.[16] In the following tables, the correlations—the degree to which the socio-economic trait predicts the pedagogic impact—are expressed numerically, and the strength of the correlation is indicated symbolically on a scale from four plus signs

16 This was done using the *eta* (η) coefficient which measures non-linear correlations between variables. When the correlation between the two variables is linear, the measure is equal in value to measures of linear correlations such as Pearson's *r*. When the connection between the variables is not linear, the ETA value will be higher than a measure of linear connections. Also, unlike measures for linear connections between variables, this measure is not symmetrical. Therefore the correlation between the variables depends on the choice of the predictor variable and the predicted variable. This choice is dependent on the researcher's theoretical model.

(a very strong correlation) through one plus sign (a weak correlation), with 0 representing a neutral relationship, or no correlation.

5.1 Familiarity with Shoah-related items. In ascertaining factors affecting cognitive learning about the Shoah, the set of socio-economic traits was considered, plus three evaluative items: students' self-perceived proficiency in Shoah studies, extent to which they consider Shoah studies relevant to their lives and extent to which they find Shoah studies thought-provoking. Since this list of items was only included in the questionnaire for 12th graders, grade level is not considered.

A number of traits emerged as strong predictors of cognitive knowledge about the Shoah. Overall, the students' traits were more strongly linked with knowledge about the Shoah than with the perception that Shoah education is relevant. In other words, the feeling that the Shoah is relevant crosses social boundaries, but social and educational background affects the level of knowledge about the subject.

There was a very strong positive connection between participating in the journey to Poland and the students' familiarity with items related to the Shoah. This shows the educational impact of the program (which will be discussed in greater detail in the chapter on the journeys). Students who lost a relative in the Shoah tended to be familiar with more of the items, and they were more likely to have participated in the journey to Poland.

Students' self-assessment of their own proficiency was a strong indicator of how many of the items in the list they could identify, showing the accuracy of the students' perception of their own level of knowledge. Additionally, those who said they found Shoah studies thought-provoking and relevant to their lives also tended to have broader knowledge about the Shoah, indicating the importance of interest in the subject for effective learning.

Strong correlations were also found with socio-economic status and ethnic background; Ashkenazi or mixed background students and those at schools of higher socio-economic status had a higher level of knowledge. Participation in a youth movement had a moderately strong correlation with knowledge. Interestingly, given the teachers' predictions, secular students had somewhat more familiarity with the subject, although school stream itself had no impact at all.

Table 16: Comparison of several possible predictors of *cognitive knowledge* assessed through *familiarity* with Shoah-related items

Predicting variable	**Correlation**	**Level of prediction**	**Category of students familiar with more Shoah-related items**
Participation in journey to Poland (yes/no)	0.274	++++	Participating students
Students' self-perceived proficiency in Shoah studies (very high/high/medium/ low)	0.247	++++	Students who feel they are proficient in the Shoah subject
Loss of relative in the Shoah (yes/no)	0.208	+++	Students who lost a relative in the Shoah
Socio-economic level (high, medium, low)	0.208	+++	Students of higher socio-economic status
Ethnic background (Ashkenazi, Mizrahi, both, other)	0.208	+++	Students of mixed or Ashkenazi origin
Shoah studies are thought-provoking (strongly agree/ agree/disagree)	0.182	+++	Students who find the subject thought-provoking
Relevance of Shoah studies to students' lives (strongly agree/agree/disagree)	0.159	+++	Students who find the subject relevant

Participation in a youth movement (leader, member, non-member)	0.137	++	Leaders, followed by members
Religious self-definition (religious, traditional, secular)	0.120	++	Secular students
School stream (general/ religious)	0.017	0	No difference

5.2 Relevance of Shoah education. Eight traits were considered, as shown in Appendix C, table r. Loss of a relative in the Shoah was the best predictor of perceived relevance of Shoah studies to students, and even this is not very strong. The weak impact of religiosity, ethnicity, type of school, grade, socio-economic level, youth movement membership, participation in the journey to Poland, or grade shows once again that the Shoah is an issue which has universal relevance to Jewish Israelis. Students from low socio-economic brackets, religious students and those at religious schools were slightly more likely to find the subject relevant to their lives.

5.3 Scope of the disaster. The same eight traits were considered in relation to students' perception of the scope of the Shoah as a disaster for all humankind or only the Jews.[17] In this case, ethnic background was the best predictor of attitude. Students of Ashkenazi or mixed origin were more likely to say they see it as a disaster for all humankind. It should be stressed, however, that the large majority students of all ethnic backgrounds said they saw it as a disaster for all humankind. The tendency to see the Shoah as a disaster for humankind was stronger among those who had lost a relative in the Shoah than among those who hadn't.

The tendency to view the Shoah as a disaster for humankind was stronger among those students who had participated in the journey to Poland. This is a very important finding as it seems to contradict critics who claim the journey to Poland instills ethnocentric values in students.

The 12th grade students were somewhat more likely to see the Shoah

17 Appendix C, Table s.

as a universal disaster, perhaps indicating a more mature understanding of the issue.

Participants in youth movements were also more likely to see the scope of the Shoah as universal.

Socio-economic level and personal religiosity had little impact, the secular students and those from medium or high socio-economic backgrounds being only slightly more likely to see the Shoah as a disaster for all humankind. School stream had no impact.

5.4. Participation in journey to Poland. Loss of a relative in the Shoah, ethnicity and socio-economic status were the strongest predictors of participation.[18] The first two are related to the degree to which the students' family was affected by the Shoah (Ashkenazi students in general and those who lost relatives). Socio-economic status is related to the ability to pay for the journey. Participants in youth movements were more likely to take part in the journey. Secular students were more also likely to go to Poland. School stream had a weaker connection to participation, perhaps because the general schools have a diverse population of secular and "traditional" students. The journey to Poland and a comparative assessment of factors affecting participation are explored in greater detail in chapter VIII.

5.5 Factor analysis. Further, a factor analysis was conducted on seven variables related to socio-demographic traits of the students and four variables related to Shoah education.[19] A factor analysis identifies categories (factors) which describe the pattern of relationships among the variables. Four factors were recognized. Two characteristics are associated with the first factor: familiarity with Shoah-related items and participation in the journey to Poland. Both of the items in this factor relate to familiarity with the history and geography of the Shoah.

Three characteristics are associated with the second factor: school stream, socio-economic status, and religiosity. This factor may be called social identity.

Three characteristics are associated with the third factor: ethnicity, loss of family member in Shoah and perceived scope of the Shoah. This factor relates to the populations involved in the Shoah. It may be noted that the variables in the second factor are sociological characteristics

18 Appendix C, Table t.

19 For results of Factor Analysis, see Appendix C, Table u.

which involve some flexibility and choice (for the students' parents, if not for the students themselves).

Two characteristics are associated with the fourth factor: involvement in a youth movement and perceived relevance of the Shoah to the students' life. These items relate to social involvement.

Shoah education as it exists in Israeli schools today is the result of decades of systematic effort and intensive discussion regarding the best way to teach this subject, whose importance is universally agreed upon. The evaluations of the principals, teachers and students attest to the fruits of these efforts. Shoah education is widely viewed as effective and relevant. It impacts students cognitively and affectively. Their knowledge of the subject is broad. Their understanding of it is intertwined with their social identities as Jews and Israelis. Students are highly interested in learning about the persecution Jews suffered in Europe and their resistance to their persecutors. Interest in and attachment to the subject is somewhat stronger among those with more direct family connections (relatives of survivors and victims and Ashkenazi Jews in general), but is far from limited to these students.

Among the varied activities available, the high school students rated the journey to Poland as the most effective. The next chapter looks in-depth at this distinctive aspect of Shoah education.

VIII. THE JOURNEY TO POLAND

> You can't "visit" Auschwitz ... and only reading about it is not enough. We must see and know, know and see, inextricably. It is heartbreaking work.—*Claude Lanzmann*[1]

> Every student must go on the journey to Poland to understand the meaning of being a proud Israeli Jew with political independence.—*Male high school principal*

> We shouldn't leave the journey crying or broken, but stronger.—*Male student*

> In my opinion the most important questions regarding the subject of the Shoah and the journey to Poland are universal questions regarding human nature, his ethics, his connection to others and especially those who are different from him.—*Female student*

• A significant and growing number of 12th graders go to Shaoh sites in Poland on school-sponsored journeys, which represent a sort of civil-religious pilgrimage.

• Specific orientation activities offered through the school are augmented by the structural preparation received through years of Shoah education.

• Groups hold ceremonies at former death camps and cemeteries and visit sites related to Jewish community life before the Shoah.

• Public expressions of Jewish and Israeli identity at Shoah sites are a feature of the journeys.

• The itineraries are designed to teach about the Shoah, impart strong emotional experiences and involve particpants in commemorative symbolic actions. '

---

1 Lanzmann, in Müller, 1980.

• As with Shoah education at large, a combination of Zionist, Jewish and universal messages and values are imparted.

• Meetings with Polish youth have been incorporated into the journey. These are not as highly regarded by the Israeli youth as are the other aspects of the journey.

• The return to Israel is an important conclusion to the journey. Participants share their experiences with their classmates, serving as as witness-ambassadors.

* * * * * *

The phenomenon of Israeli students visiting Shoah sites in Poland is multi-faceted and complex. Its many nuances and meanings are difficult to capture in one simple term. Just as various terms for the historical events being studied (Shoah, Holocaust, annihilation, genocide), each denotes a certain view, so also the terms for this educational program such as tour, trip, journey, *voyages de mémoire*,[2] pilgrimage, and excursion carry distinct connotations.

Two main Hebrew terms are used in describing the program in Israel. *Masa* (מסע) may be translated as journey or voyage. It does not have the connotations of a pleasure trip. Another term used to describe the student program is *mishlachot* (משלחות), or delegations, implying the participants are viewed as ambassadors bringing a message as well learning. The journeys have certain characteristics of a pilgrimage, or more accurately a civil-religious pilgrimage. Civil religious pilgrimages have become a feature of modern travel, through which sites related to national identity, whether at home or abroad, have become "hallowed" and the visit is undertaken as part of creating collective memory, exploring identity and expressing solidarity. However, the term pilgrimage can also be problematic, as it invokes movement from the mundane to a spiritual center, whereas the journey from Israel to Poland and back to Israel has a distinctly different dynamic.[3] In this book I mainly use the term "journey" while recognizing that no choice is neutral or

2 This term, translatable as "remembrance trips" was used by the organizers of a conference of Lacaune-les-Bains in September 2011, at which presenters spoke about various populations of Jews and non-Jews visiting Shoah sites. http://h-net.msu.edu/cgi-bin/logbrowse.pl?trx=vx&list=H-Soz-u-Kult&month=1101&week=a&msg=LBt2T0znQRk9zQBF96ZxRg&user=&pw=.

3 Campo, 1998; Cohen, 1992; Feldman, 2008; Lazar et al., 2004a; West, 2008.

completely sufficient in capturing the complexities of the experience.

The journeys simultaneously encompass different kinds of travel: educational tourism, heritage tourism, and dark tourism, civil-religious pilgrimage and more. Starting from Boorstin's classic distinction, these Israeli students are not pleasure-seeking tourists content with "pseudo-events," but are closer to his concept of travelers, seeking authentic experiences, knowledge, and self-development.[4] In Cohen's typology of tourist experiences, the journeys to Poland may be considered experiential and experimental; they are not meant to be recreational or diversionary, even if some diversionary and recreational time is included in the itinerary to give the students some relief from the heavy subject. Cohen's "existential" category, which refers to tourists who find a new spiritual center in the visited sites; while it is exceedingly rare for Israeli students to experience Poland as a spiritual center, those with families from Poland may have some sense of connection to the land of their ancestors. More commonly the existential aspect of the journey may be the rediscovery of the spiritual center in Israel upon return.[5] Additionally, it has been suggested that journeys to Shoah sites in Europe may represent an existential pilgrimage to the destroyed Yiddish culture, an aspect of Shoah education which has been largely overshadowed by the emphasis on Zionist or religious aspects in Israeli schools.[6]

The school journeys are part of a growing trend of Shoah tourism among Jews around the world, itself part of an even larger phenomenon of "dark tourism." Dark tourism refers to voluntary visits to sites related to death and disaster, such as battlefields, graves, and sites of natural disasters. Dark tourism may be linked to the visitors' national, religious or ethnic heritage, as in the case of African-Americans who visit sites along the slave route, or visitors to memorials of the genocides in Rwanda and Cambodia. Dark tourism which is connected to visitors' heritage and history provides a way to commemorate victims and ensure that the circumstances in which they died are not forgotten. If done in a way which is educational, dark tourism can help visitors understand historical events and try to draw some meaning from them.[7]

---

4 Boorstin, 1964.

5 Cohen, E., 1979.

6 Ernst, 2008.

7 Ashworth, 2002; Bruner, 1996; Caplan, 2007; Cohen, 2011c; Kugelmass, 1994; Lennon and Foley, 2000; Stone, 2006; Thurnell-Read, 2009.

In addition to the many Diaspora Jews and Israelis who visit Shoah sites as part of general tours in Europe, there are a number of programs bringing groups of Jewish adults and students on organized tours of sites related to the Shoah and to Jewish life in Europe before World War II. A program sponsored by the Israel Defense Forces, "Witnesses in Uniform," launched in the 1990s sends groups of army officers to visit Shoah sites in Europe. Over the past decade there have been over 25,000 participants in the program, which is intended as an educational experience to strengthen officers' commitment to the State of Israel, the Jewish People, and universal human values. In recent years, groups of Israeli police officers have also participated in the Witnesses in Uniform program.[8]

The March of the Living and some Israel Experience tours combine the pilgrimage to Shoah sites with a subsequent trip to Israel, thus mirroring the route of the Israeli student groups and the implicit message that the Jewish state is necessary in preventing a future Shoah. The culmination in Israel is way of ending the trip on a note of hope and national pride and the contrasting experiences in Poland and Israel make a deep impression on participants, as expressed in the following quote of an American March of the Living alumnus:

> As I stood next to the Kotel with my hand upon its wall, I listened, absorbed, imagined, remembered, and prayed. Standing there, a flood of warmth and comfort filled my body. I was In Israel. I was safe.—*Sarah Marlin, San Antonio, Texas*

> I was deeply and personally affected by the journey to Poland, although I believe it awakened things that were already inherent in me.—*Male student*

Public schools in Europe also bring students to Shoah sites. These may be much shorter tours, even day trips, facilitated by their geographical proximity. At the same time, some European students (such as in Italy

8 Levinson, 2012; see also website of Israeli Defense Forces: http://www.aka.idf.il/edim/main/; a blog (in Hebrew) of a participant can be found at http://www.leumiblog.co.il/madim. On police officers in the Witnesses in Uniform program see: http://www.police.gov.il/mehozot/agafAME/education_history_legacy/Pages/edimbemadim.aspx (in Hebrew).

and France) elect to take part in lengthy Shoah-study programs which include visits to Shoah sites.[9] The experiences of European students to these visits to Shoah sites are highly impacted by the general attitudes in their home countries regarding their country's role in the World War Two and the Shoah, and current attitudes towards the Jews as well as larger issues such as immigrants and national identity.[10]

A. The Nature of the Journey

The journeys to Poland last between a week and ten days. The journeys may be organized directly by the Ministry of Education or by the schools with the support of the Ministry's special committee for this program. The latter is the more common option. According to the Ministry of Education, 90% of the journeys are organized by the school. Of the schools which sent groups to Poland (half the surveyed sample), 62% sent groups on journeys organized by the school and 38% on journeys organized directly by the Ministry of Education.

1. Preparation for the journey.

1.1 *Orientation*. The educational experience of the journey to Poland begins well before students board the plane. All the surveyed principals from schools that sent groups to Poland said that an orientation program was offered before the journey; about half said that the orientation was mandatory for participating students. The Ministry of Education recommends that preparation begin five months prior to the journey, with an orientation program that includes 40 hours of study and discussion, offered during and/or after school hours. In practice, the orientation varies from school to school, with some holding meetings regularly for the entire year leading up to the trip, and others meeting only a few times.[11] Program organizers and accompanying teachers are mainly responsible for the orientation. A Ministry of Education survey found that just over three quarters of participating students took part in such an orientation.[12] In some schools, the orientation activities were open to students not intending to join the journey to Poland—or not sure

9 Doerry, 2011; Fontanesi, 2011.
10 Doerry, 2011; Heimberg, 2002.
11 Feldman, 1999; Israel Ministry of Education, 2011.
12 Israel Ministry of Education, 2011.

yet whether or not they would—and thus the orientation functioned as a sort of recruitment and selection tool. For example, the orientation program may provide an opportunity for teachers to observe the level of maturity and emotional readiness expressed by students.[13] The use of the orientation program as a sorting process was more common in the general schools, according to the surveyed principals.

Most of the principals and teachers felt the orientation process was necessary and beneficial, although one (who was critical of the journey and advocated terminating it) said during the preparation adults imposed their views on the students, preventing the possibility of revelation and discovery.

> Our school has a long orientation process; nine meeting conducted at the school and at relevant museums. It is organized by the guides and chaperoning teachers and includes both theoretical study and personal emotional preparation.—*Female high school principal*

1.2. *Structural preparation*. The formal orientation is only one aspect of preparation for the journey. By 12th grade, students have received years of cumulative preparation. The knowledge of the subject they gain over time through various sources may be called "structural preparation," which convinces participants of the importance of undertaking the journey, and provides them with cognitive and affective tools to understand the experience.[14]

An indicator of the extent of this structural preparation is the high percentage of 9th graders (80%) who said that they intend to participate in the journey when they reach 12th grade. Almost half indicated that they "absolutely" intend to go. Even several years before they are able to participate, students are already interested in undertaking the journey. This indicates that the journeys are given a high degree of emphasis within the school culture and that the education they receive in junior high school encourages the students to think about the trip to Poland and to want to participate.[15] The decisions being made regarding subsi-

13 Riki Mandel, Ministry of Education, personal communication, 2011.

14 I have also noted the importance of structural preparation among Diaspora youth coming on group tours to Israel (Cohen, 2008; 1999).

15 These figures may suggest the possibility of increasing the number of participants in upcoming years.

dies and support for the journeys carry great importance for the next waves of students hoping to participate.

Another aspect of structural preparation pertains to the emotional readiness of students for such an experience. Some of the teachers questioned the appropriateness of such a trip for 12th grade students for a journey of this sort was also questioned by some of the teachers and principals, some of who suggested that such a journey is more appropriate for post-army or college-age young adults. On the other hand, some European public schools bring students (mainly non-Jewish) to Shoah sites at a much younger age, as young as 13. During school trips to Auschwitz and to Izieu House in France (a museum built on the site of an orphanage from which Jewish children were deported to Auschwitz), some French students aged 13-15 were apparently unable to understand the import of what they were seeing, making comments for example about the hairstyles of the children in the portraits. There is no definitive agreed-upon minimum age for such visits, though it has been found that in order to prevent either trauma or indifference due to a lack of understanding, younger students should be brought in smaller groups and given age-appropriate preparation.[16]

> The journey to Poland doesn't have to be for all students, only those who are really interested and who have the emotional strength needed to cope with it.—*Ephrat Balberg-Rotenstreich, teacher at Yad Vashem and the Kerem Institute of teacher training*

> I'm not sure this is the appropriate age or the proper framework for such an experience. The students are involved in social issues no less than with what they are seeing...it has turned into a long annual class outing.—*Male high school vice principal*

2. Itinerary of the journey. Journeys organized by the schools have more flexibility in terms of choice of sites to visit, though their itineraries are coordinated with the Ministry. The basic itineraries of both models are similar. Groups travel in bus convoys, accompanied by

16 Biscarat, 2010, 2011.

chaperoning teachers, tour guides, and Israeli security guards. Many groups have survivor/witnesses who join them for part or all of the time in Poland.[17]

The sites include one or more of the former death camps (visiting Auschwitz-Birkenau is mandatory; many also visit others such as Majdanek and Treblinka), the Warsaw Ghetto, former synagogues and cemeteries. Often a Shoah survivor speaks to the group. Group ceremonies are held at several sites, during which participants typically say *kaddish* (the traditional Jewish prayer in memory of the deceased) for the victims and sing the Israeli national anthem *HaTikva*. A notable feature of the Ministry-organized tours is an emphasis on joint activities and ceremonies bringing together groups from different types of schools: religious, general, large cities, development towns, special needs, etc. In some cases, the group ceremonies bring together Israeli students and Diaspora Jewish youth participating in the March of the Living. These large ceremonies are a distinctive feature of the journeys organized by Israeli schools and programs for Jewish-Diaspora students, illustrating the goal of fostering group identity among the participants. In contrast, European public schools tend to bring small groups of students, sometimes recruiting individuals from various schools; fostering national identity is not a goal of such programs, and may even be perceived as contrary to the purpose of learning about the Shoah.[18]

Social or recreational activities are included, mainly in the evenings, to allow the participants relief from the heavy and emotional tone of the experience. This is spent almost exclusively with the group of students traveling together.

For most groups, there is little interaction with Poles or contemporary Polish culture. However, in recent years this has begun to change, partly in response to criticism of the insularity of the tours (voiced both by Israeli pedagogic analysts and the Polish hosts). Greater interaction between Polish people and Israelis has been enabled, in part, by changes in the attitudes regarding the Shoah held by people in Poland.[19] Many journeys now include Polish cultural events (concerts, dances) or visits

---

17 Israel Ministry of Education, 2011.

18 Fontanesi, 2011.

19 Prof. Israel Gutman, personal communication, 2009.

to sites of Polish history and culture. An increasing number of groups have facilitated meetings with Polish high school students.[20] This innovation has met with positive feedback, despite logistical, pedagogic and ideological challenges and the Ministry of Education now recommends all groups dedicate some time to such meetings.[21] However, of the various components of the journey, the meetings with Polish youth were perceived by the students as far less important than the tours of Shoah sites and ceremonies. The reaction to the exposure to Polish culture and the meetings with Polish youth differed dramatically among participants from general and religious schools: about half of those from general schools said the cultural events were very important aspects of the journey, whereas less than a quarter of those from the religious schools thought so. One student from a religious school suggested that meetings between Israeli general and religious school students should take preference over the meetings with Polish youth, saying "We need to meet the people from our own country."

20 Barkat, 2005; Feldman, 1999; Israel Ministry of Education, 2010, 2011; Kuleta-Hulboj, 2011; Moshe, 2011.

21 Israel Ministry of Education, 2011.

Figure 7: Map of sample itinerary, general school

Figure 8: Map of sample itinerary, religious state school

Map data ©2013 Google

3. Follow-up activities after the return to Israel. The journey to Poland is viewed as one significant activity within the ongoing project of Shoah education. A significant part of the educational impact of the journey is expected to occur after the students return. The itinerary is full and much of the cognitive and emotional processing of what was seen, felt, and learned will necessarily occur after the journey. The Ministry of Education emphasizes that there be meetings—preferably several—which will ensure the students receive the support and guidance they need to understand the experience. Further, the students who took part in the program are expected to serve as "witnesses" for others (classmates who didn't join the journey as well as younger students in the school who may take part in the future). Alumni of the journey may share what they experienced with the school through presentations (especially at *Yom HaShoah* events), displays at the school, slide shows of the journey, and so forth. The Ministry of Education specifies that follow-up activities are an integral part of the journey. The vast majority of participants said they were able to cope with the emotional difficulties of the experience, despite concerns expressed beforehand: personal inner strength and the support of friends and family were most important, though the school and staff were seen as playing a role in providing emotional support. Some of the staff exceeded students' expectations in this respect: upon returning students said the guides and the Shoah survivors who accompanied their groups were more important in providing emotional support than they had anticipated.[22]

> After the journey we designate time for processing and internalizing the journey. Graduates tell us that even years after the journey what a positive impact it had on their spiritual and national worldview.—*Male high school principal*

B. Objectives of the Journey

The Ministry of Education has a specified set of cognitive and affective objectives for the journeys. Despite the fact that the journey to Poland

22 Israel Ministry of Education, 2011.

clearly includes the behavioral dimension (walking, touching, seeing, visiting) this is not explicated by the Ministry of Education. It may be that this dimension is considered self-evident and therefore is not recognized.

The Ministry's goals include both the national and the universal: 1) strengthening the feeling of connection to the Jewish people and the State of Israel; 2) gaining knowledge about the connection between the Shoah and Jewish national identity; 3) gaining knowledge about the history of Jewish communities; 4) gaining knowledge about universal values in the context of the Shoah; 5) gaining knowledge about the nation and people of Poland today.[23] Participants are expected to learn about subjects such as Jewish history and life in pre-war Poland and during the war; the rise of Nazi ideology; the Zionist movement; and relations between Jews and non-Jews including the notion of Righteous among the Nations. They are also expected to enable students "feel and try to comprehend" the destruction and loss of European Jewry, the moral depravity of the Nazis, and the significance of resistance against the Nazis.[24] Minister of Education Gideon Sar considers the journeys important because they "...contribute to the strengthening of Jewish identity and the feeling of commitment to the memory of the Shoah and to the existence of the State of Israel as the nation of the Jewish People."[25]

As the journey to Poland is a component of the larger Shoah education program, the teachers' and principals' goals for the journey reflect their larger objectives for Shoah education, as discussed in chapter V.

1. Students' motivations. In an open question, students who went to Poland were asked to give their two main motivations for going on the journey (some students gave only one answer). A dozen recurring core reasons were given by the overwhelming majority (87%) of the respondents. They are summarized in Table 17.

---

23 Israel Ministry of Education, 2011.

24 Israel Ministry of Education, 2008 http://cms.education.gov.il/EducationCMS/Units/Bitachon/MishlachotLechul/MishlachotLepolin/Klali.htm

25 Gideon Sar, quoted in Maniv, 2011.

Table 17: Students' reasons for participating in journey to Poland

Reason	# of students citing this as their primary reason for going to Poland	# of students citing this as their secondary reason for going to Poland	Total # of students citing this as a reason for going to Poland
To see for myself	61	127	188
Family connection	113	60	173
To deepen knowledge	92	43	135
Linked to Jewish identity	58	47	105
Interest	57	21	78
For the experience	39	36	75
To try to understand	27	33	60
Social reasons (friends going)	22	35	57
Awareness of history	11	38	49
General importance	24	11	35
Curiosity	16	3	19
National (Israeli) identity	8	6	14

The most commonly given reason referred to a desire to "see for myself" or "...to really see how they lived there and what happened to them..." This indicated a strong motivation to ground in reality the material learned in the classroom.[26] The second most common reason, and the one which was most often cited as the primary reason for going, was related to a family connection with the Shoah: "... my grandfather went through the Shoah..."

A desire to deepen their knowledge about the Shoah "...to learn about the Shoah in a deeper way..." was another common reason. This was noted by a large number of students as their primary reason for going, indicating that educational goals were vital to many of the participating students.

The educational importance of the journey is particularly clear when we consider together the number of students who said they wanted to deepen their knowledge and those who wanted to "see for themselves" what they learned about in class.

Many students also gave reasons related to Jewish identity: "...I think as a Jew there is a responsibility to go to Poland and see what happened..."

It is interesting to note that reasons related to Jewish identity were far more common and much more likely to be listed as the primary reason than those related to Israeli identity. In fact, although the journeys have been criticized as emphasizing Zionist ideology over education, relatively few students cited reasons related to nationalism, such as "... to show the Nazis that even though they tried to destroy us, now we're walking with the Israeli flag..."

The 2011 Ministry of Education survey found a similar pattern for students' reasons for participation; they noted that girls were more likely than boys to say they were motivated by an emotional need to 'deal with' the issue of the Shoah. This was also true of students who had Shoah survivors or victims in their families.

2. Barriers to participation. 12th grade students who did not go to Poland were asked to give their reasons for not participating. These were far less varied. The most common reason by far was financial. Another barrier was that more than half the schools surveyed (55%) did not offer

26 As we found quite similar motivations among different groups of students, we do not indicate their gender and type of school.

the program; many students at these schools expressed a wish that they had the chance to participate. The emotional difficulty of the journey was mentioned by some students "...I didn't feel ready..." wrote one; another said "I didn't feel I could handle that kind of knowledge..."

A small number of the students said they didn't go because their parents objected. A few said they didn't think going to Poland with their class would be a meaningful way for them to learn about the Shoah. However, it is clear that the cost of the journey was the greatest obstacle and that many more students would go if they could receive financial support.

Table 18: Reasons given by students who didn't go to Poland for decision not to participate

Reason	# of students citing this as their **primary** reason for not going to Poland	# of students citing this as their **secondary** reason for not going to Poland	**Total** # of students citing this as a reason for not going to Poland
Financial (too expensive)	111	14	125
Too emotionally difficult	48	11	59
School-related reasons	23	4	27
Framework of journey not suitable	9	4	13
Parents or family reasons	8	2	10
Social reasons	1	8	9

C. Participation in the Journey

Since 1988, the Ministry of Education has sponsored educational journeys to key Shoah sites for groups of high school students.[27] In the past two decades, hundreds of thousands of students have taken part, and the program has expanded yearly. In just the five years between 2003 and 2007, almost 1500 groups comprising over 115,000 students and their teacher chaperones took part.

Table 19: Number of participants in school journeys to Poland 2003-2007[28]

	2003	**2004**	**2005**	**2006**	**2007**	**2008**
Number of participants (including teachers)	22,500	20,200	21,500	25,400	27,300	27,000
	2009	**2010**	**Total**			
	27,000	25,000	195,900			

Of the 12th grade students surveyed in 2007-2009, 44% said they had participated in a journey to Poland.[29] The vast majority went during their senior year, although 30% of the principals said the program was open to 11th graders from their schools as well, so some may have participated the previous year. Of the students who went to Poland, 87% were students in general schools and 13% in religious schools. This is similar to their proportion in the population of 12th graders at large,

27 Following the Six Day War, Poland (and many of the Eastern Bloc states) severed diplomatic relations with Israel. The journeys only became possible following the fall of the Communist government and restoration of diplomatic relations (Govrin, 2011).

28 Vargen, 2008, Israel Ministry of Education, 2011a (rounded figures).

29 According to Ministry of Education data about 33% of 12th grade students participated in journeys to Poland, thus this population is somewhat over-represented in the current study sample. This does not affect the accuracy of the comparison of participants and non-participants within the surveyed sample.

the students in religious schools being slightly under-represented (83% students in general schools, and 17% in religious schools).

1. Traits of participants and non-participants. A comparison of the 12th graders who participated in the journey to Poland and those who did not reveals much about motivations and goals prior to the journey and its impact on them.[30]

We found that the students who participated in the journey to Poland had greater exposure to all of types of information about the Shoah, in school and out. They embarked on the journey with a high level of familiarity and interest. They attended orientation sessions, and may have taken part in other non-compulsory activities. They were more likely to say they were very good or excellent students and with a stronger interest in history in general and in learning more about the Shoah in particular. Additionally, their greater exposure to the issue of the Shoah may reflect a difference between schools that sponsor journeys to Poland and those that do not. Schools sending students to Poland tend to have overall richer and more varied Shoah education programs. The principals of high schools that send groups to Poland indicated a higher number of hours dedicated to the subject in all grade levels (10th–12th). They were more likely to say that teachers outside the history program (art, literature, etc.) were involved in Shoah education and that their school offered activities outside the history requirements (visits to museums, informal activities). The schools sending groups to Poland were far more likely to have a coordinator dedicated to organizing the Shoah education program and teachers at these schools (whether or not they were chaperones) were more likely to attend the enrichment courses.

Since a greater percentage of participants had been members of youth movements (72% compared to 54% of those who didn't go) they were more likely to have taken part in Shoah-related activities (visits to museums, seeing movies) in this informal framework.[31] Further, participants were also more likely to have learned about the Shoah with their families. For example, they were more than twice as likely as non-participants to have gone to a memorial museum or watch documentaries and movies about the Shoah with their families. This reflects a stronger con-

---

30 For characteristics of participants and non-participants in journey to Poland, with comparison by school stream, see Appendix C, Table v.

31 See also Lazar et al., 2004b.

nection of their families to the issue. Those with relatives from Europe were more likely to go to Poland: three quarters of the participants said they were of Ashkenazi or mixed background, an over-representation of the 60% of the student sample who came from such backgrounds. Over half the participants had Shoah survivors and/or victims in their families, compared to a third of those who did not join the journey. In the religious schools impact of family background was even greater.

To deepen understanding of the connection between participation in the journey to Poland and the various socio-economic characteristics of students, an SSA was conducted on this data. A holistic portrait of the student body was created using seven basic traits as primary variables:

1) youth movement membership
2) ethnicity (Ashkenazi, Sephardi-Mizrahi, or mixed);
3) level of religiosity (secular, traditional, religious);
4) socio-economic level of the school (high, medium, low);
5) gender;
6) school stream (general, secular);
7) whether or not someone in the student's family was killed in the Shoah.

With these variables, a basic structural picture of the student body was drawn. The variables form a circle around an empty center, showing distinct differences between sub-populations. On the upper left-hand side are traits of being religious, of Sephardi-Mizrahi background, students in religious schools, attending schools in which the majority of students come from the lower two economic brackets, and not having lost a relative in the Shoah.

On the upper right are the traits of being secular, learning at a general school, having Ashkenazi or mixed background, attending schools in which the majority of students come from the highest economic bracket, and having lost a relative in the Shoah. Additionally, those who were members or leaders in youth movements are at the top and those who never were members are at the bottom.

Sub-populations of 12th grade students who did and did not participate in the journey were introduced as external variables. They are quite far from each other in the map, indicating a recognizable difference in the demographic make-up of the two populations. Participants are clearly in the right hand side of the figure, non-participants in the left. The ellipses drawn into the map, roughly encircling the axis between the participants and non-participants, indicate which items are more strongly associated with participation, namely: having lost family in the Shoah and having Ashkenazi ancestry (even if mixed). Having Sephardi-Mizrahi ancestry and not having lost family in the Shoah are most strongly correlated with non-participation. These traits play a stronger role than religiosity or even socio-economic class (although on an individual level the price of the trip was the greatest barrier to participation).

Gender is not linked to participation, male and female students being equally likely to join the program. Though participants were more likely to be youth movement members, this seems only marginally linked to participation in the journey.

Figure 9: Relationship between demographic characteristics of students, teachers' approach to Shoah studies, and participation in journey to Poland

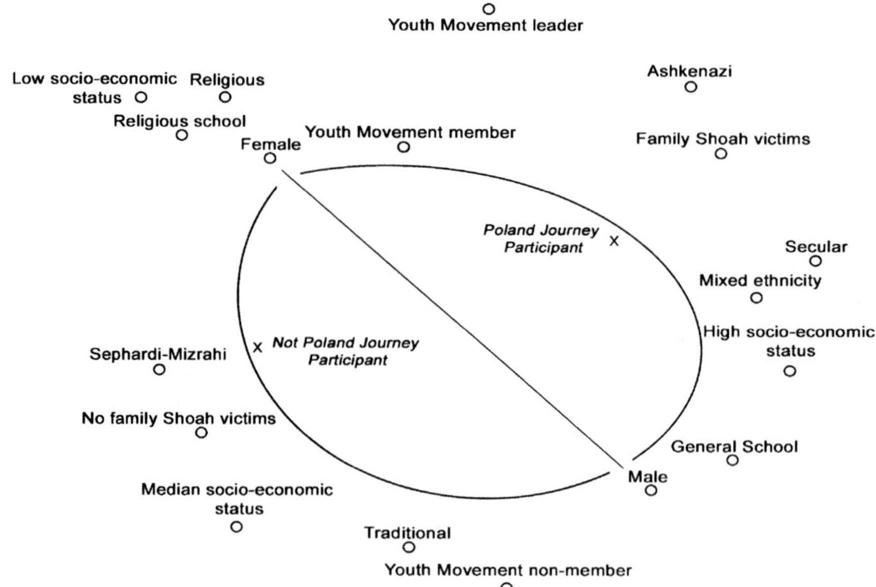

2. Participation of teacher chaperones. As the Ministry of Education requires two teachers to accompany every group of 32 students, thousands of teachers have also made the journey to Poland. The professional and personal impact on the teacher chaperones is an important aspect of the program, and one which has been given little attention in previous research.

Among the surveyed teachers, about half (51%) have accompanied groups to Poland. The teachers in the religious schools were only slightly less likely to have participated in a journey to Poland. Three quarters of the teachers who accompanied journeys to Poland taught history (either alone or in addition to other subjects). Teachers who chaperoned trips to Poland were more likely than those who didn't to participate in other enrichment activities such as ceremonies and field trips. The chaperones were more likely to have taken professional training courses on the Shoah, particularly at Yad Vashem.

The values of the chaperoning teachers were similar to those of their colleagues. However, they were somewhat more likely to stress the importance of universal values and democracy.

D. Debates and Controversies surrounding the Journey to Poland

This program has become not only one of the most important but one of the most controversial components of the Shoah educational program. It has been discussed and debated in the Ministry of Education, in the media, even in the Knesset (Israeli Parliament). We heard a number of questions and critiques voiced in the interviews, focus groups and open questions of this research. The main areas of concern are financial, educational and ideological.

1. Financial. As noted by the students, expense was the greatest barrier to participation. The cost of the journey runs from about $1400 to almost $2000 per student. The financial aspect of the program has been discussed in the Ministry of Education, the Knesset and the media. Some feel the gap created between students whose families can afford to send them to Poland and those whose families cannot is detrimental. Subsidies from the government and private foundations are available, either directly or through work-exchange. Virtually all of the principals (97%) said that at least some of the students at their schools received financial aid to make the journey to Poland, although about two thirds indicated that subsidies were available for only a small minority of the participants.[32]

Between 2004 and 2007, the Ministry of Education provided about $750,000 of subsidies for more than 3500 participants. In addition, 6,750 students received financial aid from the Claims Conference, representing (a total of $2.8 million). However, together these grants represent subsidies for less than 10% of the total number of students who participated in the journeys: about 3% of the students received funding from the Ministry of Education and about 6% from the Claims Conference. Additionally, the distribution of the funds did not apparently reach those most in need. Several of the surveyed principals said their schools enable students to work in exchange for financial support for the journey.

Interestingly, the principals of schools with students mainly in the median socio-economic level offered aid to a larger percentage of students than those with students mainly in the lowest bracket. Of the principals of schools in the median bracket, 28% said a majority of their students receive aid for the journey, compared to 19% of the principals of the lowest bracket schools.

> Not all schools are able to organize the journey, due to many existing issues. I write this as someone who has participated in four journeys in various frameworks, yet now am director of a school that isn't able to send delegations to Poland because of the limited financial situation of the student population.—*Female high school principal*

> I've gone to Poland with students eight times. In our school ... there is no student that doesn't go for financial reasons. Students who need support can do work exchange such as helping with repairs to the school during the summer vacation or tutoring younger students.—*Male high school principal*

---

32 For principals' assessment of financial support for journey to Poland available to students, with comparison according to schools' socio-economic level, see Appendix C, Table w.

Data provided by the Ministry of Education shows that between 2003 and 2007, three quarters of the groups sent to Poland were from schools whose student body came mostly from families in the upper socio-economic brackets. However, when only the Ministry-organized journeys are considered, the gap is much smaller; that is, almost half of the groups which went to Poland on Ministry-organized journeys were from schools in the lower socio-economic brackets. In stark contrast, 90% of the groups which went to Poland on school-organized journeys were from the upper brackets.

Similarly, a recent report issued by the government comptroller found that two-thirds of participants were from families in the upper third of Israel's economic spectrum, and a disproportionate number from the wealthiest 5% of the population, while only a small minority (6%) of participants were from families in the bottom third socio-economically.[33]

In response to this report, the Ministry of Education approved additional subsidies, graduated according to income, with up to 70% of the cost covered for students from families of the lowest economic percentiles.[34] This follows a subsidy made several years ago, when a cost increase forced some 1000 students to cancel their participation.[35] They also launched a special public committee to review the situation and make recommendations, further attesting to the level of importance attached to the program. Several municipalities with large populations of lower-income families have considered offering shorter journeys to Poland—even as short as one day—in order to lower the cost of the journey enough to make it available to more students.

While there are some decision-makers and educators who question whether subsidizing journeys to Poland for large numbers of students represents a good use of resources, and if the educational impact justifies the cost, there is widespread support for the program and a desire to make it available to a greater number of students. One principal of a junior high school suggested creating some type of alternative Shoah education experience for students not able to go to Poland.

---

33 Drockman, 2011.
34 Maniv, 2011.
35 Waldocks, 2008.

> After our trip to Poland last summer, we reached the conclusion that there is a need to bring as many students as possible to Poland; it gives the subject a different meaning in the eyes of the students. One of the central problems in bringing students to Poland is financial. To the extent that there is a change from the government offices and bigger budgets are given, we could bring many more students to Poland and give the subject primary importance.—*Male principal of a religious high school of median socio-economic level*

> It would be great if every student could take part in the journey to Poland. It would be worth shortening the journey to 5-6 days, and finding ways to expand financial support for those in need.—*Male high school principal*

2. Educational. Another area of debate concerns the unique educational contribution of the journey. If the journey offers the possibility of an important educational experience, do the students take it seriously, or do they see it as a recreational tour? Does visiting the physical sites of the Shoah offer something which cannot be achieved in other ways? Some of the experts interviewed suggested fundamentally revising the structure of the journeys (for example bringing smaller groups of students who receive more intimate and intensive preparation, or putting less emphasis on the ceremonies and show of Israeli flags).[36] Some said the multi-sensory experience of being at the sites had inherent educational value not accessible in classroom lessons or books, making the history real for students and enabling them to understand it on a deeper level.[37] Dr. Jackie Feldman describes the journey as a rite of transformation through which students move from being passive spectators to actively identifying witnesses, a process difficult to reproduce in the classroom.[38]

An underlying concept behind visiting the sites is to make the his-

---

36 Dr. Avner Ben-Amos, Dr. Amos Goldberg, Ephrat Balberg-Rotenstreich, Dr. Daniel Blatman, Riki Mandel, Dr. Nili Keren, Dr. Tom Segev, personal communication, 2009.

37 Dr. Ben-Sasson, Inbal Ben-Dov, Dr. Yisrael Rosenson, Dr. Tom Segev, Malka Tor, personal communication, 2009.

38 Feldman, 1999, 2008.

torical events more "real" to the students, but ironically it can have the opposite effect. A survey of (mainly non-Jewish) Belgian public school students visiting Auschwitz, for example, found the renovated camps gave the students a less "authentic" image of the horrors of the Shoah than documentaries or photos from the time.[39] Dr. Nili Keren of the Massuah Institute cautioned that students who visit the death camps may have a distorted perception that standing in the physical spot is enough to "know" what happened there.[40]

> The students are busy taking pictures and the camera distances them from what they are seeing. They take in very little "spiritual food" and it is difficult get them to take even a brief moment to look deeply, investigate, critique.—*Male coordinator of a high school*

3. Ideological. The most contentious area of debate surrounding the journey to Poland is ideological, reflecting the conflicting ideas regarding Shoah education as a whole.

In the early years of the program, the ideological tone was strongly Zionist. A Ministry of Education handbook issued in 1988 included a quote from then-mayor of Tel Aviv Shlomo Lahat, who left his native Germany in 1933 to join the Haganah in British Palestine: "Poland is the most tragic example of the impossibility of Jewish existence without a homeland. In that sense it is also the most convincing evidence for the basic truth of Zionism." A later Ministry handbook *Looking for My Brothers* states, "If there is a meaning to the journey to Poland, it is first and foremost to emphasize our Israeliness and a total negation of the Diaspora."[41] This view still has much support in the Israeli educational system and society. At a Yom HaShoah speech in 2001, Limor Livnat, then head of the Ministry of Education, said, "What separates them [Shoah victims] from us [Israelis] is not that we are some new sort of Jew. The main difference is external: we have a state and a flag and an army; caught in their tragedy, they lacked all three."[42]

Many of the interviewees reacted against such nationalist overtones

39 Grandjean et al., 2011.

40 Dr. Nili Keren, personal communication, 2009.

41 Quoted in Hazan, 2001, 46.

42 Livnat, 2001, quoted in Feldman, 2002.

of the journeys to Poland or what they saw as appropriation of the memory of the victims for political aims.[43] A smaller number said the element of strengthening and uniting the identity of the students was a valuable aspect of the journey.[44]

> To my dismay, the journey to Poland has largely overturned the goal of using the presentation to transmit universal educational messages.... The message of the price of hatred of the Other is pushed aside.—*Male high school coordinator*

E. Evaluation of the Journey to Poland

Within the educational system, we found that virtually everyone—students, teachers, principals, experts in the field, and decision-makers in the Ministry of Education—saw the journey to Poland as an educationally important and emotionally powerful experience for participants.

1. Satisfaction. Students and teachers who participated in the journey were asked to rate their level of satisfaction, taking into account all aspects of the journey. Almost all (96%) of the participating students said they were satisfied with the journey. The students were more enthusiastically positive about the journey than the teachers; two thirds of the students said they were "very satisfied" with the journey, compared to 40% of the participating teachers.

> The trip to Poland was very important to me ... during the time in Poland, which was not an easy experience, I was able to make some sort of order in my mind, and to answer for myself questions which had been open for a long time...—*Female 12th grade student in religious high school of low socio-economic level*

Of the teachers who went to Poland, 89% said they were satisfied

---

43 Dr. Manuela Consonni, Prof. Hanna Yablonka, Prof. Eyal Naveh, Prof. Eliezer Schweid, Shalvit Gross, personal communication.

44 Prof. Hanna Yaoz, Prof. YechiamWeitz, personal communication, 2009.

and 40% were "very satisfied." Of the teachers who did not go, 68% were satisfied with the program and only 15% very much so.[45]

The non-history teachers were more enthusiastic about the journey than the history teachers; 37% of the non-history teachers said they were "very satisfied," compared with 28% of those who taught only history. This seems to indicate that the journey was appreciated more by the teachers with an emotional-affective approach to Shoah teaching. The history teachers, who tend to place more value on cognitive learning, were a bit more cautious in their evaluations of the journey to Poland.

One of the criticisms raised by the teachers pertained to the students' behavior; some reported, for example, that students had parties in the evenings or slept during films and presentations. Such an atmosphere on an educational journey pertaining to the Shoah would disappoint teachers. It would be less likely to be seen as a weakness in the program by high school students, although in the open comments, some of the participants said they had been disturbed that their peers seemed mainly interested in shopping or otherwise treated the journey as a tourist excursion.

2. Educational impact. The principals saw the journey as education both in terms of the students gaining both knowledge and an important personal experience, with more emphasis on the latter. An equivalent percentage answered that the journeys are both knowledge and experience-oriented, but a far higher percentage (63%) said they are geared towards experience to a "very high degree" than said they were knowledge-oriented to a "very high degree" (17%). Principals of religious schools gave even more emphasis to the personal experience aspect than did the principals of the general schools, though their emphases on knowledge acquisition during the journeys were similar.

Almost all the students who went to Poland (99%) said that the journey was effective in teaching them about the Shoah; 91% said it was "very effective." The participants rated the journey as the best means of teaching about the Shoah; school trips to memorial museums in Israel, in comparison, were rated as "very effective" by 57% of journey participants. Hearing the testimonies of survivors was rated as the second

45 For satisfaction with the journey to Poland among participating students and teachers see Appendix C, Table x.

most effective type of Shoah education, considered "very effective" by 76% of participants. Those who went gave a stronger endorsement of hearing testimonies than did their peers who did not go to Poland. It is likely that hearing survivors speak in the context of the journey to Poland has an exceptionally strong impact. Additionally, alumni hearing survivors speak after their return may be more strongly affected than their peers who did not go.

The participants were more likely to say they felt proficient in the subject: 74% of the students who went to Poland compared to 62% of those who didn't. They also demonstrated broader knowledge, recognizing a greater number of the items in the list. The knowledge gap between participants and non-participants was greater regarding the less widely known items. For example, while virtually all the 12th graders, whether they went to Poland or not, have heard of Auschwitz, a far greater percentage of those who went to Poland knew of Himmler. It is impossible to say whether or not the students learned these specific pieces of information *during* the trip to Poland; participants may have been more motivated prior to the trip and more attentive to lessons afterwards. Nevertheless, the journey seems to have a positive correspondence to cognitive learning about the Shoah, an interesting and important finding in light of the concerns voiced in the interviews, focus groups and open questions regarding the educational value of the program. A prior evaluation among a smaller survey population of Israeli general high school students also found that those who participated in school-sponsored journeys to Poland had greater knowledge about the Shoah and were more sensitive to the subject than their peers who did not.[46]

3. Impact on teachers' proficiency. Participating in the tours has a strong impact on accompanying teachers as well. Those who went to Poland were more likely to say they felt *very* proficient in all aspects of Shoah education. In particular, the teachers who went to Poland felt more proficient regarding historical background of the Shoah, Nazi ideology, and the struggle of the Jews against the Nazis. They felt their convictions regarding the importance of preserving the memory of the Shoah had been strengthened. The teachers' increased knowledge and enthusiasm may be transmitted to their students, including those who

46 Romi and Lev, 2003.

did not participate in journeys themselves, thus expanding the impact of the journey.

Table 20: Recognition of selected items related to Shoah by students who went to Poland and those who did not (see Appendix E for descriptions of terms)

	Recognized by students who went to Poland	**Recognized by students who did not go to Poland**
Molotov-Ribbentrop pact	91%	78%
Operation Barbarossa	89%	73%
German Operation (Aktion)	81%	56%
Himmler	73%	49%
Mordechai Anielewicz	72%	43%
Anschluss	61%	46%
Babi Yar	50%	33%
Einsatzgruppen (task forces/ Uzvot Mivza)	54%	37%
Goebbels	46%	36%

Table 21: Self-perceived proficiency in aspects of Shoah education among teachers who accompanied a journey to Poland and those who did not—percentage answering they feel proficient "to a very great extent"

	Teachers who went to Poland	Teachers who didn't go to Poland
Shoah in general	35%	21%
Historical background	60%	44%
Nazi ideology	63%	49%
Struggle of Jews vs. the Nazis	50%	35%
Jewish life before the Shoah	22%	17%
Jewish life during the Shoah	25%	22%
The destruction process	67%	51%
Influence of the Shoah on the Jewish world and Israel	40%	33%

4. Impact on attitudes and beliefs. One of the key goals of the Jewish tour-pilgrimages to former death camps is to transform participants into "witnesses" of the Shoah.[47] We observed that during memorial ceremonies at schools, alumni of the program spoke or made presentations to their classmates which emphasized their role as witnesses, for example by repeating phrasing such as "this happened, this really happened…."

The vast majority of the principals, teachers and students agreed the

47 Feldman, 1999.

experience of going to Poland strengthened students' commitment to remembering what happened to the Jews of Europe during the Nazi era. The principals were the most likely to say the journey strengthens this commitment "to a very great extent" (72%). The teachers who *did not* participate in the journey were the least likely to say so (39%). The students had a more positive impression of the journey's impact on them than did the teachers who accompanied them indicating that the experience affects the students more deeply than is apparent to the teachers. 61% of the participating students said the journey had a great impact on their commitment to remember the Shoah.[48]

There was little difference in the Jewish and Israeli identity between the students who went to Poland and those who didn't. The students were essentially all proud to be Jewish and Israeli, the journey alumni very slightly more so. Those who went to Poland were more likely to select "remembering the Shoah" as a reason to be Jewish and to say that the Shoah affects their worldview. They were slightly more critical of the treatment of Shoah survivors in Israel, indicating they were more sensitive to and aware of this issue. The journey alumni were more likely to say they thought there could be another Shoah somewhere in the world, but less likely to think it could happen in Israel. At the same time, the journey did *not* increase their conviction that Israel represented an 'answer' to the Shoah; in fact, the non-participants were very slightly more likely to absolutely agree with this premise. The program alumni were also more likely to say the Shoah was a tragedy for all humankind, not just the Jews.

48 For perception of extent of impact of the journey to Poland on students' commitment to remembering the Shoah, with comparison between responses of principals, participating students, chaperoning teachers, and non-chaperoning teachers, see Appendix C, Table y.

Table 22: Attitudes regarding the Shoah among 12th graders who went to Poland and those who did not—percentage answering affirmatively (percentage answering "absolutely" in parentheses)

	12th graders who went to Poland	12th graders who didn't go to Poland
Proud to be Jewish	95% (76%)	92% (73%)
Proud to be Israeli	91% (66%)	87% (61%)
The Shoah affects my worldview	81% (41%)	75% (29%)
The State of Israel is an "answer" to the Shoah	86% (47%)	86% (49%)
Another Shoah could happen in the world	78% (35%)	67% (29%)
Another Shoah could happen in Israel	21% (7%)	27% (10%)
The State of Israel treats Shoah survivors well	17% (4%)	26% (7%)
Shoah was a tragedy for all humankind	89%	80%
Remembering the Shoah is a reason to be Jewish	51%	40%

The journey to Poland strengthened participants' commitment to universal values as well as their Israeli and Jewish identities in both types of schools, though the impact of the journey on participants from religious schools was greater; that is, there was a larger gap between participants and non-participants from the religious schools. At the same time, there was a significant gap between the views of non-participants in religious and general schools, indicating the journey slightly strengthens predispositions rather than radically altering them. This confirms previous studies which found that the journey to Poland did not cause a great change the participants' social, religious, or national identities. Since identity formation is a long and multifaceted process, a single experience, even an intense experience such as the journey to Poland, is unlikely to cause a major change, though it may reinforce existing attitudes.[49] Interestingly, a survey of army officers who took part in the Witnesses in Uniform program found in some cases nationalist attitudes were diminished slightly after the experience.[50] The impact of visiting Shoah sites on Israeli nationalist attitudes appears to be quite complex and deserving of further study.

The 2011 Israel Ministry of Education survey compared participating students' feelings before and immediately after the journey. These students reported the journey simultaneously strengthened their sense of connection to the Jewish People (87%), their understanding of the impact of violent racism (87%) and their understanding of the need for a strong State of Israel (83%). The weakest impact by far was in terms of increasing familiarity with Polish culture and people: only 45% said they learned about contemporary Poland and 30% felt they had made connections with Polish youth.[51] However, although the students said that the journey strengthened their feelings about the Shoah, the comparison of their views as stated before and immediately after the journey showed little or no change in basic attitudes. The students' statements following the journey that going to Poland impacted their feelings regarding Jewish and Israeli identity and universal values matched, almost exactly, their expectations prior to the journey that the experience *would* impact these feelings. Actual changes in attitude, however, were extremely slight.

---

49 Lev and Romi, in press; Romi and Lev, 2003, 2007; Schechter, 2002. Another subject of Schechter's study was the influence of the journey to Poland on students' feelings regarding Israeli Arabs. As this is not the subject of the current report, that aspect of the study is not addressed here.

50 Levinson, 2012.

51 Israel Ministry of Education, 2011b.

Table 23: Comparison of Jewish, Israeli and universal values among participants and non-participants in the journey to Poland, by type of school

	Non-participants from general high school	Participants from general high school	Non-participants from religious high school	Participants from religious high school
I *absolutely* feel a sense of identification with survivors of the Shoah	28%	35%	49%	60%
I am *absolutely* committed to preserving the memory of the Shoah	59%	74%	73%	88%
"Remembering the Shoah" is a reason to be Jewish	42%	51%	33%	51%
Israeli/Zionist aspects				
I am *absolutely* committed to the existence of the State of Israel	48%	58%	63%	78%
Universal/humanist aspects				
I *absolutely* identify with universal values'	30%	40%	36%	46%
I *absolutely* identify with democratic values	44%	52%	39%	48%

Upon their return, the students in the religious schools were slightly more likely than those in the general schools to say the journey gave them some insight into Jewish life in Europe before the Shoah, while those in the general schools were more likely to say they learned about modern-day Poland, reflecting some difference in the itineraries of the two school streams.

It is notable that the Ministry's survey found that participants' feelings of hatred and negative attitudes towards Polish people were diminished following the journey.[52]

5. Impact on perceived relevance of Shoah studies at large. While participants and non-participants were equally satisfied with their Shoah education overall, the students who went to Poland were more likely to say that Shoah studies were thought-provoking and relevant to their personal and family lives. Again, it is difficult to determine cause and effect; that is, whether students who felt a prior personal connection signed up for the trip, or if the experience made subsequent lessons more meaningful.

Table 24: Poland journey and perceived relevance of Shoah studies—percentage answering affirmatively (percentage answering "very true" in parentheses)

	12th graders who went to Poland	**12th graders who didn't go to Poland**
Shoah studies make me think	88% (38%)	84% (32%)
Shoah studies are relevant to my life	82% (28%)	77% (23%)
Shoah studies answer personal questions I have	62% (18%)	53% (13%)
Shoah studies are relevant to my family life	43% (14%)	29% (9%)

52 Israel Ministry of Education, 2011.

These findings are important in the context of the critique expressed in the various qualitative aspects of the research, that the journeys may be used to instill what some consider ethnocentric expressions of Jewish and Israeli ideologies. Some oppose the journeys to Poland on these grounds. The empirical data indicates that the students' Jewish and Israeli identities are strengthened but not radically altered by the journey to Poland, and that their identification with universal values is equally strengthened. These findings are congruent with another study which found that Israeli teenagers have a strong sense of Jewish Israeli national identity, whether or not they participate in a school journey to Poland and that there is a complex interplay between Jewish, Zionist and universal lessons of the Shoah.[53]

There are several possible explanations for this. One, students' social identities are largely formed by the 12th grade. Second, the Shoah plays a central role in contemporary Israeli society, and ideological messages regarding the Shoah, Jewish identity and Zionism which are delivered during the journey to Poland have already been received in other frameworks. Third, in looking at the messages teachers emphasize in Shoah education (addressed in depth in a subsequent chapter), we found that the teachers who accompanied student journeys to Poland attach great importance to goals and messages related to universal values, democracy, and fighting racism; even more than the teachers who do not go on the trip.

The data for the whole population of 12th graders indicate that the main impact of the journey for the majority of participants is on attitudes directly related to the Shoah—perceived relevance of Shoah studies, familiarity with key items, commitment to remembering the events. The journey strengthens Jewish, Israeli and universal values relative to the views expressed by non-participants in the same school stream, but differences expressed by non-participants in the two types of schools remind us that there are many other impacts on these values.

A survey of alumni who participated in the journey during the past ten years and a control group of non-participants and found the journey had a greater long-term impact on identity among participants who did *not* have a direct family connection to the Shoah. Among those who did have Shoah survivors or victims in their families, the long-term impact

53 Lazar et al., 2004a.

of the journey was negligible. This seems to point to the relative role of the journey among other sources of information. Jews with a direct family connection to the Shoah are more likely *a priori* to have a high level of sensitivity to the issue, and the impact of the journey as a single influence is relatively smaller. Those with no family connection apparently undergo a greater change in attitude.[54]

This finding is highly significant in the context of the socio-demographics of the journey among Israeli students. Parallel to this, Sephardi-Mizrahi students with no direct family connection—those alumni who were most strongly affected by the journey—are less likely to participate. Making Shoah education and commemoration relevant to Sephardi-Mizrahi students has become an area of interest in recent years, with efforts to broaden the scope of the subject and instill a sense of shared fate among Jews from all backgrounds.[55]

F. The "Poland Experience"

In studying and analyzing the journey to Poland, it became increasingly apparent that there are numerous parallels between this and another example of Jewish heritage tourism I studied in depth, namely, the group tours to Israel for Diaspora youth. A longitudinal study of the Israel Experience tours found that the sojourn in Israel strengthens Jewish identity and the link to Israel—it does not create Jewish identity and a link to Israel where none existed before.[56]

There are other similarities between the two phenomena of Diaspora youth tours to Israel and Israeli student journeys to Poland. In both cases, structural preparation—values and knowledge received from their school, family, friends, and community—convinces potential participants that the experience will be important and meaningful for them. Before going to Poland, Israeli youth have already learned about the history of the Shoah, they have heard repeatedly and from many sources that it is important to remember what happened to the Jews of Europe. They have learned to link the attempted genocide of European Jewry

54 Evron, 2011.
55 Yablonka, 2008, 2009.
56 Cohen, 2008.

with the importance of the State of Israel and pride in being Jewish. The time in Poland strengthens these attitudes.

Similarly, research on the Israel Experience tours repeatedly found that before deciding to join a tour to Israel, Diaspora youth have a strong sense of Jewish identity and a feeling of connection to Israel. Even the Taglit-birthright tours, which attempted to recruit participants from the periphery of the Diaspora Jewish world by offering free tours, largely attracted youth with at least some degree of prior interest in and connection to Judaism and Israel. Again, participants' identities, beliefs and values were strengthened by the experience; not created or changed.

The barriers which prevent youth from taking part in the journey to Poland or an educational tour to Israel may be cultural, religious or economic. Among Diaspora youth, the main barriers against participating in a tour to Israel were cultural and religious since the free Taglit tours largely removed the financial barrier, bringing over 210,000 North American youth to Israel, (between 15% and 25% of American youth).[57] Diaspora youth who were not educated to think that Judaism and Israel are relevant to them are unlikely to want to join a tour to Israel, regardless of financial considerations.

The situation is different for Israeli youth and the journey to Poland. In this case, the greatest barrier to participation is financial. As we saw, 80% of the 9th graders said they intend to go to Poland in the future. The structural preparation is conducted through the school system and throughout Israeli society, in which there is widespread consensus that learning about and remembering the Shoah is crucial. The attitudes regarding the Shoah among students from the lower socio-economic brackets are similar to those of their peers from more affluent backgrounds. They are just as likely to want to go to Poland. They are less likely to go because they simply cannot afford it.

In both the case of the Diaspora youth's tour to Israel and the Israeli student's journey to Poland, more realistic expectations and a more delicate model for interpreting the impact of the experience are necessary. While some people may expect dramatic, almost magical transformations among participants, this is rarely the case. There is a cumulative

57 According to the estimate of between 900,000 and 1.2 million Jewish-American young adults aged 18-26, the target cohort of Taglit-birthright.

contribution of educational project.[58] A journey to Israel or to sites of the Shoah is an intensive experience, but it is one part of a cumulative educational process. The data here show that the students are satisfied with the journey to Poland and they see it as the most effective tool for learning about the Shoah. Further, it strengthens their commitment to remembering the Shoah, they recognize a greater number of Shoah-related items and feel more proficient in the subject, and Shoah studies are more relevant to them.

58 Ritterband (1986) describes the interactive and cumulative impact in identity-related education as "the more, the more."

IX. IMPROVING SHOAH EDUCATION

• How to further develop Shoah education is given a great deal of serious thought and consideration, attesting to the importance attributed to the subject.

• Teachers' most common requests were for more classroom time and professional training courses.

• Teachers and principals advocate adding informal, experiential activities to enrich cognitive learning.

• In terms of ideologic approach, there is greater variation. Overall, teachers and principals would like to see the Zionist message emphasized more. Those in the religious stream also want more specifically Jewish content. Teachers who are secular and teach in the general stream are most likely to recommend increasing universal aspects.

* * * * * *

The importance attributed to the subject of the Shoah in Jewish-Israeli society also means its teaching is given a great deal of serious critique. This is not a topic to be taught simply to fulfill a requirement. It is also among the most difficult subjects to address. Shoah education is fraught with potential pitfalls. There are real dangers of misrepresentation, of trivializing on the one hand or becoming voyeuristic toward the horrors on the other. The ideological presentation must be carefully considered. It could become overly nationalistic or so universalized that the specific historic context is lost. The methods and materials must be well-developed and chosen with care so as to be appropriate for the students' ages and levels of maturity. The teachers must be adequately trained to deal with students' inevitably difficult questions.

Throughout the research, I was continually impressed by the depth of thought given to Shoah education by the academic experts, Ministry of Education officials, principals, teachers, and no less by the students themselves. There is a generally high level of satisfaction with Shoah education as it currently exists. This current state of Shoah education, it should be remembered, has come about through decades of deep thought, debate, education many suggestions for how it can be further enhanced and developed. This chapter examines the challenges to Shoah education and the recommendations for its improvement.

> The curriculum as it exists today has undergone serious improvement ... but there are still two main problems. The first is that it is often not taught in the proper historical context of World War II ... the second problem is not exactly with the curriculum itself, but that museum visits sometimes take the place of teaching.—*Professor Neima Barzel*

> The curriculum is fine, it touches on all the important topics.... If there was enough time to teach the curriculum as it is meant to be taught, it would be fine.—*Henya Weintraub*

A. Challenges to Shoah Education

Teachers were given a list of potential challenges and asked to what extent each interfered with their ability to teach the subject to their full potential.[1] Insufficient time was seen as the greatest obstacle, cited by two thirds of the teachers. As noted earlier, except for the 11th grade, when students are preparing for matriculation exams, the hours allotted for Shoah studies are quite limited.

The next greatest request on the part of the teachers was for additional enrichment courses; 42% expressed this opinion. As noted earlier, over half the teachers attended such courses mostly within the previous few years. Less than a quarter said lack of training was a problem that interfered with their ability to teach the Shoah. Also, half the teachers said they received support for attending these courses. Therefore, the high percentage who said there was a "need for further professional development" should not be seen as expression of a lack. Rather, it shows their level of enthusiasm and desire to learn so as to be able to teach

1 For assessment of extent of difficulties faced by teachers in Shoah education see Appendix C, Table z.

the subject better. Specifically, teachers said they would like to learn more about life of the Jewish community before and during the Shoah. "You cannot teach about the murder of European Jewry without teaching about what was lost, the physical and spiritual wealth of European Jewry before the Shoah," as Professor Yablonka said.

Less than a quarter of the teachers said lack of professional support was a problem for them. Although almost all admit encountering problems (less than 10% said they never did), they turned for help to other teachers or the coordinator of the history program at their school.

B. *Recommendations for Improving Shoah Education*

A list of possible recommendations was compiled based on advice of the interviews with experts, the focus groups with principals and teachers, and relevant literature published by other researchers in the field. This list was included in the questionnaires distributed to principals and teachers. For each area of possible change in Shoah education, respondents were asked whether they would suggest a great increase, a small increase, no change, a small decrease, or a large decrease.

As seen in Table 25, the strongest recommendation by both the principals and the teachers was to make the Shoah studies more informal and experiential. This finding raises an important question: to what extent are the principals and teachers trained and prepared to provide and address the informal and experiential aspects of Shoah education?

The recommendation to increase the informal and experiential approach does not imply a suggestion to reduce the emphasis on classroom teaching or on cognitive knowledge. The teachers, in particular, strongly recommend increasing the number of hours allocated to teaching the Shoah and putting more emphasis on knowledge.

> Teaching the Shoah in the framework of preparing for matriculation exams is seriously damaging. I think we have to continue to make it more meaningful and experiential.—*Female history teacher*

Over a third of the principals and 43% of the teachers said they think the journey to Poland should be given more emphasis that it is currently given. Less than 10% suggested de-emphasizing the journey. The remainder suggests continuing the current level of emphasis.

Table 25: Recommendations of principals and teachers, by percentage. "In your opinion, Shoah education should ..."

	Principals		Teachers	
	More / Much more	Much more	More / Much more	Much more
Didactics and activities				
Include informal activities	88%	**43%**	87%	**53%**
Emphasize experiential	83%	**39%**	79%	**41%**
Emphasize knowledge	61%	**14%**	68%	**27%**
Emphasize the journeys to Poland	37%	**14%**	43%	**21%**
Time/intensity				
Hours	72%	**33%**	79%	**52%**
Intensive	51%	**14%**	57%	**20%**
Values/messages				
Be Jewish	56%	**22%**	47%	**21%**
Be Universal	57%	**19%**	60%	**26%**
Be Zionist	78%	**33%**	67%	**33%**

Of the three value-approaches (Jewish, Zionist, and universal), both the teachers and principals gave the strongest recommendation for making Shoah education more Zionist. The principals were a little more likely to recommend making Shoah education more Jewish; the teachers were somewhat more likely to suggest giving more emphasis to universal values. In general, we can say that the teachers and principals would like to see Shoah education include a combination of all three types of values, with a little more emphasis on the Zionist message. The principals and teachers of the religious schools were significantly more likely to recommend increasing the emphasis to Judaism and Zionism.

That teachers who teach about the Shoah recommend increasing the number of hours dedicated to the subject is not surprising; what is more significant is that the request is strongly reinforced by the principals. The need for more time was particularly stressed in the junior high schools: 78% of principals and 87% of teachers requested more hours dedicated to Shoah education.

> The subject of Shoah education is very valuable, both Jewishly and universally. I think it is important to allot regular hours for Shoah education in junior high school.—*Male principal of general junior high school of very high socio-economic level*

History teachers were more likely to recommend increasing the number of hours. Non-history teachers involved in Shoah education were more likely to encourage intensifying the experiential aspects of the curriculum (including, especially, the journey to Poland), which are the educational activities with which they were more likely to be involved.[2]

1. A typology of teachers based on their recommendations. Based on analysis of the patterns of the teachers' recommendations, it emerged that their recommendation to increase Jewish and/or universal aspects were most instructive in differentiating between teachers' approach to the subject. A typology of the teachers with four types was developed: 1) those who suggest increasing the Jewish and Zionist aspects; 2) those who suggest increasing the universal aspects; 3) those who suggest increasing both the Jewish-Zionist and the universal as-

---

2 For means of principals' and teachers' recommendation see Appendix C, Table aa.

pects; and 4) those who don't suggest increasing either.[3]

Table 26: Characteristics of teachers according to the typology of recommendations

	Recommend increasing **universal** aspects of Shoah education	Recommend increasing **Jewish** aspects of Shoah education	Recommend increasing **both** universal and Jewish aspects of Shoah education	Recommend increasing **neither** Jewish nor universal aspects of Shoah education
Number (%)	*147 (34%)*	*85 (19%)*	*113 (26%)*	*89 (21%)*
Teaches in general school	41%	10%	26%	23%
Teaches in religious school	7%	54%	26%	13%
Teacher is secular	52%	6%	19%	23%
Teacher is traditional	22%	14%	42%	22%
Teacher is religious	5%	54%	27%	14%

As seen in Table 26, of the teachers who teach in the general schools, the largest percentage (41%) recommend increasing the universal aspects, the smallest percentage (10%) recommend increasing the Jewish aspects. In contrast, among the teachers in the religious schools, the largest percentage (54%) recommends increasing the Jewish aspects and the smallest percentage (7%) recommends increasing the universal

3 The analysis was conducted using a multi-dimensional technique known as Partial Order Scalogram Analysis, which ranges profiles of surveyed individuals and identifies which variables are most useful in discriminating between profiles in order to portray the structural relationships among them. For a full explanation of this procedure see Amar, 2005; Cohen, 2011d; Levy, 1994.

aspects. The pattern is similar when we consider the teachers' self-definition: the religious teachers were most likely to recommend increasing Jewish aspects and the secular teachers were most likely to recommend increasing the universal aspects, the teachers who define themselves as traditional were most likely to recommend increasing both Jewish and universal aspects. The teachers' self-definition of their level of religiosity was more significant than the stream of the school in which they teach.

Moreover, we found that there was a dramatic difference between younger teachers and older ones, as seen in Table 27. The older teachers were much more likely to recommend increasing universal aspects of Shoah education; younger teachers were significantly more likely to recommend increasing Jewish aspects. This again reflects a larger trend in Israeli society, mentioned earlier, in which the younger generation is giving more emphasis to Jewish aspects of identity.[4]

Table 27: Typology of teachers according to their age[5]

	Recommend increasing **universal** aspects of Shoah education	Recommend increasing **Jewish** aspects of Shoah education	Recommend increasing **both** universal and Jewish aspects of Shoah education	Recommend increasing **neither** Jewish nor universal aspects of Shoah education	Total
Under 30	6%	56%	28%	11%	100%
30-39	29%	26%	28%	17%	100%
40-49	34%	18%	24%	24%	100%
50 and older	42%	12%	24%	22%	100%

4 Auron, 1993a; Liebman and Yadgar, 2004.

5 Some caution must be taken due to the relatively small number of teachers who are younger than 30 years old. Nevertheless, the trends are clear. For instance, those recommending the universal aspects of Shoah education, who represented 42% of the 50 and older teachers, fall to 34% for the 40-49, and to 29% for the 30-39.

2. Structural analysis (SSA) of teachers' recommendations. To better perceive the overall picture of how teachers would improve Shoah education, a structural analysis using the Smallest Space Analysis technique was conducted on the teachers' recommendations for improving Shoah education. This analysis found there were two basic orientations among the recommendations. One concerns the values emphasized in Shoah studies, with a spectrum between the recommendation to make Shoah studies more universal and the recommendation to make it more Jewish and Zionist. The second concerns the way in which the Shoah is taught, with a spectrum ranging between the recommendation to increase the emphasis on knowledge and the recommendation to increase the informal/experiential aspects.

There are two axes which represent two directions of recommendations. The horizontal axis runs between the recommendation to make Shoah education more universal (on the left-hand side of the figure) and the recommendation to make it more Jewish and Zionist (on the right-hand side of the figure). The vertical axis runs between the recommendation to increase knowledge about the Shoah (above the center) and the recommendation to increase the informal/experiential aspects of Shoah education (below the center).

In addition to this structure of two intersecting axes, there is also a structure from center to periphery of three concentric circular regions. These move from most concrete, in the center, to more abstract around the periphery. In the center are two items: "increase number of hours" and "increase intensity." The placement of these recommendations in the center indicates that they were strongly correlated with all the other recommendations. In other words, teachers who suggested making Shoah education more universal and those who suggest making it more Zionist were equally likely to recommend adding hours and increasing the intensity of the educational program. Hours and intensity of the program represent tangible resources. The middle circle encompasses the pedagogic approaches, and the journey to Poland.

Various sub-groups of the teachers were introduced as external variables, showing their relative positions to the recommendations. Religious teachers are closest to the recommendation to increase the Jewish and Zionist orientation of Shoah education. Secular teachers are closer to the recommendation to increase the emphasis on universal lessons and values. Teachers who define themselves as "traditional" are closer to the recommendation to increase the informal and experiential aspects and to increase journeys to Poland.

Ashkenazi and mixed-ethnicity teachers are at the top of the map, with the recommendation to increase cognitive knowledge; Mizrahi teachers are at the bottom of the map, with the recommendation to emphasize the experiential-informal nature of Shoah education.

Figure 10: SSA of teachers' recommendations, with sub-groups of teachers as external variables

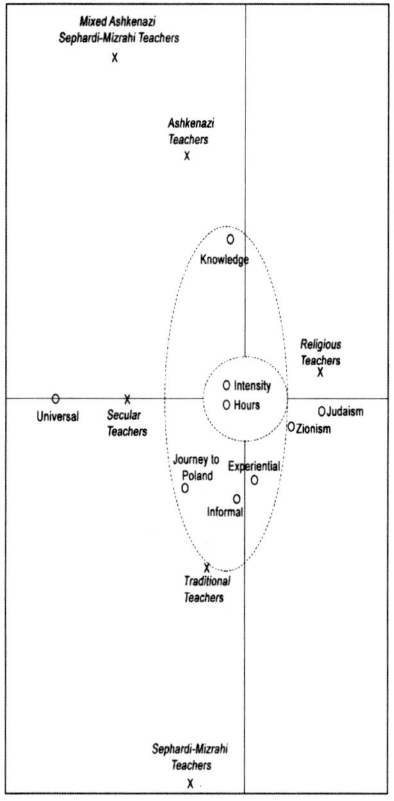

In this SSA map of the teachers' recommendations, it is possible to recognize several basic sets of conceptually related elements—"facets" in the terminology of Facet Theory. First, there is a clear differentiation between educational resources (hours, intensity), pedagogic approach (cognitive, experiential) and ideological goals (universal, Jewish,

Zionist). This facet is organized in concentric circles, with the resources in the inner circle. A second facet distinguishes between cognitive-knowledge based modes of learning (north region) and affective modes (south region). The third facet differentiates between various ideological approaches. The Universal approach is at the western part of the map and the Jewish and Zionist approaches are in the eastern part of the map. Interestingly, this last facet could be more detailed in a sequential logic from the most particularistic (Jewish), to less particularistic (Zionism), towards the most universalistic, through an intermediary ideological activity (journey to Poland), which we found in the research shares these various ideologies. Taken together, these facets impact the evaluation and recommendations.

X. REFLECTIONS AND PROVISIONAL CONCLUSIONS

• Shoah education as manifest in the Israeli school system is a unique pedagogic event, in that a population identifying with the victims of a genocide have the opportunity, through a national school system, to design and implement a curriculum teaching the era from their perspective. This presentation, further, has impacts on Shoah education in other educational systems.

• Development of this educational phenomenon has been an extended process, reflecting fundamental changes in Israeli society.

• This national pedagogic process resembles the individual psychological process of mourning.

• The diverse populations within Jewish-Israeli society have a common interest in perpetuating memory of the Shoah. At the same time, they have different ways of presenting the subject.

• This has not led to uniformity in presentation of the subject; even within the framework of the national school system, Shoah education is multi-faceted and allows for various teaching styles and ideological approaches.

• The Shoah impacts the worldview of Jewish Israelis, but it is not the basis of Israeli-Jewish identity.

• Shoah education among other populations in Israel—particularly the ultra-Orthodox and Israeli Arabs, has yet to be researched in depth; it may be expected that even more divergent ways of presenting the Shoah are to be found in these streams of the school system.

* * * * * *

A. Shoah Education: A Unique Pedagogic Event

One of the central issues explored in this book was whether or not the Shoah should be taught as a unique historical event. I offered an in-depth exploration of this thorny issue, presenting various sides of the argument from the perspectives of many people involved at all levels of the educational system. It is not my intention to attempt to offer a definitive answer. What I would like to propose, rather, is that Shoah *education* is a unique phenomenon. In particular, an undertaking such as Shoah education in Israel is absolutely unprecedented. While other groups of people, undeniably, have suffered violent racism, mass murder, and genocide (whether or not on a scale or of a nature comparable to that of the Shoah), no other people has implemented a system-wide educational project for the study and commemoration of their experience. They have lacked either the means or the motivation. Native Americans do not have the political power to insist their history be taught in all US schools, nor do the Aboriginals in Australia. The Armenians are not in a position to write curricula for Turkish schools that acknowledges their massacre at the hands of Ottoman Empire. In Rwanda and Cambodia, where mass murders were committed by the government or in civil wars and the descendants of perpetrators and victims are co-citizens, commemoration is highly sensitive and teaching the subject in the school fraught with difficulties.[1]

Only in Israel has a people slated for extermination achieved political independence in another land, where they then had the opportunity to create and implement curricula for the public school system, build memorial museums and institutes of study, dedicate a national day of commemoration, and commit budgets from the Ministry of Education for the study of the genocide perpetrated against them. The study of this inarguably unique educational project has yielded many insights, which may guide its continuation in Israel and guide the study of the Shoah in other countries and genocide education at large.

B. The Work of Shoah Memory in Jewish-Israeli Society

Even given that both the means and the motivation are clearly available to develop Shoah education in Israel, the process has been neither simple nor straightforward. A number of sociologists have recognized that an important part of creating coherent group identity rests on the collective "work of memory." The concept of the "work of memory," which was coined by Paul Ricoeur in 2000 as the French *travail de mé-*

1 Caplan, 2007; Taum, 2005.

moire, quite accurately describes what has gone on, and continues to go on, in Israel regarding the Shoah. Work—*travail*—indicates an explicit effort in remembering, and even pain in the effort. The intellectual work is accompanied by emotional effort. Memory must be more than a ritual of commemoration; it must be an active creative process. Through the "labor pains" of memory something new is brought to life.[2]

The strength and depth of commitment among Israeli Jews to preserve and transmit the memory of the Shoah drive this work. In a recent survey by the Israel Democracy Institute and Avi Chai Foundation, 98% of Israelis said remembering the Shoah was a "very important" or "fairly important" principal in their lives.[3] Essentially everyone in the Israeli public education system, it can be said with confidence, sees Shoah education as vital, interesting, engaging, worthwhile, and deserving of even more time and attention. The students were no less concerned and thoughtful than their teachers, principals, and the educational experts—a fact it seems safe to assume would apply to few if any other school subjects. The passion of the opinions on how the memory of the Shoah should be transmitted further attests to the intensity of feeling on the issue. Therefore a great deal of thought is given at all levels of the educational system to the best ways to teach the Shoah, the messages to be imparted, the activities and lessons to be offered. Because it touches so deeply issues at the core of Jewish-Israeli identity the work of preserving the memory of the Shoah is undertaken with great seriousness. For the same reason, opinions on how that memory should be presented and what lessons should be drawn from it are diverse and passionately debated. The concept of work of memory includes not only the duty of remembering but also the work of inquiry. There has been much effort put into deep inquiry of this topic, from many angles.

C. Diversity and Complexity within Unity

The Shoah is an inherently complex subject, presenting some of the most persistently difficult questions of our age. It is unsurprising that there

2 Ricoeur, 2000, 36; for others using the term "work of memory" see Booth, 2008; Confino and Fritzsche, 2002; Ernst, 2008; Slyomovics, 2012.

3 Arian, 2012.

should be a range of opinion on its messages and meanings. Indeed, too uniform a perspective would have been puzzling and somehow troubling, indicating an authoritarian and dogmatic approach. This is not the case. During the process of the research and preparation of this book, I had occasion to read and hear many opinions regarding the direction of Shoah education in Israel. Some feel universal messages are being ignored while others object to the uniquely Jewish nature of the Shoah being marginalized. Some assert the Shoah is being used as a justification for nationalist views or promoting the same type of ethnocentrism, which, ultimately, led to the Shoah; others think that the necessity of the State of Israel needs to be reinforced against anti-Semitism and anti-Israel sentiment in the world. Some asserted that Shoah education should focus on historical fact and not engage in drawing "messages" from it, while others felt, equally strongly, that a dry historical approach is inappropriate and that there must be time allotted to exploring ethical implications. In short, there is no lack of controversy and no lack of ardent opinion on the subject.

That such a full range of opinion was voiced by experts in the field, principals, and teachers and no less by the students—students as young as age fifteen—indicates that, beyond the consensus that the Shoah must not be forgotten, there is lively debate within the educational system regarding its presentation and interpretation. This is a crucial point. If one were to propose that all aspects of Shoah memory are important—the universal and the particular, historical fact and ethical implications, spirituality and politics—then this broad overview of the educational system in Israel has found all the pieces of the puzzle exist. Many sides of this complex issue are under exploration and discussion.

That is not to say that all these pieces, all the divergent views, are presented in equal balance in all settings. Various segments of Israeli society and its school system, as well as individual principals and teachers, place the emphasis on different aspects. Educational materials, guest lecturers, survivors telling their stories, museums, books, movies, and artwork all may provide a wide range of perspectives on the subject. To the extent that students are exposed to teachers with different viewpoints and diverse materials, they may get a broad understanding of the subject. Students whose education is limited to teachers tending to emphasize a certain aspect (i.e. religious or Zionist) will as a result hold a view that is more slanted in one direction or another. In other words,

Israelis as a whole hold a wide range of views on the Shoah; Israelis as individuals may focus on a narrower part of this complicated topic. Ideological fragmentation is undoubtedly a feature of the Israeli social landscape, with deep philosophical and political rifts between segments of the population. Shoah education, even with all its variegations, provides a platform of relative agreement.

While there is a range of opinion regarding the ideological aspects of Shoah education to be emphasized, the messages and meanings to be derived from it, we found that the commonalities and similarities outweighed the differences. Some individuals felt strongly that certain messages should be given predominance, but looking at the Hebrew-language state school system as a whole there emerges a picture in which universal, national-Zionist and religious-Jewish messages are all included.

D. An Educational Process of Mourning

It is possible to see the development of Shoah education in Israel as part of a collective psychological processing of this immense tragedy. Before proceeding, it is worth reiterating that this type of psychological interpretation is itself characteristic of our times.[4] Social, political and economic considerations are equally important, as has been discussed throughout this book. That said, it is compelling to observe how each of the stages in Kübler-Ross's well-accepted model of mourning are reflected in the diverse and evolving attitudes surrounding the Shoah and transmission of its memory.

The first stage of mourning in Kübler-Ross' model is *denial*. This should not be confused in any way with denial that the Shoah occurred. One trait of the psychological stage of denial is a feeling that the world has become meaningless. This may be expressed as inability, reluctance, or refusal to find any meaning in the Shoah. This was a not uncommon response, as noted, in the first decade following the Shoah. As Theodor Adorno famously declared in 1949, "To write poetry after Auschwitz is barbaric."[5] Over six decades later, some of the interviewees in the current

4 Illouz, 2003.

5 Adorno, 1949, quoted in Adorno and Tiedmann, 2003, 162. Adorno later reconsidered this

research voiced the feeling that finding "meaning" in the Shoah demeans the victims. Another characteristic of the stage of denial is simply trying to get through each day, without facing the enormity of the loss. This was seen during the nation-building stage of Israel, when energy and attention were put on practical issues rather than emotional processing. Also among the survivors themselves, in Israel and in other countries, the immediate focus was frequently put on starting a new life. This type of denial may be played out anew as each generation learns about the Shoah. The industrialized murder of so many people and the destruction of entire communities are incomprehensible, and are therefore not comprehended. Students may not know how to respond. Social pressure for students to express "appropriate" responses such as crying conflicts with what Kübler-Ross presents as a natural first response. Indeed, in past generations there was not such an expectation that students would cry during memorial ceremonies, field trips or other school activities related to the Shoah.

The second stage is *anger*. Anger may have many targets: the perpetrator (when there is one); the victim, for not saving himself somehow; oneself (for not being able to save the victim); God, for allowing the tragedy to happen. We can see each of these types of anger manifest in Jewish discourse about the Shoah. Anger is not limited to the Nazis, their collaborators and the countless bystanders. There was much anger directed at the victims for "going like sheep to the slaughter." In some circles today one may hear accusations at various groups of Jews for their purported role: members of the *Judenräte* councils for collaborating; religious leaders for encouraging their followers to stay in Europe rather than escape to "impure" environments; Zionists for abandoning religious Jews who didn't fit their criteria of the new Israeli Jew, and so on. Survivor guilt, too, was manifest among those who survived, escaped, or spent the years of the war outside Europe. Anger at God was expressed in the writings of many survivors, such as in Elie Wiesel's book *The Trial of God*, in which he wrote (through his fictional character) "...it is as a Jew that, with my last breath, I shall shout my protest to God ... I'll tell Him that He's more guilty than ever!"[6] In the context of Shoah

dictum. Theodor Adorno was the son of a German-Jewish father and Catholic mother. He left Germany in 1934 for the United States, where he became a professor of philosophy and social critic.

6 Wiesel, 1977, 165

education, teachers and students may express anger directed inward, outward, or heavenward in various ways.

The third stage is *bargaining*. This is an attempt to restore order and meaning to the world and life. The various moral lessons being drawn from the Shoah may be seen as representing this stage of mourning. A strong State of Israel, subsequent generations of Jews giving birth to Jewish children, preservation of Jewish tradition, or a world free of racism will somehow rescue, if not the victims from death then at least their deaths from meaninglessness.

Depression is the fourth stage. There are now collective rituals of mourning such as on *Yom HaShoah*, at Yad Vashem and other museums, or at ceremonies during the journey to Poland. It took Israelis several decades to reach this stage. Though there are those who criticize the openly emotional nature of the ceremonies, they may be seen as an outlet for the depression which would necessarily emerge following such a tragedy. At the same time, since not everyone reaches this stage simultaneously, there is the danger of "enforcing" crying as the only acceptable response and eliciting emotions not genuinely felt.

The final stage is *acceptance*, recognition of the new reality in which one must necessarily begin to function. Kübler-Ross wrote, "Healing looks like remembering, recollecting, and reorganizing." For sixty-five years the Jewish People have been "reorganizing" their world, finding a way to accept living in the post-Shoah world. For sixty-five years, they have been finding ways to remember and recollect. All the many faces of Shoah education are an important part of this, and the dedication to preserving the memory of the Shoah is part of this stage of mourning. Another manifestation of this stage is the perceived responsibility to act as a "witness"; the acceptance of a new role vis à vis the tragedy.[7] The psychological approach to the Shoah, in addition to reflecting the larger tone of modern society, fits well into this stage of mourning; there is collective desire to find meaning in the Shoah if not an explanation for it.

In understanding this communal process of mourning, it is instructive to look at other major tragedies which the Jewish People have suffered over their long history, and the "readjustments" which were necessarily made following these tragedies. Two thousand years ago, the Roman Empire overthrew the ancient kingdoms of Israel and Judea, de-

7 Kübler-Ross, 1969; Kübler-Ross and Kessler, 2005.

stroyed the Temple in Jerusalem, and exiled the population. The entirety of Jewish life was overturned. It took literally centuries for the Jewish collective to address the social, cultural, and ideological consequences of this. Similarly, the Expulsion of the Jews of Spain in 1492 set off a course of events whose repercussions are still being felt today.

E. Jewish Identity after the Shoah

The depth and breadth of the "reorganization" the Shoah forced the Jewish world to undergo can hardly be overstated. Demographically the Jews have not yet recovered from the murder of six million Jews and the loss of countless descendants who were never born: there are still fewer Jews in the world today (13.4 million) than there were in 1939 (16.7 million).[8] The destruction of centuries-old Jewish communities across Europe, and their distinctive cultures including the Yiddish language and the rich literature in it, the emigration of survivors and their resettlement in Israel, North and South America, Australia. These represent only part of the cataclysmic change. The Shoah engendered fundamental shifts in Jewish identity. The Jewish people have had to come to terms with a world that includes the memory of Auschwitz and the recognition that there are those who wish for a "final solution" to the problem of Jewish existence.

Other more subtle shifts in perception of the world were equally disturbing. In the century prior to Word War II, Europe had undergone a process of modernization that included a change in attitude towards minorities in general and Jews in particular. In the emergent "liberal" worldview, group distinctions were to disappear and the Jews as individuals were to be treated as equal citizens. Many Jews embraced this ideology and assimilated or acculturated into the dominant societies of the countries where they lived. The Nazis violently reinstated the concept of an inescapable group identity that overrode individual identity, an idea which modern Europe had long struggled to overturn. As the French-Jewish writer Shmuel Trigano noted, "...at Auschwitz, the Jews once again collectively faced their existence as a people. Moreover, they did so under the pressure of necessity and not as a matter of ideological

8 DellaPergola, 2010; Jewish Virtual Library, 2012.

choice or commitment."[9] No Jew, no matter how completely integrated into non-Jewish society, no matter how alienated from the Jewish community, was exempt in the Nazis' worldview.[10] Collective identity was reimposed, and this has had lasting impacts. Disillusioned with the promise that group distinctions would disappear, Jews re-embraced their collective identity, reformed and revised it in the post-Shoah world. It must be clarified, however, that while the Shoah inevitably impacts the Jews' perception of their group identity, their Jewish *identity* consists of far more than just a reaction to the Shoah.

F. Worldview and Identity

This distinction between the impact of the Shoah on Israeli Jews' worldview and the role of the Shoah in their personal-social identity as Jews emerged clearly in this survey. This seems a subtle point, but it must be stressed, as there have been analyses and critiques based on the premise that the Shoah has become the predominant feature of many contemporary Jews' identity and education, overriding other aspects of affiliation.[11] The large majority of respondents said their worldview is influenced by their knowledge of the Shoah. However, only a small minority selected memory of the Shoah as one of the foundational components of their Jewish identity. Knowledge of the extent to which the Nazis went in their attempt to wipe out the Jewish People, the support they got from many and the indifference of much of the world has been impressed on the collective Jewish psyche quite deeply. Further, the Shoah impacted the contemporary Jewish world in myriad ways. This is understood by Israelis, even those of a quite young age. This does *not* mean that their identity as Jews is built on the Shoah, which would imply, perversely, that Jewish identity is based on its attempted destruction. Some, indeed, have claimed that without anti-Semitism Jewish identity would not continue to exist.[12] However, this is not

9 Trigano, 1997, 301.

10 See for example the memoirs of Auschwitz survivor Améry (1980).

11 See for example Novick, 1999; Neusner, 1997; Segev, 2000.

12 Sartre, 1948. Sartre's book is an impressive philosophical study of anti-Semitism and the liberal approach illustrating how both call for the end of the Jewish People, albeit from different sets of preconceptions. Sartre revisited later this point of view, especially after he met French-Jewish philosopher Benny Levy.

what the research shows. Some of the interviewees clearly stated that Jewish identity should not be based on the Shoah or anti-Semitism. The students indicated that their Jewish identity (like their peers I have surveyed in Jewish communities around the world) is primarily based on a family connection, followed by aspects such as religion, culture, education, language and other *positive* elements. At the same time they are highly aware of the Shoah and their worldview has been inescapably impacted by it.

G. Towards the Future

While Shoah education has been offered in the schools for many decades, and has been continually expanding and intensifying, there was not, prior to this survey, a solid data base by which it could be evaluated. Now that basic information exists, and may be used to methodically and rationally assess the progress which has been made and the challenges and opportunities still ahead.

There is much left to learn. There are major populations in Israel whose attitudes have not yet been systematically surveyed. One of these is the ultra-Orthodox (*haredi*) Jewish community. This segment of the population is growing and an increasing percentage of school children (particularly in certain areas of the country) are enrolled in independent religious schools. The pilot survey in the teachers' colleges training women to teach in this school system (and who were themselves educated in this system) gave a first indication of the distinct style of Shoah education in this system. The subject is attributed a great deal of importance, but from a religious perspective that is distinctly different from that presented in either the general or the religious-national public schools. Also yet to be surveyed on the subject of Shoah education are the 1.5 million Arab citizens of Israel, whose children mostly learn in a separate track of Arab language state schools. How students and teachers in the Arab sector perceive the Shoah and its relationship to controversial issues of national identity, religious values, democracy, and collective memory would make a fascinating and vitally important study. Yet another avenue of study would be an international comparison of Shoah education in both private Jewish schools and public schools around the world. Based on published literature, this book presented some points of similarity and difference in how the subject is treated in Israel and abroad, but there has yet to be a systematic survey with parallel questions yielding truly comparable data.

The culmination of one research project almost inevitably reveals new areas to be explored. It is hoped that this contribution in the ongoing study of Shoah education will help pave the way for continued study of this important and fascinating field.

Appendix A: List of experts interviewed

Date of interview	Status	Affiliation	Name
11.07.08	Researcher	Arizona University	Prof. Shlomo Aronson
25.11.07	Researcher	Hebrew University of Jerusalem	Dr. Yael Nidam-Orvieto
13.11.08	Researcher	Open University	Prof. Yair Auron
07.10.08	Guide for groups traveling to Poland	Yad Vashem	Gila Oren
30.07.07	Researcher	Hebrew University of Jerusalem	Prof. Sidra Ezrahi
30.07.07	Pedagogic administrator of the main school for Holocaust education in Yad Vashem	Yad Vashem	Shulamit Imber
17.09.07	Researcher	Hebrew University of Jerusalem	Prof. Yehuda Bauer
15.07.07	Researcher	Yad Vashem	Prof. Zvi Bachrach
18.05.07	Teacher	Yad Vashem, Kerem Institute	Ephrat Balberg-Rotenstreich
27.06.07	Researcher	Hebrew University of Jerusalem	Prof. Daniel Blatman
29.07.07	Manager of the guidance course	Yad Vashem	Inbal Kwiti-Ben Dov
25.06.07	Researcher	Tel Aviv University	Dr. Avner Ben-Amos
15.07.07	Researcher	Hebrew University of Jerusalem	Dr. Havi Dreifuss (Ben Sasson)
17.07.07	Researcher	Hebrew University of Jerusalem	Prof. David Bankier
11.07.07	School principal	Be'er Tuvia Regional High School	Aryeh Barnea

05.12.07	Researcher	Yad Yizchak Ben-Zvi	Dr. Mordechai Bar-On
06.11.08	Researcher	Oranim College	Prof. Neima Barzel
18.08.08	Researcher	Hebrew University of Jerusalem	Prof. Yisrael Gutman
17.06.07	Researcher	Hebrew University of Jerusalem	Dr. Amos Goldberg
14.05.07	Teacher	Pelech High School	Shalvit Gross
30.07.07	Manager of in-service teacher training program	Yad Vashem	Dr. Haim Gertner
19.10.07	Researcher	Tel Aviv University	Prof. Yuval Dror
30.07.07	Head of teachers seminars	Yad Vashem	Dina Drori
18.09.07	Teacher	Ramat Gan City High School for Girls	Henya Weintraub
04.07.07	Researcher	Haifa University	Prof. Yechiam Weitz
18.08.08	Researcher	Basel University	Prof. Idit Zartal
30.08.07	Researcher	Ben Gurion University	Prof. Hanna Yablonka
05.02.08	Researcher	Bar Ilan University	Prof. Hanna Yaoz
05.09.07	Film Maker	None	Yaron Kaftori
28.05.07	Researcher	Hebrew University of Jerusalem and Yad Vashem	Dr. Zeev Mankowitz
17.07.07	Researcher	Bar Ilan University, Yad Vashem	Prof. Dan Michman

17.09.09	Trip to Poland Guide	Ministry of Education	Riki Mandel
28.08.07	Head of the International School for Holocaust Studies at Yad Vashem	Yad Vashem	Dorit Novak
03.09.08	Researcher	Tel Aviv University	Prof. Eyal Naveh
10.07.07	Researcher	Tel Aviv University	Prof. Dina Porat
05.12.08	Researcher	Ben-Gurion University of the Negev	Dr. Jackie Feldman
09.10.07	Researcher	Western Galilee College	Dr. Uri Fargo
02.11.08	Researcher	Mofet Institute	Dr. Tova Perlmutter
20.11.08	Researcher	Tel Aviv University	Prof. Moshe Zuckermann
16.07.07	Head of Yad Ben Zvi	Yad Ben Zvi	Dr. Zvi Zameret
12.06.07	Researcher	Hebrew University of Jerusalem	Dr. Manuela Consonni
16.07.07	Teacher	Rene Cassin	Savi Klor
22.07.07	Researcher	Massuah Institute	Dr. Nili Keren
05.11.07	Historian	Efrat Seminary	Prof. Yisrael Rosenson
09.09.08	Researcher	Hebrew University of Jerusalem	Prof. Eliezer Schweid
05.09.07	Historian and journalist	Ha'aretz Newspaper	Dr. Tom Segev
09.07.07	Teacher	Yad Vashem	Malka Tor

Appendix B: English translations of questionnaires for principals, teachers and students

Questionnaire for school principals

(Items included only in the questionnaire for high school principals or only for junior high school principals are indicated)

A research project on Shoah education is currently being conducted. Your school was selected as part of a sample of schools. The viewpoint of the school is critical to understanding the subject. This is why we are interested in learning about your perception of the subject in a deeper manner. Please fill out the questionnaire with care. The principal of the school may answer this questionnaire him\herself or appoint someone from management to answer instead of him\her. The questionnaire was created so that it could be filled out quickly. The questionnaires will be statistically analyzed for the entire population of subjects without noting the name or the school of any specific people. We thank you for our cooperation.

Dr. Erik Cohen, Director of Research

Note: when the word "school" appears in the questionnaire with no extra description, we are referring to the school in which you work.

Name of the respondent: ______________________
Job description: ______________________
Email : ______________________
Name of School : ______________________
District : ______________________
School telephone number : ______________________

Sector (*circle the answer*): 1. General (*Mamlachti*) 2. Religious (*Mamlachti-Dati*)

School type (*circle the answer*):
1. Academic (*Iyuni*)
2. Vocational (*Miktzoi*)
3. Comprehensive (*Mekif*)
4. Other: ____________

In your opinion, the school is:
1. Excellent
2. Very good
3. Good
4. Average

School: General Aspects

In your opinion, how important is it that your school educates students for the following subjects:

	To a very great extent	To a great extent	To some extent	Not at all
Absorption of immigrants (*olim*)	1	2	3	4
Social equality	1	2	3	4
Zionism	1	2	3	4
Judaism	1	2	3	4
Adherence to the law	1	2	3	4
Democracy	1	2	3	4
Human dignity	1	2	3	4
General culture	1	2	3	4
Israeli culture	1	2	3	4
Jewish culture	1	2	3	4
Excellence	1	2	3	4
Self-realization	1	2	3	4
Art	1	2	3	4
Science and technology	1	2	3	4
Development of personal skills	1	2	3	4
Torah and religious laws	1	2	3	4
Ambitiousness	1	2	3	4

Which methods of education are used frequently in your school?
(*Please circle all applicable answers*)

1. A teacher in front of the class (frontal lecture)
2. Independent work
3. Group work
4. Art, creative drama

To what extent is each of the following issues a goal of your school?

	To a very great extent	To a great extent	To some extent	Not at all
Instilling learning skills	1	2	3	4
Enriching the world of the student	1	2	3	4
Instilling manners	1	2	3	4
Instilling the student with religious values	1	2	3	4
Ensuring equal opportunity	1	2	3	4
Helping the student get to know him/herself	1	2	3	4
Helping the student succeed in society	1	2	3	4
Instilling universal values	1	2	3	4
Preparing the student for life	1	2	3	4
Instilling the student with Zionism	1	2	3	4
Developing personal skills	1	2	3	4
Instilling the student with knowledge and content	1	2	3	4

Shoah Education in School

How important is it that the teachers emphasize each of the following subjects when teaching about the Shoah?

Content	To a very great extent	To a great extent	To some extent	Not at all	I don't know
Historical background	1	2	3	4	5
Nazi ideology	1	2	3	4	5
The cultural and spiritual wealth of the Jewish communities before the Shoah	1	2	3	4	5
The life of the Jewish communities during the Shoah	1	2	3	4	5
The Jewish struggle against the Nazis	1	2	3	4	5
The destruction process	1	2	3	4	5
Other: ______________					
Educational messages					
Identification with the destiny of the Jewish people	1	2	3	4	5
Commitment to the continuation of the Jewish legacy	1	2	3	4	5
Commitment to the memory of the Shoah	1	2	3	4	5
Universal-humanistic values	1	2	3	4	5
Fighting racism of any kind	1	2	3	4	5
Protecting the democratic regime	1	2	3	4	5
Bravery, heroism, and dedication	1	2	3	4	5
Belonging to the Israeli nation	1	2	3	4	5
Commitment to the existence of an independent Jewish state	1	2	3	4	5
Other: ______________					

If you know, please write the number of hours dedicated to teaching about the Shoah (including teaching, ceremonies, seminars, and so on) throughout the school year for each grade level.

7th: _____ 8th: _____ 9th: _____
10th: _____ 11th: _____ 12th: _____

In comparison to the time dedicated to other subjects, do you think the time dedicated to Shoah education is:

1. Not enough time 2. Enough time 3. Too much time

In the following list, circle the teachers that teach or are involved in Shoah education (*please circle all applicable answers*):

1. History teachers 3. Homeroom teachers 5. Art teachers
2. Literature teachers 4. English teachers 6. Other: ____________

Is there anyone in school who coordinates and manages Shoah education?

1. Yes 2. No

If so, please note his\her name: ______________________

How many teachers are involved in Shoah education in your school
(if the number is unknown, please write an estimate)? _________________

How many teachers teach in your school? ____________________

In the last two years, how many teachers have participated in professional advancement programs in Shoah education? (*If the number is unknown, please write an estimate)* _______

Educational programs and activities about the Shoah in school

Which programs and activities (not including regular teaching) about the Shoah take place? (*please circle all applicable answers*)

1. General enrichment hours and seminars
2. Visits to institutes commemorating the Shoah
3. Ceremonies
4. Museum or memorial site in school
5. Journey to Poland [*only included in questionnaire for high school principals*]
6. Other programs

Is there an attempt to integrate the classes for Shoah education with other activities dedicated to the subject in school?

1. Yes 2. Partially 3. No

Are students <u>required to</u> participate in activities about the Shoah other than the actual classes?

1. Yes 2. No

Do a large <u>majority</u> of the students participate in activities about the Shoah other than the actual classes?

1. Yes 2. No

Is there cooperation between the history teachers and other teachers involved in Shoah education?

1. Yes, absolutely 2. Yes 3. No 4. Not at all

Which methods of education are used frequently when dealing with <u>the subject of the Shoah</u> in school? (*Please circle all applicable answers*)

1. A teacher in front of the class (frontal lecture) 3. Group work
2. Independent work 4. Art, creative drama, ...

In your opinion, does exposure to the subject of the Shoah strengthen the students' Jewish identity?

1. Absolutely 2. Yes 3. No 4. Absolutely not

In your opinion, does exposure to the subject of the Shoah strengthen the students' Israeli identity?

1. Absolutely 2. Yes 3. No 4. Absolutely not

In your opinion, does exposure to subject of the Shoah strengthen the students' universal values?

1. Absolutely   2. Yes   3. No   4. Absolutely not

How satisfied are you with Shoah education in your school?

1. Very satisfied   2. Satisfied   3. Dissatisfied   4. Very dissatisfied

In your opinion, how important are each of the following activities in teaching the students about the Shoah?

	To a very great extent	To a great extent	To some extent	Not at all
History classes in school	1	2	3	4
Other classes in school	1	2	3	4
Memorial ceremonies	1	2	3	4
Journey to Poland *(high school only)*	1	2	3	4
Seminars	1	2	3	4
Films	1	2	3	4
Visiting institutes for Shoah commemoration	1	2	3	4
Plays	1	2	3	4
Testimonies	1	2	3	4
Other: ____________				

(for junior high school principals only)

In your opinion, to what extent do the different activities about the Shoah in your school prepare the students for learning about the Shoah in high school?

1. To a very great extent   2. To a great extent   3. To some extent   4. Not at all

(for junior high school principals only)

In your estimation, to what extent are students who do not continue to high school familiar with the subject of the Shoah?

1. To a very great extent   2. To a great extent   3. To some extent   4. Not at all

The following is dedicated to schools which participate in the journey to Poland as part of the Shoah educational programs *[only included in questionnaire for high school principals]*

What is the status of the delegations to Poland that are organized by the school?

1. National delegation   2. Private delegation

Is there a selection process for choosing the students who go to Poland? 1. Yes   2. No

Is there a preparation process before going on the journey? 1. Yes   2. No

Does the preparation process also function as a sorting tool? 1. Yes   2. No

Is the preparation process before the journey delivered solely by the school?

1. Yes   2. No

Are all the students who are participating in the journey obligated to take part in the preparation process?

1. Yes 2. No

How many students participated in the journey last year?
*(If the exact number is unknown, please write an estimate)*____________

In which grade are the students going on the journey? 1. 11th grade 2. 12th grade

How long is the journey? ______ days.

Is financial aid given to students so they might participate in the journey?

1. Yes, to the majority
2. To a substantial part
3. To a minority
4. To none of the students

In your estimation, who is the most dominant element in the journey?

1. Teachers 2. Guides 3. Witnesses

How knowledge-oriented is the journey?

1. To a very great extent 2. To a great extent 3. To some extent 4. Not at all

How experience-oriented is the journey?

1. To a very great extent 2. To a great extent 3. To some extent 4. Not at all

In your estimation, to what extent did the journey strengthen the students' commitment the memory of the Shoah?

1. To a very great extent 2. To a great extent 3. To some extent 4. Not at all

Is there an educational process for processing and summarizing after the journey?

1. No 2. One night 3. A whole day 4. A series of meetings

Are there any specialty programs in your school that <u>are not</u> related to the Shoah?

1. No 2. Yes, please elaborate: a. ____________________________
b. ____________________________

Are there any alternative programs available to students who do not participate in the journey? 1. Yes 2. No

The following is dedicated to schools who do not participate in the journey to Poland as part of the Shoah educational programs.

Why doesn't your school participate in the journey to Poland? Please note the two main reasons:

A. ______________________________

B. ______________________________

Shoah Education: Your recommendations for the future

With your help, we would like to find way to improve and strengthen Shoah education in schools around the country. Please circle your recommendation about each of the following criteria.

In your opinion, in the near future Shoah education should be:

Number 3 Means you do not recommend any change in the situation.

With more teaching hours	1	2	3	4	5	With less teaching hours
More intensive	1	2	3	4	5	Less intensive
More knowledge oriented	1	2	3	4	5	Less knowledge oriented
More experience oriented	1	2	3	4	5	Less experience oriented
More Judaism oriented	1	2	3	4	5	Less Judaism oriented
More Zionism oriented	1	2	3	4	5	Less Zionism oriented
More journeys to Poland	1	2	3	4	5	Less journeys to Poland
More universal oriented	1	2	3	4	5	Less universal oriented
More informal activity hours	1	2	3	4	5	Less informal activity hours

We would appreciate it if you could take several minutes of your time to write down your comments on all subjects connected with the questionnaire:

____

____

____

____

____

____

____

____

Thank you for your participation

Questionnaire for the teachers involved in Shoah teaching

A research project on Shoah education is currently being conducted. We are interested in the opinions of the teachers who are involved with this subject. Your opinions are critical to understanding the subject. Please fill out the questionnaire with care. The questionnaire was created so that it could be filled out quickly. The questionnaires will be statistically analyzed for the entire population of subjects without noting the name or the school of any specific people. We thank you for our cooperation.

Dr. Erik Cohen, Director of Research

[*Please refer to the school through which you are filling out this questionnaire*]

Sector (*circle the answer*): 1. General (*Mamlachti*) 2. Religious (*Mamlachti-Dati*)

School type (*circle the answer*): 1. Academic (*Iyuni*) 2. Vocational (*Miktzoi*) 3. Comprehensive (*Mekif*) 4. Other: ____________

In your opinion, the school is: 1. Excellent 2. Very good 3. Good 4. Average

In which framework do you teach or are you involved in Shoah education at your school (*please circle all applicable answers*):

1. History teacher
2. Literature teacher
3. Homeroom teacher
4. English teacher
5. Art teacher
6. Other: __________

Shoah Experience and Training

Where have you acquired your knowledge concerning the Shoah?
(*Please circle all applicable answers*)

1. History studies in college
2. History studies in university
3. Professional advancement program on the subject
4. Personal reading
5. Other: ____________

In general, taking into account your professional training in the subject, are you:
1. Very satisfied 2. Satisfied 3. Dissatisfied 4. Very dissatisfied 5. I received no training

Please note the professional advancement programs in Shoah education that you have attended in the last three years

1. Sponsorship: _______________ Length: ____________
2. Sponsorship: _______________ Length: ____________

Does the school encourage participation in professional advancement programs in Shoah education?

1. To a great extent 2. Quite a bit 3. Somewhat 4. Very little

In general, when taking into account all the components of the professional advancement programs in Shoah education, are you:

1. Very satisfied 2. Satisfied 3. Dissatisfied 4. Very dissatisfied 5. I received no training

In general, what do you feel is your level of knowledge in each of the following subjects within the field of Shoah education:

	Completely proficient	Proficient to a great extent	Moderately proficient	Proficient to a small extent
Historical Background	1	2	3	4
Nazi ideology	1	2	3	4
Jewish opposition to the Nazis	1	2	3	4
Jewish community life before the Nazis	1	2	3	4
Jewish community life during the Shoah	1	2	3	4
The destruction process	1	2	3	4
The influence of the Shoah on the Jewish world and Israel	1	2	3	4

How much do you feel the need for more knowledge in each of the following subjects?

	To a very great extent	To a great extent	So, so	To some extent
Historical Background	1	2	3	4
Nazi ideology	1	2	3	4
Jewish opposition to the Nazis	1	2	3	4
Jewish community life before the Nazis	1	2	3	4
Jewish community life during the Shoah	1	2	3	4
The destruction process	1	2	3	4
The influence of the Shoah on the Jewish world and Israel	1	2	3	4

In general, how proficient do you feel you are in the Shoah as a subject?

1. Completely 2. To a great extent 3. Moderately 4. To a small extent

Involvement

With which school programs concerning the Shoah are you involved?

1. Classroom teaching
2. General enrichment activities
3. Ceremonies
4. Visits to institutes for Shoah commemoration
5. Museum or memorial in school
6. Journey to Poland
7. Other

Do you attempt to integrate the classes for Shoah education with other activities dedicated to the subject in school?

1. Yes, absolutely 2. Yes, partially 3. Not usually 4. There isn't a need for it

In your opinion, the time mandated for teaching about the Shoah is:

1. Not enough time 2. Enough time 3. Too much time

Educational Approach and the Curriculum

What do you think are the purposes of Shoah education?

		To a very great extent	To a great extent	To some extent	Not at all
A	Strengthening identification with the destiny of the Jewish people	1	2	3	4
B	Strengthening the commitment to remembering the Shoah	1	2	3	4
C	Strengthening the commitment to fighting racism	1	2	3	4
D	Strengthening Jewish identity	1	2	3	4
E	Strengthening Israeli identity	1	2	3	4
F	Strengthening the democratic regime	1	2	3	4
G	Strengthening universal values	1	2	3	4
H	Strengthening the commitment to the existence of an independent Jewish state	1	2	3	4
I	Strengthening the knowledge of Shoah history	1	2	3	4

Which of these goals are the most important to you? *(Note the letter of the relevant item)*

First Goal: |__| Second Goal: |__|

There are many different aspects to Shoah education. Please mark the level of importance that you attribute to each one of the following aspects in your work:

	To a very great extent	To a great extent	So, so	To some extent
Historical background	1	2	3	4
Nazi ideology	1	2	3	4
Jewish opposition to the Nazis	1	2	3	4
Jewish community life before the Nazis	1	2	3	4
Jewish community life during the Shoah	1	2	3	4
The destruction process	1	2	3	4
The influence of the Shoah on the Jewish world and Israel	1	2	3	4
The place of the individual during the Shoah	1	2	3	4

Which methods of education do you use frequently when dealing with <u>the subject of the Shoah?</u> (*Please circle all applicable answers*)

1. A teacher in front of the class (frontal lecture)
2. Independent work
3. Group work
4. Art, creative drama, …

Which educational materials do you use when teaching about the Shoah?

1. Historical sources
2. Films
3. Literature
4. Memorial books
5. Testimonies
6. Plays
7. Websites
8. Other ________

Which textbook do you use when teaching about the Shoah? ______________________

Do you use any material other than what is provided by the Ministry of Education?
1. Yes 2. No
If so, elaborate: ______________________________

Have you written educational material on the subject? 1. Yes 2. No

In general, when you take into account Shoah education as it exists in Israel are you:
1. Very satisfied 2. Satisfied 3. Dissatisfied 4. Very dissatisfied

Do you draw a connection between the Shoah and current events?
1. Often 2.Occasionally 3.Rarely 4. Never

Do you think the public discussion about the Shoah affects what is taught in the classroom?
1. To a very great extent 2. To a great extent 3. To some extent 4. Not at all

How much do you emphasize the <u>knowledge</u> (historical, cultural...) when you teach about the Shoah?
1. To a very great extent 2. To a great extent 3. To some extent 4. Not at all

How much do you emphasize the <u>experience</u> (emotions, identification...) when you teach about the Shoah?
1. To a very great extent 2. To a great extent 3. To some extent 4. Not at all

How much do you encourage debates on issues of values\ morals\ education when teaching about the Shoah?
1. To a very great extent 2. To a great extent 3. To some extent 4. Not at all

Do the students raise religious\theological questions while learning about the Shoah?
1. Often 2. Occasionally 3. Rarely 4. Never

If the students do raise religious\theological questions, do you feel comfortable with such questions?
1. Absolutely 2. Yes 3. No 4. Not at all

Difficulties in Shoah Education

How often have you encountered the following problems?

	All the time	Often	Occasionally	Never
Too few teaching hours	1	2	3	4
Inadequate training	1	2	3	4
Need for further professional development	1	2	3	4
Inadequate professional support	1	2	3	4
Inadequate learning materials	1	2	3	4

Other. Elaborate: ______________

When encountering these problems, to whom did you turn?
(Please circle all applicable answers)

1. To my principal
2. To the history coordinator in school
3. To other teachers involved in the subject
4. To the Ministry of Education
5. To institutes that deal with the Shoah
6. To someone else. Elaborate: ____________
7. To no one
8. I have not encountered any problems

Personal Opinions

Do you think the creation of the state of Israel is the answer to the Shoah?

1. Absolutely 2. Yes 3. No 4. Not at all

Do you think the Shoah was a disaster only for the Jewish people or a disaster for all humanity?

1. Jewish people only 2. All humanity

Does the Shoah affect the way you view the world?

1. Absolutely 2. Yes 3. No 4. Not at all

The Journey to Poland

Have you participated in the journey to Poland? 1. Yes 2. No

In general, when taking into account all the components of the journey to Poland, are you:

1. Very satisfied 2. Satisfied 3. Dissatisfied 4. Very dissatisfied

In your opinion has commitment to memorializing the Shoah been strengthened in students who have participated in the journey to Poland?

1. To a very great extent 2. To a great extent 3. To some extent 4. Not at all

Student Relationship to the Shoah Issue

Do you feel there is a difference between students who belong to different groups in how they relate to the Shoah issue:

For each of the following populations, circle the one you feel expresses more interest and identification with the issue of the Shoah. If you think there is no difference, circle X.

	No difference	
Students from Ashkenazi origins	X	Students from Sephardic origins
Boys	X	Girls
Students from high socioeconomic background	X	Students from low socioeconomic background
Traditional and religious students	X	Secular students

Personal Background and Connection to Shoah Education

Surname *(Optional)*: ______________ **First Name***(Optional)*:_____________

Country of Birth:_________________ **Year of Aliya**: |__|__|__|__|

Age: 1. Under 30 2. 30-39 3. 40-49 4. 50 and up

Sex: 1. Female 2. Male

Name of School: ______________________________

How many years have you been teaching? |__|__|

How many years have you worked in this school? |__|__|

Which classes do you teach?
(*Please circle all applicable answers*)
1. 7th grade 2. 8th grade 3. 9th grade 4. 10th grade 5. 11th grade 6. 12th grade

Which subjects do you teach? 1.____________ 2.____________ 3.____________

Education: Please circle the highest degree you have received:

1. High school diploma (*Bagrut*)
2. Teacher Seminar graduation
3. Yeshiva
4. BA\BED
5. MA
6. PHD
7. Rabbinical diploma
8. Other:__________

You would define yourself as:

1. Secular Jew
2. Traditional Jew
3. Religious Jew
4. Other

What is your ethnic origin?

1. Ashkenazi
2. Oriental
3. Ashkenazi and Oriental
4. Other ethnicity (which?)________

Is anyone in your family a Shoah survivor? 1. Yes 2. No

Have you lost relatives in the Shoah? 1. Yes 2. No

Your Recommendations for the Future

With your help, we would like to find way to improve and strengthen Shoah education in schools around the country. *Please circle your recommendation about each of the following criteria. Number 3 Means you do not recommend any change in the situation.*

In your opinion, Shoah education in the near future should be:

With more teaching hours	1	2	3	4	5	With less teaching hours
More knowledge oriented	1	2	3	4	5	Less Knowledge oriented
More experience oriented	1	2	3	4	5	Less experience oriented
More Intensive	1	2	3	4	5	Less Intensive
More Judaism oriented	1	2	3	4	5	Less Judaism oriented
More Zionism oriented	1	2	3	4	5	Less Zionism oriented
With more journeys to Poland	1	2	3	4	5	With less journeys to Poland
More universal oriented	1	2	3	4	5	Less universal oriented
More informal activity hours	1	2	3	4	5	Less informal activity hours

We would appreciate it if you could take several minutes of your time to write down your comments on all subjects connected with the questionnaire:

____

____

____

____

____

____

____

____

Thank you for your participation

Questionnaire for Students

[*Some items were only included in questionnaire to 12th graders or only in questionnaire to 9th graders, as indicated*]

As a part of Shoah education research we are passing out the following questionnaire to students from around the country. The purpose of the questionnaire is, for the most part, to get to know you and your opinions about Shoah education. The data from the questionnaire will be used solely for research purposes and your privacy is guaranteed.

We thank you for your cooperation.

School

How important to you are each of the following things in school?

	Extremely important	Quite important	Not so important	Not important at all
Being with friends	1	2	3	4
Getting good grades	1	2	3	4
Being the best in class	1	2	3	4
Learning interesting subjects	1	2	3	4
Learning things for future use	1	2	3	4
Having fun	1	2	3	4
Personal development	1	2	3	4
Being part of a group of friends	1	2	3	4
Contributing to my class	1	2	3	4
Learning in a pleasant environment	1	2	3	4

How important is it for you to learn each of the following subjects?

	Extremely important	Quite important	Not so important	Not important at all
English	1	2	3	4
Math	1	2	3	4
Science	1	2	3	4
Tanakh (Bible)	1	2	3	4
Jewish Studies	1	2	3	4
Art	1	2	3	4
History	1	2	3	4
Computers	1	2	3	4
Literature	1	2	3	4
Sport	1	2	3	4

Leisure Time Activities

Are you a member of a youth movement?

1. Yes, as a counselor 2. Yes, as a member 3. Yes, I was in the past 4. I've never been

Do you do volunteer work as part of your school requirements (personal commitment)?

1. Yes 2. No

The Shoah Subject in School (History, Literature, Ceremonies, Visiting memorial institutes)

How true or false are the following things about you:

	Very True	True	False	Completely false
The subjects learned in class have meaning in my life	1	2	3	4
The subjects learned in class are connected to personal questions I have	1	2	3	4
The subjects learned in class are connected to my family life	1	2	3	4
The subjects learned in class make me think	1	2	3	4

In comparison to the time dedicated to other subjects, do you think the time dedicated to learning about the Shoah is:

1. Too much time 2. About right 3. Too little time

In general, how proficient do you feel you are in the Shoah subject?

1. Completely 2. To a great extent 3. Moderately 4. Little

Please mark the activities that you have been exposed to and in which framework (mark an X). You may, of course, mark more than one activity and framework.

Type of activity	Framework		
	Family	School	Youth movements
Plays	☐	☐	☐
Visiting Shoah memorial institutes	☐	☐	☐
Documentary films	☐	☐	☐
Feature films	☐	☐	☐
Nonfiction books	☐	☐	☐
Fictional literature	☐	☐	☐
Memory books	☐	☐	☐
Internet	☐	☐	☐
Survivor testimony	☐	☐	☐
Ceremonies	☐	☐	☐

In your opinion, how successful are each of the following activities in educating you about the Shoah?

	To a very great extent	To a great extent	To some extent	Not at all
History classes in school	1	2	3	4
Other classes in school	1	2	3	4
Memorial ceremonies	1	2	3	4
The journey to Poland	1	2	3	4
Films	1	2	3	4
Visiting Shoah memorial institutes	1	2	3	4
Plays	1	2	3	4
Testimonies	1	2	3	4
The internet	1	2	3	4

How much does each of the following subjects interest you within the Shoah field?

	To a very great extent	To a great extent	To some extent	Not at all
The battle of the individual versus adversity	1	2	3	4
Questions of religion and faith	1	2	3	4
General historical knowledge	1	2	3	4
The implications of the Shoah to the Jewish people and the state of Israel	1	2	3	4
The horrors of the destruction of the Jews	1	2	3	4
The power and cruelty of the Nazi regime	1	2	3	4
Physical battle against the Nazis	1	2	3	4
The return to life of the survivors	1	2	3	4

Are there more or less discipline problems in classes that deal with the Shoah as opposed to other classes?

1. More in classes that deal with the Shoah
2. No difference
3. Less in classes that deal with the Shoah

The following part is intended for students who have participated in the journey to Poland
[only included in questionnaire for 12th graders]

Within which framework did you attend the journey to Poland? *Mark all that apply*

1. School 2. Youth movement 3. Family 4. Other____________

Why did you participate in the journey to Poland? Please note the two main reasons:

A. ____

B. ____

In general, when taking into account all the components of the journey to Poland, are you:

1. Very satisfied 2. Satisfied 3. Dissatisfied 4. Very dissatisfied

How much did the journey strengthen your commitment to the memory of the Shoah?

1. To a very great extent 2. To a great extent 3. To some extent 4. Not at all

<u>The following part is intended for students who have not participated in the journey to Poland</u> *[only included in questionnaire for 12th graders]*

Why didn't you participate in the journey to Poland? Please note the two main reasons:

A. ______________________________

B. ______________________________

[only included in questionnaire for 9th graders]

Do you plan to go on the journey to Poland in the future?

1. Definitely
2. Yes
3. No
4. Definitely not

Opinions

If you could be reborn, what would you choose to be?

1. A Jew in Israel
2. A non-Jew in Israel
3. A Jew abroad
4. A non-Jew abroad
5. Identity and location are not important to me

There are many different reasons for being Jewish. Out of the following list choose all the reasons that you are Jewish:

1. Birth
2. Commitment
3. Culture
4. Family
5. Loyalty
6. Shoah
7. Choice
8. Education
9. Religion
10. Israel
11. Hope
12. Anti-Semitism
13. Hebrew\Jewish language
14. Other Jews around the world
15. Destiny
16. I don't define myself as a Jew

If a relative of yours would be interested in marrying a non-Jew, how would you react?

1. There's nothing wrong with it
2. I would have mixed feelings about the situation
3. I would object somewhat to it
4. I would object vehemently

Have you celebrated a bar or bat mizva? 1. Yes 2. No

Do you observe Jewish traditions?

1. I observe all the traditions religiously
2. I generally observe the traditions
3. I observe the traditions to some extent
4. I am completely nonobservant

Do you keep kosher? 1. At home and out 2. At home but not out 3. Nowhere

Do you fast on Yom Kippur?

1. Always
2. Often
3. Rarely
4. Never

How do you feel about the State of Israel? 1. Very connected 2. Quite connected 3. A bit distant 4. Very distant

Are you positive that you will stay in Israel?

1. Positive
2. Almost sure
3. Possibly, but am not sure
4. I think not, but am unsure
5. Almost definitely not

Is it good to live in Israel? 1. Definitely 2. Yes 3. No 4. Definitely not

How true are the following things about you?

	Absolutely True	True	False	Completely false
It is important to me to be part of the Jewish people	1	2	3	4
I am proud to be a Jew	1	2	3	4
I am proud to be an Israeli	1	2	3	4
I feel a connection to Jews abroad	1	2	3	4
In my opinion, the establishment of the state of Israel is an "answer" to the Shoah	1	2	3	4
The Shoah affects the way I see the world	1	2	3	4
In my opinion another Shoah could happen in the world	1	2	3	4
In my opinion another Shoah could happen in Israel	1	2	3	4
In my opinion, the state of Israel treats Shoah survivors well	1	2	3	4

After learning what you have about the Shoah, how true are the following things about you?

	Very True	True	False	Completely false
I am interested in religious questions	1	2	3	4
I am interested in ethical questions	1	2	3	4
I empathize with Shoah survivors	1	2	3	4
I empathize with the Jewish people	1	2	3	4
I am committed to the existence of the state of Israe	1	2	3	4
I empathize with universal values	1	2	3	4
I am committed to the memory of the Shoah	1	2	3	4
I empathize with democratic values	1	2	3	4
I am committed to fighting racism	1	2	3	4

[only included in questionnaire for 12th graders]

The history of the Shoah includes a multitude of events, people, and places of all types and everyone isn't familiar with all of them. Before you is a list of events, places, and people connected to the history of the Shoah. Out of the list, please mark only the ones that are familiar to you.

1. Auschwitz\Birkenau
2. Schnellbrief
3. Eichmann
4. Anne Frank
5. Aktzia
6. Babi Yar
7. Goebbels
8. Ghetto
9. General Government
10. Anschluss
11. Heydrich
12. Himmler
13. Munich Agreement
14. The Ribbentrop-Molotov Pact
15. The Final Solution
16. The Wannsee Conference
17. The Sanctification of Life
18. Nuremberg Laws
19. Hannah Szenes
20. Righteous among the Nations
21. Janusz Korczak
22. Judenrate
23. Kristallnacht
24. Operation Barbarossa
25. Concentration Camp
26. Warsaw Ghetto Uprising
27. Mordechaj (Mordecai) Anielewicz
28. Einsatzgruppen (Task Forces)
29. Emmanuel Ringelblum
30. Partisans
31. Raoul Wallenberg
32. The Rabbi of Piaseczno

Do you plan on serving in the Israel Defense Forces?

1. Definitely 2. Yes 3. No 4. Definitely not

How satisfied are you with the way the Shoah subject is taught in your school?

1. Very satisfied
2. Moderately satisfied
3. To some extent satisfied
4. Not satisfied

How much more would you like to learn about the Shoah?

1. Much more 2. More 3. Not much more 4. Not at all

Do you think the Shoah was a disaster only for the Jewish people or a disaster for all humanity?

1. Jewish people only 2. All humanity

In the last few years images from the Shoah have been used in public and political events (prisoners' clothes in demonstrations; comparing the Shoah to difficult events in Israel; use of the word "Nazi" as a slur for political or other rivals and so on). How appropriate do you feel this is?

1. Very appropriate
2. Appropriate
3. Mostly inappropriate
4. Inappropriate
5. I have no opinion

How important are each of the following things to you?

	Extremely Important	Quite important	Not so important	Not important at all
Enjoying beauty	1	2	3	4
Respecting parents	1	2	3	4
Working hard	1	2	3	4
Making a lot of money	1	2	3	4
Behaving according to emotions	1	2	3	4
Enjoying life	1	2	3	4
Learning and reading in order to broaden horizons	1	2	3	4
Serving in the IDF	1	2	3	4
Learning *Tanakh* (Bible)	1	2	3	4
Doing volunteer work	1	2	3	4
Being at peace with one's self	1	2	3	4
Believing in God	1	2	3	4
Being a religious person	1	2	3	4
Helping the needy	1	2	3	4
Understanding other people's perspective	1	2	3	4

In your opinion, what sort of student are you?

1. Excellent 2. Very good 3. Good 4. Mediocre 5. Difficult

In general, would you consider yourself:

1. Very happy 2. Happy 3. Not so happy 4. Completely unhappy

Personal Details

Gender: 1. Male 2. Female **Year of Birth:** 19|__|__|

Country of Birth: ____________________ **Year of Aliya:** |__|__|__|__|

You would define yourself as:

1. Secular Jew 2. Traditional Jew 3. Religious Jew 4. Other:________

How would you define your home environment?

1. Secular Jew 2. Traditional Jew 3. Religious Jew 4. Other:________

Is anyone in your family a Shoah survivor? 1. Yes 2. No 3. I don't know

Have you lost relatives in the Shoah? 1. Yes 2. No 3. I don't know

What is your ethnic origin? 1. Ashkenazi 3. Ashkenazi and Oriental
2. Oriental 4. Other ethnicity which?)_________

We would appreciate your comments on any subjects connected with the questionnaire
(You may add an extra page for notes if necessary)

Thank you for your participation

Appendix C: Supplemental data

Table a: Students' participation in Shoah-related educational activities, by framework

Type of activity	Framework		
	Family	School	Youth movement
Ceremonies	26%	95%	22%
Documentary films	10%	73%	54%
Feature films	8%	62%	59%
Fiction books/literature	3%	56%	24%
Internet	4%	39%	60%
Memoirs	6%	54%	26%
Nonfiction books	5%	62%	28%
Performances and presentations	8%	82%	13%
Survivors' testimonies	10%	78%	29%
Visits to institutions for Shoah commemoration	9%	85%	26%

Table b: Exposure to types of Shoah-related educational activities with school, by school stream and grade level

	General schools		**Religious schools**	
	9th graders	**12th graders**	**9th graders**	**12th graders**
Ceremonies	94%	96%	92%	95%
Documentary films	62%	82%	64%	80%
Feature films	51%	69%	51%	79%
Internet	37%	43%	33%	31%
Literature	64%	52%	49%	56%
Memoirs	55%	56%	44%	52%
Nonfiction books	60%	66%	49%	64%

Performances and presentations	84%	82%	78%	74%
Survivors' testimonies	69%	82%	78%	89%
Visits to institutes for Shoah commemoration	76%	93%	70%	91%

Table c: Methods and materials for teaching the Shoah, by subject taught—percentage indicating they are involved in or use each

	Teachers of only history	Teachers of history and another subject	Non-history teachers
Number (%)	*248 (50%)*	*129 (25%)*	*130 (25%)*
Activities of involvement			
Classroom teaching	96%	94%	45%
Visits to institutes for Shoah commemoration	58%	72%	58%
General enrichment activities	33%	67%	56%
Ceremonies	34%	55%	61%
Journey to Poland	40%	50%	34%
Museum or memorial room in school	13%	11%	12%
Teaching styles			
Frontal lectures	95%	94%	68%
Independent work	53%	52%	27%
Group work	23%	33%	39%
Creative works (art, drama, etc.)	20%	22%	26%

Materials used			
Historical sources	90%	96%	45%
Films	86%	86%	59%
Testimonies	65%	73%	56%
Internet	32%	40%	35%
Literature	33%	48%	53%
Memoirs	23%	36%	21%
Presentations/performances	17%	25%	38%
Integrate Shoah and other subjects (yes/absolutely yes)	88%	95%	89%

Table d: Teachers' academic emphases in Shoah education, by school stream—percentage of teachers indicating they emphasize each "to a very great extent" in their work.

	Teachers in general schools	**Teachers in religious schools**	**Total**
Nazi ideology	62%	40%	58%
The destruction process	58%	62%	58%
Influence of the Shoah on the Jewish world and Israel	55%	56%	55%
Struggle of the Jews against the Nazis	51%	57%	52%
Historical background	54%	37%	50%
The place of the individual during the Shoah	45%	49%	46%
Jewish life during the Shoah	31%	38%	33%
Jewish community life before the Shoah	22%	26%	23%

Table e: Didactic approach of teachers, by school stream and level—percentage indicating they emphasize each to a "great" or "very great" combined (in parenethses—percentage indicating to a "very great extent")

	Teachers in general schools	**Teachers in religious schools**	**Junior high school teachers**	**High school teachers**	**Total**
Emphasize cognitive knowledge	94% (42%)	95% (45%)	95% (44%)	96% (46%)	94% (43%)
Emphasize experiential aspects	89% (41%)	94% (44%)	99% (53%)	88% (38%)	90% (42%)

Table f: Teachers' goals for Shoah education, according to didactic approach—percentage indicating "to a very great extent"

	Emphasize **cognitive** aspects "to a great extent"	Emphasize **experiential** aspects "to a great extent"	Emphasize **both** aspects "to a great extent"	Emphasize **neither** aspect "to a great extent"
Strengthening Jewish identity	53%	62%	70%	47%
Strengthening Israeli identity	44%	48%	64%	42%
Strengthening universal values	56%	54%	57%	44%

Table g: Teachers' assessment of theological and ethical discussion in Shoah teaching

	Teachers in general schools	Teachers in religious schools	Total
Do you encourage discussions of values and ethics in the framework of Shoah education?			
To a very great extent	47%	42%	46%
To a great extent	43%	45%	44%
To a small extent/not at all	10%	13%	11%
Do the students raise theological questions in the framework of Shoah studies?			
Very often	14%	46%	21%
Often	44%	42%	44%
Rarely	34%	12%	29%
Never	7%	0%	6%
Do you feel comfortable addressing these questions?			
Absolutely	39%	52%	42%
Yes	51%	47%	50%
No/not at all	10%	1%	8%

Table h: Jewish, Israeli and universal values of students

	Positive response "true" and "absolutely true" combined)	Absolutely true
I am proud to be Jewish	94%	74%
It is important to me to be part of the Jewish people	91%	68%
I intend to serve in the Israeli army	90%	73%
I am proud to be Israeli	89%	63%
I feel a sense of identification with the Jewish People	88%	48%
I feel committed to the existence of the State of Israel	86%	51%
I feel committed to the fight against racism	86%	52%
I identify with democratic values	83%	42%
I identify with universal values	80%	32%
I would choose to be "re-born" as Jew in Israel if given choice	77%	n/a
I will stay in Israel	70%	40%
I feel connected to Jews in the Diaspora	60%	22%

Table i: Scope of the tragedy according to students

	Students in 9th grade	Students in 12th grade	Students in general schools	Students in religious schools	Total students
Shoah a tragedy for all humanity	76%	84%	81%	78%	81%
The Shoah was a tragedy only for the Jews	24%	16%	19%	22%	19%

Table j: Scope of the tragedy according to teacher

	Junior high school teachers*	High school teachers*	Teachers in general schools	Teachers in religious schools	Total teachers
Shoah a tragedy for all humanity	89%	79%	82%	85%	82%

** Many teachers work in both junior high and high schools. The data in this table includes only teachers who work in one type of school.*

Table k: Students' attitudes regarding the potential of another Shoah and protection offered by the State of Israel, by school stream and grade level—percentage answering "absolutely true"

	Students in 9th grade	Students in 12th grade	Students in general schools	Students in religious schools
State of Israel is an "answer" to the Shoah	43%	48%	44%	52%
Another Shoah could happen somewhere in the world	23%	32%	29%	25%

A Shoah could happen in Israel	9%	9%	8%	10%

Table l: Principals' evaluations of Shoah education, by school stream and level—percentage answering "satisfied" or "absolutely satisfied" combined (in parentheses—"absolutely satisfied")

	Principals of general schools	**Principals of religious schools**	**Principals of high schools**	**Principals of junior high schools**	**Total**
Satisfied with Shoah education at school	87% (20%)	78% (12%)	85% (19%)	80% (13%)	83% (17%)
Number of hours dedicated to Shoah education is:					
Not enough	41%	35%	32%	48%	39%
Sufficient	58%	60%	64%	51%	58%
Too much	1%	5%	4%	1%	2%

Table m: Teachers' satisfaction with Shoah education in Israel

	Absolutely satisfied	**Satisfied**	**Not satisfied**	**Total**
Teachers in general schools	4%	65%	31%	100%
Teachers in religious schools	4%	60%	40%	100%
Teachers in junior high schools	3%	69%	28%	100%
Teachers in high schools	4%	64%	32%	100%
History teachers	5%	67%	28%	100%

Non-history teachers	4%	54%	41%	100%
TOTAL population of teachers	4%	67%	33%	100%

Table n: Students' satisfaction with Shoah studies, by school stream and grade

	General schools 9th graders	**General schools 12th graders**	**Religious schools 9th graders**	**Religious schools 12th graders**	**TOTAL**
VERY satisfied	27%	29%	23%	41%	29%
Satisfied	54%	56%	48%	50%	54%
Minimally satisfied	15%	13%	18%	9%	14%
Not satisfied	5%	2%	10%	1%	3%

Table o: Students' perception of the effectiveness of Shoah education activities—percentage answering "to a very great extent"

	9th grade students	12th grade students
Ceremonies	44%	31%
Films	57%	55%
History lessons at school	29%	37%
Other lessons at school	9%	6%
Internet	23%	16%
Performances and presentations	34%	28%
Testimonies of survivors	62%	72%
Visits to institutions commemorating the Shoah	60%	58%
Journey to Poland (12th grade students only)[1]	n/a	78%

1 *This data refers to the entire population of 12th grade students, including those who have not participated in the journey to Poland.*

Table p: Comparison of evaluations by 9th grade students in general and religious schools—percentage answering to a "great" and "very great" extent combined

	9th graders in general school	9th graders in religious school
I feel proficient in the subject of the Shoah	63%	42%
I would like to learn more about the Shoah	40%	27%

Table q: Students' assessment of discipline in Shoah studies classes

	General schools	Religious schools	TOTAL
More discipline problems during lessons on the Shoah	9%	14%	10%
No difference	36%	41%	37%
Fewer discipline problems during lessons on the Shoah	55%	45%	53%

Table r: Socio-economic predictors of students' perceived *relevance* of Shoah studies to their lives

Predicting variable	Correlation	Level of prediction	Category of students who see Shoah studies as more relevant to their lives
Loss of relative in the Shoah (yes/no)	0.129	++	Students who lost a relative in the Shoah
Religious self-definition (religious, traditional, secular)	0.087	+	Religious students
Ethnic background (Ashkenazi, Sephardi-Mizrahi, both, other)	0.086	+	Ashkenazi and mixed origin students
School stream (general/religious)	0.072	+	Students from religious schools
Participation in a youth movement (leader, member, non-member)	0.076	+	Students who are members or leaders in youth movements
Participation in journey to Poland (yes/no)	0.075	+	Participating students
Socio-economic level (high, medium, low)	0.057	+	Students from a low socio-economic background
Grade (9th/12th)	0.019	0	No difference between 12th and 9th graders

Table s: Socio-economic predictors of students' perception of the *scope of the Shoah* as a disaster for humankind or Jews only

Predicting variable	**Correlation**	**Level of prediction**	**Category of students more likely to see the *Shoah* as a disaster for all humankind**
Ethnic background (Ashkenazi, Mizrahi, both, other)	0.185	+++	Ashkenazi and mixed origin students
Loss of relative in the Shoah (yes/no)	0.127	++	Students who lost a relative in the Shoah
Participation in journey to Poland (yes/no)	0.123	++	Participating students
Grade (9th/12th)	0.104	++	12th graders
Participation in a youth movement (leader, member, non-member)	0.104	++	Students who are members or leaders in youth movements
Socio-economic level (high, medium, low)	0.085	+	Students from medium or high socio-economic background
Religious self-definition (religious, traditional, secular)	0.080	+	Secular students
School stream (general/religious)	0.034	0	No difference

Table t: A comparison of several possible predictors of the tendency to participate in the journey to Poland

Predicting variable	Correlation	Level of prediction	The group of students who are more likely to participate in the journey to Poland
Loss of relative in the Shoah (yes/no)	**0.279**	++++	Students who lost a relative in the Shoah
Ethnic background (Ashkenazi, Mizrahi, both, other)	**0.276**	++++	Ashkenazi and mixed origin students
Socio-economic level (high, medium, low)	**0.238**	++++	As the measure gets higher
Religious self-definition (religious, traditional, secular)	0.185	+++	Secular students
Participation in a youth movement (leader, member, non-member)	0.180	+++	Students who are participating or have in the past participated in youth movements
School stream (general/religious)	0.091	+	Students from general schools

Table u: Factor Analysis of socio-demographic impacts on Shoah education[1]

	Factor			
	1) Familiarity	**2) Social identity**	**3) Populations involved in the Shoah**	**4) Social involvement**
Familiarity with Shoah-related items (Yes/no)	**.951**	-.007	.031	.056
Journey to Poland (participant/non-participant)	**.729**	-.147	-.064	-.156
School stream (general/religious)	.040	**.840**	.013	-.202
Socio-economic level of school (low/median/high)	-.228	**.741**	-.064	.046
Self-defined religiosity (secular/traditional/religious)	.098	**.626**	.432	-.055
Ethnicity (Ashkenazi/Mizrahi/mixed)	-.085	.080	**.688**	.113
Lost a relative in the Shoah (yes/no)	-.161	.144	**.667**	.268
Scope of Shoah (human-kind/Jews only)	.218	-.195	**.592**	-.389

1 Extraction Method: Principal Component Analysis. Rotation Method: Varimax with Kaiser Normalization. Rotation converged in 5 iterations.

Involvement in youth movement (counselor/ member/non-member)	-.001	-.124	.083	**.733**
Students' perception that Shoah studies are relevant to their life (very true/true/not true/not true at all)	.038	-.038	.063	**.559**
Grade (9th/12th)	-.928	-.036	.085	-.134

Table v: Characteristics of participants and non-participants in journey to Poland from religious and general high schools

	Non-participant from general high school	Participant from general high school	Non-participant from religious high school	Participants from religious high school
Someone in my family survived the Shoah	35%	52%	23%	55%
Someone in my family died in the Shoah	30%	55%	21%	65%
Ashkenazi or mixed background	52%	74%	28%	83%

Table w: Principals' assessment of financial support for journey to Poland, by socio-economic level of the school

	High socio-economic level	Median socio-economic level	Low socio-economic level	Total
Number of schools	*75*	*39*	*32*	*146*
Majority of participants receive support	3%	28%	19%	13%
Substantial percentage of participants receive support	9%	26%	25%	17%
Small percentage of participants receive support	84%	41%	56%	66%
No participants receive support	4%	5%	0%	3%

Table x: Satisfaction with the journey to Poland among participating students and teachers

	Very satisfied	Satisfied	Not satisfied	Not satisfied at all
Participating teachers	40%	49%	10%	1%
Participating students	67%	29%	3%	<1%

Table y: Principals', teachers' and students' assessment of impact of journey to Poland on strengthening students' commitment to preserving the memory of the Shoah

	To a very great extent	To a great extent	To a small extent	Not at all
To what extent do the *principals* think the journey to Poland strengthens students' commitment to remembering the Shoah? (only principals whose schools sent students to Poland)	72%	24%	3%	1%
To what extent do *students who participated* in the journey think it strengthened their commitment to remembering the Shoah?	61%	30%	8%	1%
To what extent do the *teachers who participated* in the journey to Poland think the journey strengthens students' commitment to remembering the Shoah?	48%	46%	7%	0%
To what extent do the *teachers who didn't participate* in the journey to Poland think the journey strengthens students' commitment to remembering the Shoah?	39%	48%	12%	1%

Table z: Difficulties faced by teachers in Shoah education

	Problem to a "great" or "very great" extent
Too few hours allotted	66%
Need for additional enrichment courses	44%
Insufficient training	23%
Insufficient professional support	23%
Lack of appropriate educational materials	20%

Table aa: Recommendations of principals and teachers, by means (1 = recommend much less, 2 = recommend less, 3 = recommend no change, 4 = recommend more, 5 = recommend much more)

	Principals	**Teachers**
Informal activities	4.30	4.37
Emphasis on experiential	4.20	4.15
Hours	4.05	4.30
Zionist	4.09	3.91
Emphasis on knowledge	3.72	3.94
Universal	3.67	3.72
Intensive	3.63	3.73
Jewish	3.68	3.51
Journeys to Poland	3.40	3.38

Appendix D
Structural analysis of components of Jewish identity (reasons to be Jewish), as assessed by Diaspora youth on group tours to Israel (Cohen, 2008)

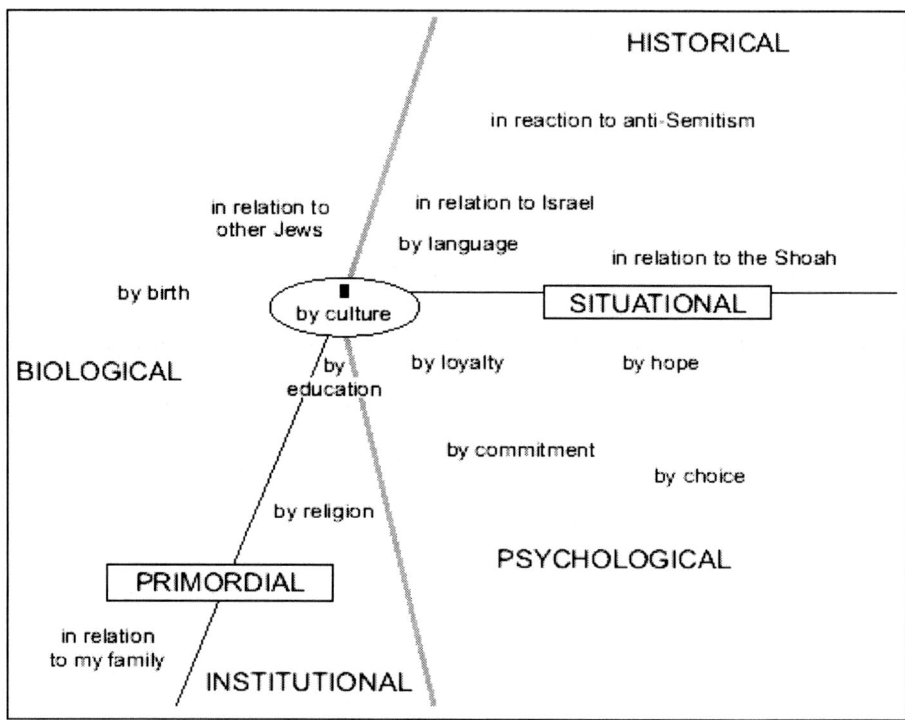

Appendix E: Brief descriptions of specific items related to the Shoah included in questionnaire for 12th grade students

1. **Auschwitz—Birkenau**
   The concentration and death camp in southwest Poland was the largest death camp erected by Nazi Germany during World War II. More Jews were killed there than in any other place during the war. Auschwitz operated from June 1940–January 1945. In Auschwitz the industrialization of mass murder reached its peak.
2. **Schnellbrief**
   The *Schnellbrief* was a formal letter sent by Reinhard Heydrich, Chief of the Reich Security Main Office, to the heads of the Einsatzgruppen forces (see #28) in occupied Poland. The letter was sent on 21 September 1939, three weeks after German forces entered Poland. The content of the letter included orders for transferring all Jews in the territories to ghettos near train stations, establishment of the Judenräte councils (see #22), sorting of Jews into groups by age and gender for forced labor, and transfer of Jewish owned lands to Polish and German farmers.
3. **Eichmann**
   Adolf Otto Eichmann (19 March 1906–31 May 1962) was in charge of the Jewish Division of the Nazi Security Police and one of the main people in charge of implementing the Final Solution of the destruction of Jews in Europe. In 1960 Eichmann was brought to trial in Israel, sentenced to death by hanging, and was executed in May of 1962.
4. **Anne Frank**
   Annelies Marie (Anne) Frank (12 June 1929–March 1945) was a Jewish girl from Amsterdam. Her family and some friends hid in an apartment, with the aid of Dutch friends. She wrote a diary about their life in hiding. After more than two years in hiding, they were denounced to the Nazis in Amsterdam. Anne's mother died in Auschwitz. Anne and her sister both died of typhus in Bergen-Belsen in March 1945. Their father, Otto, survived Auschwitz and later published Anne's diary, which became one of the most popular books worldwide, and the basis of a well-known play and movie.

5. **Aktzia**
   Aktzia (German for "operation") refers to an operation of the Gestapo and other security forces in the ghettos in order to locate, arrest, and concentrate Jews for deportation to concentration, death, or labor camps. Those resisting arrest were usually shot on the spot.
6. **Babi Yar**
   Babi Yar is a ravine north west of Kiev in Ukraine where the Nazis murdered approximately 100,000 people (most of whom were Jews) beginning on the 29th of September 1941.
7. **Goebbels**
   Paul Joseph Goebbels (29 October 1897–1 May 1945) served as minister of propaganda for the Nazi regime, and was one of Hitler's closest allies. He and his family committed suicide in Hitler's bunker.
8. **Ghetto**
   Historically the term *ghetto* referred to streets or city sections where only Jews lived. During World War II the Jews of Eastern Europe were forced to leave their homes and move to ghettos where they were held as prisoners. These ghettos were known for their extremely poor standard of living, over-crowding, hunger and deprivation, severe restrictions, exposure to abuse, and poor hygiene. The first ghetto in Poland was established in October 1939. The largest ghetto in Europe, the Warsaw Ghetto, was set up in November 1940. Ghettos were also constructed in Hungary, Amsterdam, and Theresienstadt.
9. **General Government**
   When the Germans invaded Poland in September 1939, they split the country into three parts: the western third was annexed to the Third Reich; the eastern third was occupied by the Soviet Union; and the central third was made into the General Government (GG) under German occupation. The city of Krakow was the administrative center of the GG. The GG was the source of Polish slave labor, and later was the part of Poland in which the extermination camps were built and operated. The GG had a total population of 12 million, of which 1.5 million were Jews.
10. **Anschluss**
    Anschluss refers to Germany's annexation of Austria on 13 March 1938. Austria as a state then ceased to exist and became a part of the Third Reich.

11. **Heydrich**
    Reinhard Tristan Eugene Heydrich (7 March 1904–4 June 1942), commander of the SD (the Security section of the SS), was in charge of the Final Solution of the Jewish people in Nazi occupied Europe. He was known as the "butcher from Prague," the "blond monster," and the "Hangman." Heydrich chaired the Wannsee Conference that took place on 20 January 1942 (see #16). He was assassinated by the Czechoslovak underground in Prague in 1942.
12. **Himmler**
    Heinrich Himmler (7 October 1900–23 May 1945) was the high commander of the SS, the Gestapo and the police forces of Nazi Germany. He was responsible for the death of millions of people, most of whom were Jews, in the death camps.
13. **Munich Conference**
    The Conference was held in Munich on September 28–29, 1938. In the conference, the leaders of Great Britain, France, and Italy agreed to allow Germany to annex the Sudetenland section of Czechoslovakia. No representative of Czechoslovakia was present. The conference and the agreement represent the policy of "appeasement" towards Nazi Germany and its demands. Five months later, in March 1939, Hitler broke the agreement by dismembering the rest of Czechoslovakia. As a result, the term "Munich" became a symbol of appeasement policy that eventually leads to war.
14. **The Ribbentrop-Molotov Pact**
    The Ribbentrop-Molotov Pact was an agreement of non-aggression signed between Nazi Germany and the Soviet Union on 23 August 1939. It was signed by German Foreign Minister Joachim von Ribbentrop and Soviet Foreign Minister Viacheslav Molotov, giving the agreement its code name. The pact also included a secret attachment about the division of Poland between the two countries. The pact was abruptly broken by the Germans when they invaded the Soviet Union in June 1941.
15. **The Final Solution**
    "The Final Solution of the Jewish Question in Europe" was the code name given by the Germans to their policy of physical destruction of the Jews of Europe during World War II.
16. **The Wannsee Conference**
    A meeting held at a lakeside villa in Wannsee, Berlin, on 20 January

1942, whose purpose was to discuss and coordinate the "Final Solution of the Jewish Problem" (#15). The Wannsee Conference was organized by Reinhard Heydrich (#11). Those invited to the meeting were either involved in or aware of the murder of Jews which was already taking place in Eastern Europe. At the meeting Heydrich announced that the official policy of the German government regarding the Jews would be total annihilation. The issue discussed in the conference was not *whether* to implement the policy, but *how* to implement it.

17. **The Sanctification of Life**
    The term refers to any spontaneous or planned action which undermined the Nazi's goal of exterminating all the Jews. The term is attributed to the religious Zionist leader Rabbi Yitzchak Nissenbaum (1868-1942) of the Warsaw Ghetto. As opposed to a traditional concept of sanctification of God by martyring oneself for religious beliefs, in the context of the Shoah, Nissenbaum (and others) declared the primary goal had to be survival and sanctification of life.
18. **Nuremberg Laws**
    The set of laws implemented by the German Parliament in Nuremberg on 15 September 1935 became the legal basis for the racist anti-Jewish policy in Germany. The first of the Nuremberg Laws was called the "Reich Citizenship Law," which declared that only Aryans could be citizens of the Reich. This stripped the Jews of their political rights and reduced them from citizens to state subjects. The second law, entitled the "Law for the Protection of German Blood and Honor," forbade marriages and extramarital relations between Germans and Jews, the employment of German maids under the age of 45 in Jewish homes and the raising of the German flag by Jews. The Nuremberg Laws provided the legal mechanism for excluding the Jews from mainstream German public life, culture and civil rights. On the 3rd of January 1936 the law was expanded to include Gypsies in the Reich territories.
19. **Hannah Senesh**
    Hannah Senesh (Szenes) was born in 1921 in Budapest. In 1939 she immigrated to Palestine. Senesh became a poet at a young age, writing in Hungarian at first and later in Hebrew. In 1943 Senesh volunteered to join a group of Jewish parachutists who were to be sent by the British on missions behind enemy lines in occupied Europe. In

March 1944 she parachuted into Yugoslavia. In early June 1944 she crossed the border into Hungary with a radio transmitter, and was caught immediately. Imprisoned by the Germans, she was tortured brutally but did not break. Senesh was put on trial, convicted of treason against Hungary, and was executed by firing squad on 7 November 1944.

20. **Righteous among the Nations**
    The Righteous among the Nations refers to non-Jews who saved or helped Jews in Europe during the Shoah. The title is bestowed by Yad Vashem on behalf of the State of Israel. Naming and paying tribute to the Righteous among the Nations was included in the mission of Yad Vashem's Remembrance Authority since its inception in 1953. The origin of the expression "Righteous among the Nations" comes from traditional Jewish texts, referring to non-Jews who helped Jews in times of danger. By the end of 2010 Yad Vashem had recognized 23,788 Righteous Among the Nations from 45 countries.
21. **Janusz Korczak (Yanush)**
    This is the pen name of Henryk Goldszmit (1878 or 1879–1942). He is also known as "Yanush." He was a Polish-Jewish doctor, author and educator. Born in Warsaw in an assimilated Jewish family, Korczak dedicated his life to caring for children, particularly orphans. He wrote several books for and about children, and broadcasted a children's radio program. After the establishment of the Warsaw Ghetto he continued to care for the children in the orphanage that he directed. Despite offers from Polish friends to hide him on the "Aryan" side of the city, Korczak refused to abandon the children. On 5 August 1942, the Nazis rounded up Korczak and his 200 children. They marched with Korczak in the lead to Treblinka, where they were murdered.
22. **Judenräte**
    These were councils set up in the Jewish communities of Nazi-occupied Europe to implement the Nazis' policies, such as providing lists of names of Jews. The first *Judenräte* were established in occupied Poland in 1939, on orders issued by Security Police head Reinhard Heydrich. (#11). The attempted resistance versus complicity of the Jewish members of these councils is one of the most controversial aspects of Shoah history.

23. **Kristallnacht**
German for "Crystal Night" or "Night of the Broken Glass," *Kristallnacht* refers to a physical attack on Jews carried out by the Nazis throughout Germany and Austria on the night of 9-10 November 1938. The name *Kristallnacht* refers to the glass of the shop windows smashed by the rioters. Officially, *Kristallnacht* was launched in retaliation to the assassination on November 7 of a German embassy official in Paris by a young Jewish refugee, Herschel Grynszpan. During the riots shop windows of Jewish businesses were smashed, the stores looted, hundreds of synagogues and Jewish homes were burnt down and many Jews were physically assaulted. Approximately 30,000 Jews were arrested and deported to concentration camps. Some 90 Jews were murdered.
24. **Operation Barbarossa**
Operation Barbarossa was the code name given to the German invasion of the Soviet Union during World War II which began on 22 June 1941. The operation was named after the emperor Frederick Barbarossa. The operation was the beginning of the eastern front battles, which became the largest battle ground in World War II. The success of the Red Army in fending off the Nazi invader was the major turning point in World War II. At the end of 1942, the Soviets' luck turned with their victory over the Germans at Stalingrad. Over the next two years, they pushed the German army from the areas that have been occupied in the earlier stages of the war.
25. **Concentration Camp**
A concentration camp is a large imprisonment camp for political prisoners and members of an ethnic or religious group. The Nazis imprisoned their victims in the camps without trial. Although the term "concentration camp" is often used as a term for all Nazi camps, there were several types of camps in the Nazi system; the concentration camp was one of them. Others were: hard labor camps, extermination camps, transit camps, and prisoner of war camps.
26. **Warsaw Ghetto Uprising**
The Warsaw ghetto uprising was the largest Jewish insurgency during the Shoah and became a prominent symbol of Jewish resistance. The uprising broke out on 19 April 1943, (eve of the Passover holiday) and lasted until 16 May 1943. It was organized and carried

out by two Jewish underground organizations with very limited help from the Polish underground resistance. The Warsaw Ghetto Uprising was the first uprising of an urban population in occupied Europe, and took the German army by surprise.

27. **Mordechaj (Mordecai) Anielewicz**

    M. Anielewicz (1919–8 May 1943) was the leader of the Warsaw Ghetto Uprising (#26). Anielewicz was born in Warsaw, and was a member of a Zionist youth movement. In November 1942, Anielewicz became the commander of the ZOB—the underground movement in the Warsaw Ghetto. After the fierce fighting in the Ghetto that started on 19 April 1943, Anielewicz and many of his comrades retreated to the bunker at 18 Mila Street. The bunker fell on 8 May 1943. Most of the ZOB members, including Anielewicz, were killed.

28. **Einsatzgruppen (Task Forces)**

    Einsatzgruppen is the general name for the task forces of the SD and the SIPO (police) that acted as the executioners of the destruction of the Jews of Europe. They operated as killing squads, who followed the invading army in the eastern front. Their main tactic was shooting Jews and burying them in pits. There were four Einsatzgruppen spread from north to south in the eastern front.

29. **Emmanuel Ringelblum**

    Jewish historian (1900-1944), founder and director of the secret *Oneg Shabbat* Archive in the Warsaw Ghetto. Ringelblum and his colleagues were determined to record the events for future historians. The *Oneg Shabbat* materials were preserved in three milk cans. Two of them were uncovered. The archive materials and Ringelblum's own written chronicles are the most comprehensive and valuable source of information about the Jews in German-occupied Poland. In March 1943, Ringelblum and his family escaped the ghetto and went into hiding in the non-Jewish area of Warsaw. In March 1944 their hideout was discovered. Ringelblum and his family were taken to the ruins of the ghetto and were executed.

30. **Partisans**

    The term refers to groups of organized guerilla fighters operating in occupied territories. During World War II, partisans in Nazi-occupied Europe were mainly active in Eastern Europe, but there was also partisan activity in Yugoslavia, Greece, Slovakia, and

Western European countries such as France and Italy. Many Jews joined the partisans, whether as part of individual Jewish units or as members of non-Jewish units.

31. **Raoul Wallenberg**
Raoul Wallenberg (4 August, 1912–1947, exact date of death unknown) was a Swedish diplomat in Budapest, Hungary during World War II, who used his diplomatic status to save the lives of tens of thousands of Hungarian Jews. Among other things, Wallenberg issued "protective passports" to the Jews of Budapest, established shelters under the protection of the Swedish crown as a safe haven for the Jews, put pressure on Nazi and Hungarian officials to stop the transports of Jews to Auschwitz, and even physically confronted the SS, trying to stop the deportation of Jews. At the end of the war, after his intensive work to save the Jews of Hungary, Wallenberg fell into Soviet captivity and mystery surrounds his fate. Israel, Canada, and the United States awarded him honorary citizenship. He was designated as a Righteous among the Nations (#20).

32. **The Rabbi of Piaseczno**
The Great Rabbi Klonymus Kalmish Shapira of Piaseczno (1889–1943) is the author of *Chovat haTalmidim* ("The Students' Responsibility"), *Esh Hakodesh* ("The Holy Fire") and other volumes. When World War II broke out, the Rabbi was trapped in Warsaw. His son, daughter in-law, and aunt were killed in the bombings and his mother was killed shortly after the beginning of the German occupation. Rabbi Shapira refused offers of escape and chose to remain with his followers in the Warsaw ghetto. On April 1943, after the Warsaw Ghetto Uprising, the rabbi was deported along with the remaining living Jews to Trawniki concentration camp near Lublin. He was murdered on November 1943 along with all the other Jews in the camp.

Appendix F: Correlation matrices and arrays for Smallest Space Analyses maps, Figures 4 and 8

Correlation matrix for SSA of students' beliefs, values, and attitudes towards the Shoah (Figure 4)

		1	2	3	4	5	6	7	8	9
interest-religious questions	1	100	72	40	61	47	36	49	25	25
interest-moral questions	2	72	100	43	56	57	63	61	48	47
identify with Shoah survivors	3	40	43	100	77	56	38	67	35	40
identify with Jewish People	4	61	56	77	100	84	47	74	48	36
commit-State of Israel	5	47	57	56	84	100	60	77	56	44
commit-universal values	6	36	63	38	47	60	100	63	67	53
commit-Zionism	7	49	61	67	74	77	63	100	66	62
identify with democracy	8	25	48	35	48	56	67	66	100	72
commit to fight racism	9	25	47	40	36	44	53	62	72	100

Correlation matrix for SSA of teachers' recommendations, with sub-groups of teachers as external variables (Figure 8)

		1	2	3	4	5	6	7	8	9
classroom hours	1	100	71	72	80	47	62	45	10	66
cognitive	2	71	100	56	66	49	60	38	33	35
experiential	3	72	56	100	70	56	69	61	24	71
intensity	4	80	66	70	100	56	67	61	30	55
Judaism	5	47	49	56	56	100	80	30	-5	33
Zionism	6	62	60	69	67	80	100	54	6	50
journey to Poland	7	45	38	61	61	30	54	100	40	53
universal values	8	10	33	24	30	-5	6	40	100	32
informal	9	66	35	71	55	33	50	53	32	100

Dimensionality 2
Coefficient of Alienation ...... .12382

Research Team

Prof. Erik H. Cohen, Educational sociologist, Research and project director
Dr. Einat Bar-On Cohen, Educational anthropologist, Director of the qualitative aspects of the research
Dr. David Resnick, Project consultant
Ephrat Balberg-Rotenstreich, Shoah history teacher, Consultant on Shoah teaching
Reuven Amar, Mathematician, Computer and data analysis consultant
Oshri Weiss, PhD student in cognitive sciences, Research assistant
Adam Farkash, MA student in history, Research assistant—special thanks for helping to compile the section on the history of Shoah education in Israel
Limor Zeelah, MA student in Jewish education, Research assistant
Allison Ofanansky, Research assistant and English editor
Rina Iflane, Data processing
David Meyers, Data processing

Observers and interviewers

Noémie Grynberg
Ofra Guttman
Adam Farkash
Sarit Michaelov
Allison Ofanansky
Iris Reuveni
Hilla Tsadok
Oshri Weiss
Limor Zeelah

References

Abebe, D. (2011). Eichmann witnesses meet German youth. *Israel Jewish Scene*. September 22.

Abitbol, M. (1989). *North African Jews during the Second World War*. Trans. C. Zentelis. Detroit, MI: Wayne State University Press.

Aboud, F. (1988). *Children and Prejudice*. New York: Blackwell.

Adorno, T. and R. Tiedemann, (2003). *Can One Live after Auschwitz? A Philosophical Reader*. Stanford, CA: Stanford University Press.

AFP-EJP. (2008). Sarkozy drops Holocaust education proposal—new avenues to be explored. *European Jewish Press*. February 27.

Aharon, Y. (2001). *Value-Oriented Education in General and Religious State Schools in the Context of the Holocaust*. Tel Aviv. (Hebrew).

Alderman, G. (1999). British Jews or Britons of the Jewish persuasion? The religious constraints of civic freedom. In *National Variations in Jewish Identity: Implications for Jewish Education,* ed. S.M. Cohen and G. Horenczyk, 125-135. New York: State University of New York Press.

Alexander, E. (2009). *Remembering the Holocaust: A Debate*. Oxford: Oxford University Press.

Alexander, H. (2003). Moral education and liberal democracy: Spirituality, community and character in an open society. *Educational Theory* 53(4): 367- 387.

Alexander, H., ed. (2004). *Spirituality and Ethics in Education: Philosophical, Theological and Radical Perspectives*. Brighton, UK: Sussex Academic Press.

Almog, O. (2000). *The Sabra: The Creation of a New Jew*. Berkeley: University of California Press.

Alphen, E. (1998). *Caught by History: Holocaust Effects in Contemporary Art, Literature, and Theory*. Stanford, CA: Stanford University Press.

Altman, I. (1999). *Teaching the Holocaust in Russia in the 21st Century*. Jerusalem: Yad Vashem. October 14.

Amadeo, J. et al. (2002). *Civic Knowledge and Engagement: An IEA Study of Upper Secondary Students in Sixteen Countries*. Amsterdam: The International Association for the Evaluation of Educational Achievement.

Amar, R. (2005). *HUDAP Manual*. Jerusalem: Hebrew University. http://

www.facet-theory.org/files/HUDAP%20Manual.pdf (accessed December 17, 2012).

Améry, J. (1980). *At the Mind's Limits: Contemplations by a Survivor on Auschwitz and Its Realities*. Trans. Sidney Rosenfeld and Stella P. Rosenfeld. Bloomington: Indiana University Press.

Anti-Defamation League. (2006). Teaching about the Holocaust: Why simulation activities should not be used. http://www.adl.org/education/Simulationinteachinghol.pdf (accessed December 17, 2012).

Anti-Defamation League. (2009). Holocaust and Nazi images abound at anti-Israel rallies in U.S. http://www.adl.org/PresRele/IslME_62/5431_62.htm (accessed December 17, 2012).

Arendt, H. (1951). *The Origins of Totalitarianism*. New York: Meridian Books.

Arendt, H. (1963). *Eichmann in Jerusalem: A Report on the Banality of Evil*. New York: Viking Press.

Arian, A. (2012). *A Portrait of Israeli Jews: Beliefs, Observance and Values of Israeli Jews, 2009*. Jerusalem: Israel Democracy Institute and Avi Chai Foundation.

Arian, A. and C. Gordon. (1993). The political and psychological impact of the Gulf War on the Israeli public. In *The Political Psychology of the Gulf War: Leaders, Publics, and the Process of Conflict*, ed. S. Renshon, 227-250. Pittsburgh, PA: University of Pittsburgh Press.

Aron, R. (1969). *De Gaulle, Israel and the Jews*. New York: Praeger.

Ashworth, G. (2002). Holocaust tourism: The experience of Kraków-Kazimierz. *International Research in Geographical and Environmental Education* 11(4): 363-367.

Associated Press. (2003). Germany rules animal rights group's Holocaust ad offensive. March 26.

Associated Press. (2009). Jewish leaders object to Nazi images at rallies. January 19.

Associated Press. (2012). Turkey: State TV broadcasts Holocaust documentary. January 27.

Auerbach, J. (2001). *Are We One? Jewish Identity in the United States and Israel*. New Brunswick, NJ: Rutgers University Press.

Auerhahn, N. and D. Laub. (1998). Intergenerational memory of the Holocaust. In *International Handbook of Multigenerational Legacies of Trauma*, ed. Y. Danieli, 21-42. New York: Springer.

Auron, Y. (1993a). *Jewish-Israeli Identity: Research on attitudes of future teachers of all types to Judaism in our time and Zionism*. Tel Aviv: Sifriat Poalim Publishing House. (Hebrew).

Auron, Y. (1993b). The Holocaust and me: Opinions and attitudes of education students in Israel towards the Holocaust. *Dapim* 16:37-66.

Auron, Y. (2008). The Shoah: A central factor in the Jewish-Israeli identity. In *Jewish Identity, Values and Leisure of Israeli Youth*, ed. E.H. Cohen, 153-160. Tel Aviv: The Kelman Center, School of Education, Tel Aviv University. (Hebrew).

Aviv, C. and D. Shneer. (2005). *New Jews: The End of the Jewish Diaspora*. New York: New York University Press.

Ayalon, H. and A. Yogev. (1996). The alternative worldview of state religious high schools in Israel. *Comparative Education Review* 40(1): 7-27.

Barkat, A. (2005). Youth trips to Poland: Under Polish pressure, government considering changes to camp visits. *Ha'aretz*. May 4.

Barkat, A. (2004). Settlers slammed for orange stars to protest pullout. *Ha'aretz*. December 21.

Baron, L. (2003). The Holocaust and American public memory, 1945-1960. *Holocaust and Genocide Studies* 17(1): 62-88.

Bauer, Y. (1977). Trends in Holocaust research. *Yad Vashem Studies* 12:7-36.

Bauer, Y. (1981). *American Jewry and the Holocaust: The American Jewish Joint Distribution Committee, 1939-1945*. Detroit, MI: Wayne State University Press.

Baum, R. (1996). "What I have learned to feel": The pedagogical emotions of Holocaust education. *College Literature* 23(3): 44-57.

BBC News. (2012). Israeli bill would prohibit Nazi comparisons. January 10.

Bekerman, Z. (2004). Potential and limitations of multicultural education in conflict-ridden areas: Bilingual Palestinian-Jewish schools in Israel. *Teachers' College Record* 106(3): 574-610.

Bekerman, Z. and G. Horenczyk. (2004). Arab-Jewish bilingual coeducation in Israel: A long-term approach to intergroup conflict resolution. *Journal of Social Issues* 60(2): 389-404.

Beilin, Y. (2000). *His Brother's Keeper: Israel and Diaspora Jewry in the Twenty-First Century*. New York: Schocken Books.

Beim, A. and G. Fine, (2007). Trust in testimony: The institutional embeddedness of Holocaust survivor narratives. *Archives of European*

Sociology 48:55-75.

Ben-Amos, A. and I. Bet-El, (1999). Holocaust day and memorial day in Israeli schools: Ceremonies, education and history. *Israel Studies* 4(1): 258-284.

Ben-Bassat, N. (2000). Holocaust awareness and education in the United States. *Religious Education* 95(4): 402-424.

Berkovits, E. (1973). *Faith after the Holocaust*. New York: Ktav.

Birnbaum, P. (1994). *L'Affaire Dreyfus: La République en péril*. Paris: Découverte, Gallimard.

Biscarat, P-J. (2011). *Y a-t-il un âge pour aller à Auschwitz?* (What is the age to go to Auschwitz?). Presentation at Les Voyages de Memoire de la Shoah, Lacaune, France, September 17-18.

Biscarat, P-J. (2010). *Les voyages pedagogiques en Pologne des eleves de Troisieme: Rapport d'evaluation*. Paris: Fondation pour la Memoire de la Shoah.

Bloom, B.S., et al. (1956). *Taxonomy of Educational Objectives Handbook: Cognitive Domain*, vol. 1. New York: David Mackay.

Boder, D. (1949). *I Did Not Interview the Dead*. Chicago: University of Illinois Press. [out of print]

Boorstin, D. (1964). *The Image: A Guide to Pseudo-Events in America*. New York: Harper & Row.

Booth, W. (2008). The work of memory: Time, identity and justice. *Social Research: An International Quarterly* 75(1): 237-262.

Brabham, E. (1997). Holocaust education: Legislation, practices and literature for middle-school students. *Social Studies* 88(3): 139-142.

Braiterman, Z. (1998). *(God) after Auschwitz: Tradition and Change in Post-Holocaust Jewish Thought*. Princeton: Princeton University Press.

Breitman, R. and A. Kraut. (1987). *American refugee policy and European Jewry, 1933-1945*. Bloomington: Indiana University Press.

Brody, D. (2009). Sailing through stormy seas: An Israeli kindergarten teacher confronts Holocaust remembrance day. *Early Childhood Research & Practice* 11(2): 1-13.

Brown, M. and I. Davies, (1998). The Holocaust and education for citizenship: The teaching of history, religion and human rights in England. *Educational Review* 50(1): 75–83.

Brown, T. (2006). *Confirmatory Factor Analysis for Applied Research*. New York: Guilford Press.

Bruner, E. (1996). Tourism in Ghana: The representation of slavery and the return of the black Diaspora. *American Anthropologist* 98(2): 290-304.

Burtonwood, N. (2002). Holocaust Memorial Day in schools: Context, process and content; A review of research into Holocaust education. *Educational Research* 44(1): 69–82.

Campo, J. E. (1998). American pilgrimage landscapes. *The Annals of the American Academy of Political and Social Science* 558:40-55.

Caplan, K. (2001). Have "Many lies accumulated in history books"? The Holocaust in Ashkenazi "haredi" historical consciousness in Israel. *Yad Vashem Studies* 29:321-375.

Caplan, P. (2007). "Never again": Genocide memorials in Rwanda. *Anthropology Today* 23(1): 20-22.

Cargas, H. (2003). *Problems Unique to the Holocaust*. Kentucky: University of Kentucky Press.

Carmil, D. and S. Breznitz, (1991). Personal trauma and world view: Are extremely stressful experiences related to political attitudes, religious beliefs and future orientation? *Journal of Traumatic Stress* 4(1): 393-405.

Carrington, B. and G. Short, (1997). Holocaust education, anti-racism and citizenship. *Educational Review* 49(3): 271-282.

Chanes, J. (2009). Kasztner: Hero or devil? New documentary revisits Israel's Holocaust reception. *Forward*. October 23. http://forward.com/articles/116718/kasztner-hero-or-devil/ (accessed August 1, 2012).

Chazan, B. (1981). What is informal education? *Philosophy of Education*, 241-253. Carbondale, IL: Philosophy of Education Society.

Cioflanca, A. (2004). A "grammar of exculpation" in communist historiography: Distortion of the history of the Holocaust under Ceausescu. *Romanian Journal of Political Science* 4(2): 29-46.

Cohen, A. and Y. Cochavi, eds. (1995). *Zionist Youth Movements during the Shoah*. New York: Peter Lang Publishing.

Cohen, E. (1979) A phenomenology of tourist experiences. *Sociology* 13(2): 179-201.

Cohen, E. (1992). Pilgrimage and tourism: Convergence and divergence. In *Sacred Journeys: The Anthropology of Pilgrimage*, ed. A. Morinis, 47-61. Westport, CT: Greenwood Press.

Cohen, E. H. (1997). Formal and informal Jewish education: A structural comparison. In *Sixth International Facet Theory Conference:*

Contributing to Cumulative Science, ed. M. Ito, 58-72. Liverpool: University of Liverpool.

Cohen, E. H. (2000). Mifgashim: A meeting of minds and hearts. *Journal of Jewish Education* 66(1-2): 23-37.

Cohen, E. H. (2004). Preparation, simulation and the creation of community: Exodus and the case of Diaspora education tourism. In *Tourism, Diasporas and Space*, ed. T. E. Coles and D. J. Timothy, 124-138. London: Routledge.

Cohen, E. H. (2005). *Identity, Values and Social Pursuits: Israeli Youth in the Year 2000.* Jerusalem: Avi Chai.

Cohen, E. H. (2008). *Youth Tourism to Israel: Educational Experiences of the Diaspora.* Clevedon, UK: Channel View Publications.

Cohen, E. H. (2009a). *Echoes and Reflections 2008-2009.* Yad Vashem and ADL. Unpublished Report.

Cohen, E. H. (2009b). The components of ethnic identity: A cross-cultural theory and case study of Jewish student activists. In *Educational Eclectics*, ed. S. Wygoda and I Sorek, 15-48. Jerusalem: Mandel Foundation.

Cohen, E. H. (2010). Research on Jewish identity: A state of the art. *The International Journal of Jewish Education Research* 1(1): 7-48.

Cohen, E. H. (2011a). *The Jews of France Today: Identity and Values.* Leiden, Netherlands: Brill.

Cohen, E. H. (2011b). *The Educational Shaliach 1939-2009: A Socio-history of a Unique Project in Formal and Informal Jewish Education.* Jerusalem: Lookstein Center for Jewish Education.

Cohen, E. H. (2011c). Educational dark tourism at an in populo site: The Holocaust museum in Jerusalem. *Annals of Tourism Research* 38(1): 193-209.

Cohen, E. H. (2011d). Facet Theory methods in the study of religion: A case study of symbols of Jewish identity in the US. In *The Routledge handbook of research methods in the study of religion*, ed. M. Stausberg and S. Engler, 178-203. Routledge.

Cohen, E. H. (2012). Israeli youth movements in the structure of Kahane's components of informality: A multi-dimensional and diachronic analysis, In *Between Order and Disorder*, ed. T. Rapoport and A. Kahane, 519-543. Jerusalem: Carmel Publishers. (Hebrew).

Cohen, E. H. and R. Amar. (2002). External variables as points in Smallest Space Analysis: A theoretical, mathematical and computer-based contribution. *Bulletin de Méthodologie Sociologique* 75:40-56.

Cohen, E. H. and R. Amar. (2005). External variables: Some novelties and applications. In *Facet Theory: Design, Analysis and Applications,* ed. W. Bilsky and D. Elizur, 231-240. Rome, Italy: Facet Theory Association.

Cohen, E. H. and E. Cohen. (2012). Teaching the Shoah in haredi teachers' seminars. Unpublished Report.

Cohen, H. (1966). The anti-Jewish *Farhud* in Baghdad, 1941. *Middle Eastern Studies* 3:2-17.

Cohen, S. and G. Horenczyk, eds. (1999). *National Variations in Jewish Identity: Implications for Jewish Education*. New York: State University of New York Press.

Cohen-Almagor, R. (2008). Hate in the classroom: Free expression, Holocaust denial, and liberal education. *American Journal of Education* 114:215-241.

Confino, A. and P. Fritzsche. (2002). *The Work of Memory: New Directions in the Study of German Society and Culture*. Champain, IL: University of Illinois Press.

Coombs, P. H. with C. Prosser and M. Ahmed. (1973). *New Paths to Learning for Rural Children and Youth*. New York: International Council for Educational Development.

Crawford, K. and S. Foster. (2007). *War, Nation, Memory: International Perspectives on World War II in School History Textbooks*. Charlotte, NC: Information Age Publishing.

Cywiński, P. (2011). Preface. In *Guide historique du camp d'Auschwitz et des traces juives de Cracovie*, J-F. Forges and P-J. Biscarat. Paris, France: Coedition Autrement Ministère de la Défense.

Dagan, B. (1986). The psychological-educational approach to teach the Holocaust in early childhood. *Hed haGan* 40(2): 467-474. (Hebrew).

Dagan, B. (2007). How did I tell kindergarten children about the Holocaust? *Masad: Maasaf leynyaney sifrut vehoraata* 5, 17. (Hebrew).

Dan, H. (1949). The dream and its solution. *Hapo'el Hatzair,* January 11.

Danieli, Y. (1981). *Therapists' difficulties in treating survivors of the Nazi Holocaust and their children*. PhD dissertation, New York University.

Danieli, Y. (1984). Psychotherapists' participation in the conspiracy of silence about the Holocaust. *Psychoanalytic Psychology* 1:23-42.

Darr, Y. (2010). The childlike voice as a means for a therapeutic narrative of Holocaust survivors: A new wave of Holocaust literature for children in Israel. In *Negotiating Childhoods*, ed. L. Hopkins, M. Macleod, and W. Turgeon, 221-229. Oxford: Interdisciplinary Press.

Dasberg, H. (1987). Society facing trauma or psychotherapist facing survivors. *Sihot, Israel Journal of Psychotherapy* 1:98-103.

Dashefsky, A. and C. Lebson. (2002). Does Jewish schooling matter? A review of the empirical literature on the relationship between Jewish education and dimensions of Jewish identity. *Contemporary Jewry* 23(1): 96-131.

Dawidowicz, L. (1981). *The Holocaust and the Historians*. Cambridge, MA: Harvard University Press.

Dawidowicz, L. (1990). How they teach the Holocaust. *Commentary* 90:25-31.

De Felice, R. (2001). *The Jews in Fascist Italy: A History*. New York: Enigma Books.

Debono, E. (2008). The Dynamics of Antisemitism in the Maghreb on the Eve of World War II. Paper presented at conference North Africa and Its Jews During the Second World War. Yad Vashem and the Ben Zvi Institute, April 28-30.

Dekoning, P. (1980). What psychotherapists have against working with people who were persecuted during World War II. In *Israel Netherland Symposium on the Impact of Persecution*, 49-54. Rijswijk, Holland: Ministry of Social Welfare.

DellaPergola, S. (2011). Jewish Shoah survivors: Neediness assessment and resource allocation. In *Holocaust Survivors: Resettlement, Memories, Identities*, ed. D. Ofer, F. Ouzan, and J. Baumel-Schwartz. New York: Berghahn Books.

DellaPergola, S. and U. Rebhun. (1994). *Israel-Diaspora Relationships: A First Quantitative Analysis of Social Indicators*. Jerusalem: Hebrew University of Jerusalem.

Deutsch, A. (1974). *The Eichmann Trial in the Eyes of Israeli Youngsters: Opinions, Attitudes, and Impact*. Ramat-Gan: Bar-Ilan University.

Diner, H. (2009). Immigration in U.S. history. U.S. Department of State. http://www.learnnc.org/lp/pdf/immigration-in-us-history-p5690.pdf. (accessed December 17, 2012)

Doerry, J. (2011). *Comment s'approcher d'un lieu de la Déportation et de la Shoah en Allemagne: Des séminaires pour groupes français réalisés au Mémorial de Bergen-Belsen*. Presentation at Les Voyages de Memoire de la Shoah, Lacaune, France, September 17-18.

Donnelly, (2004). *National Study of Secondary Teaching Practices in*

Holocaust Education. Arlington, VA: SRI International. http://policyweb.sri.com/cep/publications/SRI_Natl-Study_TeachingPractices.pdf (accessed December 17, 2011).

Dorst, N. (1985). Therapists' coping with treatment of Holocaust survivors. Paper presented at a meeting of the Israeli Society for Psychotherapy.

Dreyfus, J. (2011). Holocaust memory in the twenty-first century: Between national reshaping and globalization. *European Review of History* 18(1): 69-78.

Drockman, Y. (2011). The comptroller's report: Financial considerations cannot prevent the journey to Poland. *Yediot Aharanot.* May 17. http://www.ynet.co.il/articles/0,7340,L-4069129,00.html (accessed December 17, 2012).

Dror, Y. (1996). National denial, splitting, and narcissism: Group defence mechanisms of teachers and students in Palestine in response to the Holocaust. *Mediterranean Journal of Educational Studies* 1:107–137.

Dror, Y. (2001). Holocaust curricula in Israeli secondary schools 1960s-1990s: Historical evaluation from the moral education perspective. *Journal of Holocaust Education* 10(2): 29-39.

Eden, D. and R. Hertz-Lazarowtiz. (2001). The political power of school principals in Israel: A case study. *Journal of Educational Administration* 40(2): 211-229.

Eglash, R. (2011) Surviving the Shoah—and beating Israeli bureaucracy. *Jerusalem Post.* April 29.

Ein-Gil, E. and M. Machover. (2009). Zionism and Oriental Jews: A dialectic of exploitation and co-optation. *Race & Class* 50(3): 62-76.

Eitinger, L. (1961). Concentration camp survivors in the postwar world. *American Journal of Orthopsychiatry* 32:367-375

Eitinger, L. (1980). The concentration camp syndrome and its late sequelae. In *Survivors, Victims and Perpetrators: Essays on the Nazi Holocaust*, ed. J. Dimsdale, 127-162. New York: Hemisphere.

Elazar, D. (1977). *Israel-American Jewish Relation in the Context of the World Jewish Polity.* New York/Jerusalem: American Jewish Committee.

Elbaz-Luwisch, F. (2004). How is education possible when there's a body in the middle of the room? *Curriculum Inquiry* 34(1): 9-27.

Elkana, Y. (1988). The need to forget. *Ha'aretz.* March 2.

Epstein, J. and L. Lefkovitz, eds. (2001). *Shaping Losses: Cultural Memory and the Holocaust*. Urbana and Chicago: University of Illinois Press.

Ernst, S. (2008). *Quand les mémoires déstabilisent l'école. Mémoire de la Shoah et Enseignement*. Paris: Institut National de recherche pédagogique (INRP).

Ettinger, Y. (2011). New Bnei Brak center to focus on Haredi-style Shoah commemoration. *Ha'aretz*. May 2.

Evens, T. (2008). *Anthropology as Ethics: Nondualism and the Conduct of Sacrifice*. New York/Oxford: Bergham Books.

Evron, L. (2011). The influence of the journey in Poland on the Jewish identity of its participants in the range of one to ten years. Master's thesis, The School of Education: Bar Ilan University (Hebrew, with an abstract in English).

Fackenheim, E. (1982). *To Mend the World: Foundations of Future Jewish Thought*. Indiana University Press.

Fallace, T. (2006). The origins of Holocaust education in American public schools. *Holocaust and Genocide Studies* 20(1): 30-102.

Fallace, T. (2007). Playing Holocaust: The origins of the Gestapo simulation game. *Teachers' College Record* 109(12): 2642-2665.

Fallace, T. (2010). Teaching about the Holocaust in US schools. In *Teaching and Studying Social Issues: Major Programs and Approaches*, ed. S. Totten and J. Pederson, 139-152. Charlotte, NC: Information Age Publishing.

Farago, U. (1982). *A summary of Holocaust education in Israel.* Haifa: University of Haifa. (Hebrew).

Fargo, U. (1989). Jewish identity of Israeli youth, 1965-1985. *Yahadut Zmanenu* 5:259-287.

Fathi, N. (2006). Holocaust conference draws skeptics to Iran. *International Herald Tribune*. December 11.

Feldman, J. (1999). Voyages to Poland: Sensitizing educators to non-verbal elements. Paper presented at Yad Vashem. http://www1.yadvashem.org/download/education/conf/Feldman1B.pdf (accessed December 17, 2012).

Feldman, J. (2002). Marking the boundaries of the enclave: Defining the Israeli collective through the Poland "Experience". *Israel Studies* 7(2): 84-114.

Feldman, J. (2008). *Above the death pits, beneath the flag: Youth voyages to Poland and the performance of Israeli national identity*. Oxford and New York: Berghahn Books.

Finkielkraut, A. (2003). *Au nom de l'Autre: Réflexions sur l'antisémitisme qui vient.* [In the name of the Other: Reflections on the coming anti-Semitism]. Paris: Editions Gallimard.

Firer, R. (1987). The Holocaust in textbooks in Israel. In *The Treatment of the Holocaust in Textbooks*, ed. R. L. Braham, 178–188. New York: Columbia University Press.

Firer, R. (1989). *The Agents of the Lesson.* Ramat Gan: Sifriat Poalim. (Hebrew).

Fischer, C. (2002). *The Rise of the Nazis.* Manchester, UK: Manchester University Press.

Flanzbaum, H., ed. (1999). *The Americanization of the Holocaust.* Baltimore: Johns Hopkins University.

Fontanesi, A. (2011). *Un voyage d'un an: L'expérience des voyages de la mémoire d'Istoreco Reggio d'Émilie (Italie).* Presentation at Les Voyages de Memoire de la Shoah, Lacaune, France, September 17-18.

Fox, T. (1999). *Inherited Memories: Israeli Children of Holocaust Survivors.* London: Cassell Publishers.

Frankl, M. (2003). Holocaust education in the Czech Republic, 1989-2002. *Intercultural Education* 14(2): 177-189.

Freedman, S. (2011). Distinctive mission for Muslims' conference: Remembering the Holocaust. *New York Times.* September 23.

Friedman, G. (1946). Maurice Halbwachs: 1877-1945. *American Journal of Sociology* 51(6): 509-517.

Friedman, M. (1995). Life tradition and book tradition in the development of ultraorthodox Judaism. In *Israeli Judaism: The Sociology of Religion in Israel*, ed. S. Deshen, C. Liebman, and M. Shokeid, 127-148. Livingston, NJ: Transaction Publishers.

Friedman, M. (1991). *The Haredi (Ultra-Orthodox) Society: Sources, Trends, and Processes.* Jerusalem: Jerusalem Institute for Israel Studies (in Hebrew).

Friedman, P. (1951). American Jewish research and literature on the Jewish catastrophe of 1939-1945. *Jewish Social Studies*, 13(3): 235-250.

Friedman, S. (1973). *No Haven for the Oppressed: United States Policy toward Jewish Refugees, 1938-1945.* Detroit, MI: Wayne State University Press.

FSJU. (2012). Marche des Vivants 2012: 24ème edition. Fonds Social Juif Unifié. http://www.fsju.org/doc/index/israel/jeunesse/marche-des-vivants-2012-24eme-edition.html (accessed February 18, 2012).

Garber, Z. and B. Zuckerman. (1994). Why do we call the holocaust "The Holocaust"? An inquiry into the psychology of labels. In *Shoah: The Paradigmatic Genocide: Essays in Exegesis and Eisegesis*, ed. by Z. Garber, 51-66. Lanham: University Press of America.

Gelber, Y. (1996). The shaping of the "New Jew" in Eretz Israel. In *Major Changes within the Jewish People in the Wake of the Holocaust*, ed. I. Gutman, 443-462. Proceedings of Yad Vashem's 9th International Historical Conference, Jerusalem.

Gerstenfeld, M. (2008). Holocaust Trivialization. http://jcpa.org/article/holocaust-trivialization/ (accessed December 17, 2012).

Gidwitz, B. (1999). *Post-Soviet Jewry: The Critical Issues*. Jerusalem: Jerusalem Center for Public Affairs.

Gidwitz, B. (2011). Post-Soviet Jewry on the cusp of its third decade. *Changing Jewish Communities: Berman Jewish Policy Archive*, 68-69. http://www.bjpa.org/Publications/results.cfm?PublicationName=Changing%20Jewish%20Communities&VolumeIssue=Vol%2E69%2Fno%2E15 (accessed 17 December 2012).

Gitelman, Z. (1997). *Bitter Legacy: Confronting the Holocaust in the USSR*. Bloomington: Indiana University Press.

Glatthorn, A. and J. Jailall. (2008). *The Principal as Curriculum Leader: Shaping What is Taught and Tested*. Thousand Oaks, CA: Corwin Press.

Godsi, L. (1998). Development of Perceptions of Arab Groupings among Jewish-Israeli Children. MA thesis, School of Education, Tel Aviv University.

Goldberg, D. and M. Krausz, eds. (1993). *Jewish Identity*. Philadelphia: Temple University Press.

Goldhagen, D. (1997). *Hitler's Willing Executioners: Ordinary Germans and the Holocaust*. New York: Vintage Books.

Goldhirsh, O. (2008). Remembrance day for the holocaust and heroism in the kindergarten. http://cms.education.gov.il/educationcms/units/preschool/moreshet/tkasim/zicaronshoagvura.htm (accessed December 17, 2012).

Goodman, Y. and N. Mizrachi. (2008). "The Holocaust does not belong to European Jews alone": The differential use of memory techniques in Israeli high schools. *American Ethnologist* 35(1): 95-114.

Gorny, Y. (1998). *Between Auschwitz and Jerusalem*. Tel Aviv: Am Oved and Ben Gurion Research Center. (Hebrew).

Gorsuch, R. (1983). *Factor Analysis*. Hillsdale, NJ: Erlbaum.

Gouri, H. (2004). *Facing the Glass Booth: The Jerusalem Trial of Adolf Eichmann*. Trans. Michael Swirsky. Detroit, MI: Wayne State University Press. [Originally published in 1962 Tel Aviv: Hakibbutz Hame'uhad in Hebrew].

Govrin, Y. (2011). *Israel's Relations with the East European States: From Disruption (1967) to Resumption (1989-91)*. Middlesex: Vallentine Mitchell.

Graham, D. (2004). *European Jewish Identity at the Dawn of the 21st Century*. Institute for Jewish Policy Research, American Joint Distribution Committee, Hanadiv Charitable Foundation.

Grandjean, G. et al. (2011). *Les sentiers de la memoire: Paroles des jeunes*. Editions de l'Université de Liège.

Greene, N. (1999). *Landscapes of Loss: The National Past in Postwar French Cinema*. Princeton: Princeton University Press.

Gross, Z. (2003). State-religious education in Israel: Between tradition and modernity. *Prospects* 33(2): 149-164.

Gross, Z. (2010). Holocaust education in Jewish schools in Israel: Goals, dilemmas, challenges. *Prospects* 40:93–113.

Gur Ze'ev, I. (1999). *Philosophy, politics, and education in Israel*. Haifa: Haifa University Press. (Hebrew).

Gur-Ze'ev, I. (2000). Defeating the enemy within: Exploring the link between Holocaust education and the Arab/Israeli conflict. *Religious Education* 95(4): 373-401.

Gur-Ze'ev, I. (2001). The production of self and the destruction of the other's memory and identity in Israeli/Palestinian education on the Holocaust/*Nakbah*. *Studies in Philosophy and Education* 20:255–266.

Guttman, L. (1968). A General nonmetric technique for finding the smallest co-ordinate space for a configuration of points. *Psychometrika* 33:469-506.

Guttman, L. (1986). Coefficients of polytonicity and monotonicity. In *Encyclopedia of Statistical Sciences volume* 7, ed. S. Kotz, N. Johnson, and C. Read, 80-87. New York: John Wiley and Sons.

Gutwein, (2008). *L'individualisation de la Shoah: Politique, mémoire et historiographie*. *Revue d'histoire de la Shoah* 188:417-452.

Hadid, D. and I. Barzak. (2011). Hamas protests UN plans to teach Holocaust in Gaza. *Associated Press, Washington Post*. March 22.

Hakohen, D. (2003). *Immigrants in Turmoil: Mass Immigration to Israel and Its Repercussions in the 1950s and After.* Syracuse, NY: Syracuse University Press.

Halbwachs, M. (1950 [1992]). *On Collective Memory.* Trans. and ed. L. Coser. Chicago: University of Chicago Press. Originally published as *La mémoire collective*, Paris, Presses Universitaires de France.

Hancock, I. (1988). Uniqueness of the victims: Gypsies, Jews and the Holocaust. *Without Prejudice: The EAFORD International Review of Racial Discrimination* 1(2): 45-67.

Haron, M. (1981). The British decision to give the Palestine question to the United Nations. *Middle Eastern Studies* 17(2): 241-248.

Harrow, A. (1972). *A Taxonomy of Psychomotor Domain: A Guide for Developing Behavioral Objectives.* New York: David McKay.

Hayes, P. (1991). *Lessons and Legacies: The Meaning of the Holocaust in a Changing World.* Evanston, IL: Northwestern University Press.

Hazan, H. (2001). *Simulated Dreams: Israeli Youth and Virtual Zionism.* Oxford: Berghahn Books.

Hazan, K. (2005). *L'enseignement de la Shoah dans les écoles juives. Les Cahiers de la Shoah* 8:87-117.

Heilman, S. (1992). *Jewish Unity and Diversity: A survey of American Rabbis and Rabbinical Students.* American Jewish Committee, New York.

Heimberg, C. (2002). *Le rapport Bergierà l'usagedes élèves. La Suisse, le national-socialismeet la Seconde Guerre mondiale, la question des réfugiés.* Deuxième éditionaprès la publicationdu rapport final. Cycle d'orientation de Genève.

Heinman, R. (1999). The Alternative Agents for Holocaust Education. Master's thesis, School of Education, Tel Aviv University.

Helmreich, W. (1986). The *World of the Yeshiva: An Intimate Portrait of Orthodox Jewry.* New Haven, CT: Yale University Press.

Helmreich, W. (1991). *Don't Look Back: Holocaust Survivors in the US.* Jerusalem Center for Public Affairs.

Helmreich, W. (1994). *The March of the Living: A Follow-up Study of its Long Range Impact and Effects.* New York: Department of Sociology, City College of New York.

Helmreich, W. (2005). *Long Range Effects of the March of the Living on Participants.* New York: Department of Sociology, City College of New York.

Herman, S. (1977). *Jewish Identity: A Social Psychological Perspective.*

Beverly Hills: Sage Publishers.

Holocaust Educational Trust. (2009). *Evaluation of the Holocaust Educational Trust's Lessons from Auschwitz Project: Final Report.* London: University of London.

Hilberg, R. (1979). The Judenrat: Conscious or unconscious tool. Patterns of Jewish Leadership in Nazi Europe, 1933-1945. *Proceedings of the Third Yad Vashem International Historical Conference.* Jerusalem: Yad Vashem.

Hill, M. and M. Augoustinos. (2001). Stereotype change and prejudice reduction: Short- and long-term evaluation of a cross-cultural awareness programme. *Journal of Community & Applied Social Psychology* 11:243–262.

Honig, F. (1954). Reparations agreement between Israel and the Federal Republic of Germany. *The American Journal of International Law* 48(4): 564-578.

Horowitz, B. (2000). *Connections and journeys: Assessing critical opportunities for enhancing Jewish identity.* New York: UJA-Federation of New York.

Horowitz, T., et al. (1971). Volunteers for Israel during the Six Day War: Their motives and careers. *Dispersion and Unity* 13:68-115.

Ichilov, O., G. Salomon, and D. Inbar. (2005). Citizenship education in Israel: A Jewish-Democratic state. *Israel Affairs* 11(2): 303-323.

Ijaz, M. and I. H. Ijaz. (1981). A cultural program for changing racial attitudes. *The History and Social Science Teacher* 17:17-20.

Ikor, R. (1968). *Peut-on être Juif aujourd'hui?* [Is it Possible to be Jewish Today?] Paris: Editions Grasset.

Illouz, E. (2003). *Oprah Winfrey and the glamour of misery: An essay on popular culture.* New York: Columbia University Press.

Insdorf, A. (1983). *Indelible Shadows: Film and the Holocaust.* Cambridge, UK: Cambridge University Press.

Ioanid, R. (2000). *The Holocaust in Romania: The Destruction of Jews and Gypsies under the Antonescu Regime, 1940-1944.* Chicago: Ivan R. Dee.

Iram, Y. and M. Shemida. (1998). *The Educational System of Israel.* Westport, CT: Greenwood Publishing Group.

Israel Central Bureau of Statistics. (2011). Immigrants by period of immigration, country of birth and last country of residence. *Statistical Abstract of Israel,* 233-234.

http://www.cbs.gov.il/reader/shnaton/templ_shnaton.html?num_

tab=st04_04&CYear=2011 (accessed December 17, 2012).

Israel Central Bureau of Statistics. (2010). Students in secondary education, by supervision (Hebrew education), Table 8.19. *Statistical Absract of Israel 2010.*

http://www1.cbs.gov.il/reader/shnaton/templ_shnaton.html?num_tab=st08_19&CYear=2010 (accessed December 17, 2012).

Israel Ministry of Education. (2011). *Evaluation of Youth Journeys to Poland in the Year 2009: Cognitive, Emotional and Axiological Impacts.* Jerusalem: Rama.

Israel Ministry of Education. (2010). *Social and Informal Education: Youth Delegations to Poland.*

http://cms.education.gov.il/EducationCMS/applications/mankal/arc//se4bk7_6_10.htm (accessed December 17, 2012).

Israel Ministry of Education. (2008). Goals of the student delegations to Poland. (In Hebrew). http://cms.education.gov.il/EducationCMS/Units/Bitachon/MishlachotLechul/MishlachotLepolin/Klali.htm (accessed December 17, 2012).

Israel Ministry of Education, Culture, and Sport. (2009). Minutes from conference on Shoah education in Jewish and Arab sector schools. http://www.knesset.gov.il/mmm/data/pdf/m02376.pdf (accessed December 17, 2012).

Israel Ministry of Education. (2011a). Evaluation of Youth Journeys to Poland. http://cms.education.gov.il/NR/rdonlyres/EDFB2F83-BA42-4706-A7D7-95638E02BB76/139929/polin_2009_f.pdf (accessed December 17, 2012).

Israel Ministry of Education, Special Needs Branch. (2011b). Learning kit on the subject of the Shoah for special education. http://cms.education.gov.il/EducationCMS/Units/Special/ChadashVemeanyen/HadashAlHamadaf.htm (accessed December 17, 2012).

Isserman, N. (2009). Political tolerance and intolerance: Using qualitative interviews to understand the attitudes of Holocaust survivors. *Contemporary Jewry* 29(1): 29-47.

ITF. (2004). *Country Report on Holocaust Education in Task Force Member Countries: United States.* Task Force for International Cooperation on Holocaust Education, Remembrance and Research.

ITF. (2005). *Country Report on Holocaust Education in Task Force Member Countries: Israel.* Task Force for International Cooperation on Holocaust Education, Remembrance and Research.

ITF. (2006a). *Country Report on Holocaust Education in Task Force Member Countries: Germany*. Task Force for International Cooperation on Holocaust Education, Remembrance and Research.

ITF. (2006b). *Country Report on Holocaust Education in Task Force Member Countries: France*. Task Force for International Cooperation on Holocaust Education, Remembrance and Research.

ITF. (2006c). *Country Report on Holocaust Education in Task Force Member Countries: Croatia*. Task Force for International Cooperation on Holocaust Education, Remembrance and Research.

ITF. (2006d). *Country Report on Holocaust Education in Task Force Member Countries: Lithuania*. Task Force for International Cooperation on Holocaust Education, Remembrance and Research.

ITF. (2006e). *Country Report on Holocaust Education in Task Force Member Countries: United Kingdom*. Task Force for International Cooperation on Holocaust Education, Remembrance and Research.

ITF. (2009). *Country Report: Austria*. Task Force for International Cooperation on Holocaust Education, Remembrance and Research.

ITF. (2010). *United Kingdom Country Report, 2010*. Task Force for International Cooperation on Holocaust Education, Remembrance and Research.

ITF. (2011). *Italy Country Report*. Task Force for International Cooperation on Holocaust Education, Remembrance and Research.

Jahanbegloo, R. (2006). Holocaust Denial in Iran and Anti-Semitic Discourse in the Muslim World. In "Muslim-Jewish dialogue in a 21st Century world," proceedings from workshop on the comparative study of Jews and Muslims held at Royal Holloway, University of London, on April 22-23.

Jewish Black Book Committee. (1946). *The Black Book: The Nazi Crime Against the Jewish People*. New York: Jewish Black Book Committee.

Jick, L. (1981). The Holocaust—its use and abuse within the American public. *Yad Vashem Studies* 14:303-318.

Jockusch, L. (2007). *Collect and Record. Help to Write the History of the Latest Destruction. Jewish Historical Commissions in Europe, 1943-1953*. New York University.

Kahane, R. (1997). *The Origins of Postmodern Youth: Informal Youth Movements in a Comparative Perspective*. New York and Berlin: Walter de Gruyter.

Kamen, C. (1991). *Little Common Ground: Arab Agriculture and Jewish*

Settlement in Palestine. Pittsburgh, PA: University of Pittsburgh Press.

Kashti, O. (2010). OECD report shows Israeli schools lagging in student-to-computer ratio. *Ha'aretz*. December 21.

Kashti, O. (2011). Battle over civics ends in ouster of two critics. *Ha'aretz*. May 26.

Katriel, T. (1988). Gibush: A study in Israeli cultural semantics. *Anthropological Linguistics* 30(2): 199-213.

Katriel, T. and P. Nesher. (1986). Gibush: The rhetoric of cohesion in Israeli school culture. *Comparative Education Review* 30(2): 216-231.

Katz, S. (1983). *Post-Holocaust Dialogues: Critical Studies in Modern Jewish Thought*. New York: New York University Press.

Katz, S. (1996). Introduction. In I. Trunk, *Judenrat: the Jewish councils in Eastern Europe under Nazi occupation*. Lincoln, NE: Bison Books Edition, University of Nebraska.

Kaufman, B., ed. (1996). *Reflections: March of the Living 1996: Jewish Youth Confront the Holocaust*. Miami, FL: Central Agency for Jewish Education.

Keren, N. (1985) The influences of those who shape public opinion on one side and the holocaust research from the other side on the development of the educational discussion and educational programs about the holocaust in the post elementary schools and the informal education in Israel between 1948-1981. PHD dissertation. Jerusalem. (Hebrew).

Kershner, I. (2012).Israeli protest's invocation of Holocaust is condemned. *New York Times*. January 1.

Klein, H. (1973). Children of the Holocaust: Mourning and bereavement. In *The Child in his Family: The Impact of Disease and Death*, ed. E. J. Anthony and C. Koupernik, 393-409. New York: John Wiley.

Klein, H. and A. Kogan. (1987). Denial and identification processes in survivors of the Holocaust. *Sihot, Israel Journal of Psychotherapy* 1:108-111 (Hebrew).

Kochan, L. (1989) Life over death. *Jewish Chronicle*. December 22.

Kochavi, A. (2001). *Post-Holocaust Politics: Britain, the United States and Jewish Refugees, 1945-1948*. Chapel Hill, NC: University of North Carolina Press.

Kohlberg, L. (1981). *Essays on Moral Development, Vol. I: The Philosophy of Moral Development*. San Francisco, CA: Harper & Row.

Kolb, D. (1984). *Experiential Learning: Experience as the Source of Learning and Development*. Englewood Cliffs, NJ: Prentice-Hall, Inc.

Konopniki, G. (2011). Le nouvel enseignement du mépris. *Aschkel*. July 23. http://www.aschkel.info/article-le-nouvel-enseignement-du-mepris-par-guy-konopnicki-80067923.html (accessed December 17, 2012).

Kopelowitz, E. (2003). *Between Mifgash and Shlichut Paradigms in Contemporary Zionist Education and the Question of the Ideological Relationship between Israel and Diaspora*. Jerusalem: Jewish Agency for Israel.

Kraemer, D. (2000). *The Meanings of Death in Rabbinic Judaism*. London and New York: Routledge.

Krathwohl, D. (2002). A Revision of Bloom's Taxonomy: An Overview. *Theory into Practice* 41(4): 212-218.

Krathwohl, D., B. Bloom, and B. Masia. (1964). *Taxonomy of Educational Objectives: The Classification of Educational Goals. Handbook II: Affective Domain*. New York: David McKay Co., Inc.

Krichevsky, L. (2005). Russia's Jewish day schools increase but enrollment still slow. *Jewish Telegraphic Agency*. April 15.

Kriegel, A. (1984). *Réflexion sur les questions juives*. Paris: Hachette, Collection Pluriel.

Kübler-Ross, E. (1969). *On Death and Dying*. London: Tavistock Publications Limited.

Kübler-Ross, E. and D. Kessler. (2005). *On Grief and Grieving*. New York: Simon & Schuster.

Kugelmass, J. (1994). Why we go to Poland: Holocaust tourism as secular ritual. In *The Art of Memory Holocaust Memorials in History*, ed. J. Young, 174-184. Washington, DC: Prestel.

Kuleta-Hulboj, M. (2011). *Polish-Jewish Youth Encounters*. Presented at International Council of Christians and Jews. Cracow, Poland, July 3-5.

Lacey, C., A. Saleh, and R. Gorman (1998). Teaching nine to five: A study of the teaching styles of male and female professors. Paper presented at the Annual Women in Educational Leadership Conference, Lincoln Nebraska, October 11-12.

Laird, T., A. Garver, and A. Niskodé. (2007). Gender Gaps: Understanding Teaching Style Differences between Men and Women. Paper presented at the Annual Meeting of the Association for Institutional Research, June 2-6.

Lanzmann, C. (2011). Contre le bannissement du mot "Shoah" des manuels scolaires. *Le Monde*. August 31.

Lanzmann, C. (1990). Hier ist kein Warum. In *Au sujet de Shoah*, ed. B. Cuau, 279. Trans. D. LaCapra in *History and Memory after Auschwitz*, Ithaca: Cornell University Press.

Laskier, M. (1983). *The Alliance israélite universelle and the Jewish communities of Morocco, 1862-1962*. Albany: SUNY Press.

Lavy, G. (1996). *Germany and Israel: Moral Debt and National Interest*. London: Routledge.

Lawrence, S. and B. Tatum. (1997). Teachers in transition: The impact of antiracist professional development on classroom practice. *Teacher's College Record* 99(1): 162-178.

Lazar, A., T. Litvak-Hirsch, D. Bar-On, and R. Beyth-Marom. (2009). Through psychological lenses: University students' reflections following "Psychology of the Holocaust" course. *Educational Review* 61:101-114.

Lazar, A., J. Chaitin, T. Gross, and D. Bar-on. (2004a). Jewish Israeli teenagers, national identity and the lessons of the Holocaust. *Holocaust and Genocide Studies* 18(2): 188-204.

Lazar, A., J. Chaitin, T. Gross, and D. Bar-on. (2004b). A journey to the Holocaust: Modes of understanding among Israeli adolescents who visited Poland. *Educational Review* 56(1): 13-31.

Lederhendler, E., ed. (2000) *The Six Day War and World Jewry*. Bethesda, MD: University Press of Maryland.

Lemish, D. (2002). Between here and there: Israeli children living cultural globalization. In *Children, Young People and Media Globalization*, ed. C. von Feilitzen and U. Carlsson. Göteborg, Sweden: UNESCO.

Lennon, J. and M. Foley. (1999). Interpretation of the unimaginable: The U.S. Holocaust Memorial Museum, Washington, D.C. and "dark tourism." *Journal of Travel Research* 38:46-50.

Lennon, J. and M. Foley. (2000). *Dark tourism: The Attraction of Death and Disaster*. London and New York: Continuum.

Lev, M. and S. Romi. (in press). Third-generation adolescents' journeys to Poland: Differential effects on emotions, attitudes, and values toward the Holocaust of Israeli and Canadian adolescents. In *Promoting Jewish Literacy in Educational Settings*, ed. Y. Rich., Y. Katz, Z. Mevarech, and S. Ohayon. College Park: University of Maryland Press.

Levi, P. (1958). *If This Is a Man*. London: Abacus.

Lévinas, E. (1963). *Difficile liberté: Essais sur le Judaïsme*. Paris: Editions Albin. [English edition, 1990, *Difficult freedom: Essays on Judaism*. Trans. S. Hand. Baltimore: Johns Hopkins Univ. Press].

Levinson, H. (2012). Study: IDF officers less committed to Jewish values after visits to Nazi death camps. *Ha'aretz*. January 20. http://www.haaretz.com/print-edition/news/study-idf-officers-less-committed-to-jewish-values-after-visits-to-nazi-death-camps-1.408237 (accessed January 30, 2012).

Lévy, B. (2003). *Etre Juif: Etude Lévinassienne*. Lagrasse: Editions Verdier.

Lévy, D. and N. Sznaider. (2006). *The Holocaust and Memory in the Global Age*. Philadelphia: Temple University Press.

Levy, S. (1985). Lawful roles of facets in social theories. In *Facet Theory: Approaches to Social Research*, ed. D. Canter, 73-74. New York: Springer-Verlag.

Levy, S. (1994). *Louis Guttman on Theory and Methodology: Selected Writings*. Dartmouth, MA: Aldershot.

Levy, S. (2002). Similarity and differences in the value system of youth of two generations (1975 and 1994) and in educational frameworks which differ in terms of religion. In *Values Education in Various Teaching Contexts,* ed. N. Maslovaty and Y. Iram, 179-201. Ramot: Tel Aviv University Press. (Hebrew).

Levy, S. (2005). Guttman, Louis. In *Encyclopedia of Social Measurement, volume 2*, ed. K. Kempf Leonard, 175-188. Amsterdam: Elsevier Inc.

Levy, S., and L. Guttman. (1976). *Values and Attitudes of Israeli High School Youth.* Jerusalem: The Israel Institute of Applied Social Research.

Levy, S., H. Levinson, and G. Katz. (1993). *Beliefs, Observances and Social Interaction among Israeli Jews.* Jerusalem: The Louis Guttman Israel Institute of Applied Social Research.

Lewis, B. (2005). Freedom and justice in the modern Middle East. *Foreign Affairs* 84(3): 36-51.

Liebman, C. (1993). The myth of defeat: The memory of the Yom Kippur War in Israeli society. *Middle Eastern Studies* 29(3): 399-418.

Liebman, C. and Y. Yadgar. (2004). Israeli identity: The Jewish component. In *Israeli Identity in Transition*, ed. A. Shapira, 163-184. Wesport, CT: Greenwood Publishing.

Lindquist, D. (2006). Guidelines for teaching the Holocaust: Avoiding common pedagogical errors. *The Social Studies* 97(5): 215-221.

Linn, R. and I. Gur-Ze'ev. (1996). Holocaust as metaphor: Arab and Israeli use of the same symbol. *Metaphor and Symbolic Activity* 11(3): 195-206.

Lipstadt, D. (1994). *Denying the Holocaust: The Growing Assault on Truth and Memory*. New York: Plume Publishers.

Lipstadt, D. (1995). Not facing history. *The New Republic*, 26-29. March 6.

Lipstadt, D. (1996). America and the memory of the Holocaust. *Modern Judaism* 16(3): 195-214.

Litvak-Hirsch, T., J. Chaitin, and E. Zaher. (2010). Perceptions of the holocaust of Palestinian young adults, citizens of Israel. *Peace and Conflict: Journal of Peace Psychology* 16(3): 231-252.

Loehlin, J. (2004). *Latent Variable Models: An Introduction to Factor, Path, and Structural Equation Analysis*. Mahwah, NJ: Lawrence Erlbaum Associates.

London, L. (2003). *Whitehall and the Jews, 1933-1948: British Immigration Policy, Jewish Refugees and the Holocaust*. Cambridge: Cambridge University Press.

Maitles, H. (2008). "Why are we learning this?": Does studying the Holocaust encourage better citizenship values? *Genocide Studies and Prevention* 3(3): 341-352.

Maitles, H. and P. Cowan. (2008). More open to diversity? The longer term citizenship impact of learning about the Holocaust. In *Reflecting on Identities: Research, Practice and Innovation*, ed. A. Ross and P. Cunningham, 521-530. London: CiCe.

Manfra, M. and J. Stoddard. (2008). Powerful and authentic digital media and strategies for teaching about genocide and the Holocaust. *The Social Studies*, 99(6): 260-264.

Maniv, O. (2011). Not for the rich alone: Journeys to Poland will be subsidized. *Ma'ariv*. July 25.

Mankowitz, Z. (2002). *Life between Memory and Hope: The Survivors of the Holocaust in Occupied Germany*. New York: Cambridge University Press.

Mann, M. (2005). *The Dark Side of Democracy: Explaining Ethnic Cleansing*. Cambridge: Cambridge University Press.

Marans, N. and R. Bell, eds. (2006). *The A. B. Yehoshua Controversy: An Israel-Diaspora Dialogue on Jewishness, Israeliness, and Identity*. New York: American Jewish Committee.

Marcuse, H. (2010). Holocaust memorials: The emergence of a genre. *American Historical Review* 115(1): 53-89.

Matthews, L. and G. Crow. (2009). *The Principalship: New Roles in a Professional Learning Community.* Boston: Allyn & Bacon.

Medding, P., ed. (2008). *Sephardic Jewry and Mizrahi Jews.* Oxford University Press.

Meir-Glitzenstein, E. (2004). *Zionism in an Arab Country: Jews in Iraq in the 1940s.* London and New York: Routledge.

Michael, G. (2007). Deciphering Ahmadinejad's Holocaust revisionism. *Middle East Quarterly* 14(3): 11-18.

Michlic, J. (2012). Remembering to remember, remembering to benefit, remembering to forget: The variety of memories of Jews and the Holocaust in postcommunist Poland. Institute for Global Jewish Affairs. http://www.jcpa.org/indexph.asp (accessed February 16, 2012).

Michman, D. (1996). The impact of the Holocaust on religious Jewry. In *Major Changes within the Jewish People in the Wake of the Holocaust. Proceedings of the Ninth YadVashem International Historical Conference*, ed. Y. Gutman and A. Saf, 659-707. Jerusalem: Yad Vashem.

Michman, D. (2000). From holocaust to revival! From holocaust to revival? The historiography of the consequential connection between the Holocaust and the establishment of the State of Israel: Between myth and reality. *Considerations of the Revival of Israel* 10:234-259. (Hebrew).

Michman, D. (2003). The causal relationship between the Holocaust and the birth of Israel: Historiography between myth and reality. In *Holocaust Historiography, A Jewish Perspective: Conceptualizations, Terminology, Approaches and Fundamental Issues*, ed. D. Michman, 303-328. London: Vallentine Mitchell.

Michman, D. (2008). La recherche sur la Shoah: existe-t-il une "école israélienne"? *Revue d'histoire de la Shoah* 188:93-116.

Milchman, A. and A. Rosenberg, eds. (1997). *Martin Heidegger and the Holocaust.* Amherst, NY: Humanity Books.

Miller, H. (2001). Meeting the challenge: The Jewish schooling phenomenon in the UK. *Oxford Review of Education* 27(4): 501-513.

Misco, T. (2008). "Nobody told us about what happened": The current state of Holocaust education in Romania. *International Education* 38(1): 6-20.

Mnookin, R. (2010). *Bargaining with the Devil: When to Negotiate, When to Fight*. New York: Simon & Schuster.

Morris, B. (2004). *The Birth of the Palestinian Refugee Problem Revisited.* Cambridge: Cambridge University Press.

Moshe, A. (2011). *Polish-Israeli Youth Meetings: An Overview from an Israeli Perspective*. Presented at International Council of Christians and Jews. Cracow, Poland, July 3-5.

Mudde, C. (2005). *Racist Extremism in Central and Eastern Europe*. London: Routledge.

Müller, F. (1980). *Trois ans dans une chambre a gaz d'Auschwitz: Présenté par Claude Lanzmann*. Paris: Pygmalion.

Nadel, M. and S. Frost. (1981). Teaching the Holocaust in the Jewish school. *Journal of Jewish Education* 49(1): 30-33.

Neher, A. (1962). *L'existence juive: Solitude et affrontements*. [Jewish Existence] Paris: Seuil.

Neistat, A. (2011, November 12). ADL slams movie that compares Holocaust to abortion. *Ha'aretz*.

Neuberger, B. (2007). Education for democracy in Israel: Structural impediments and basic dilemmas. International Journal of Educational Development 27(3): 292-305.

Neusner, J. (1981). *Stranger at Home: The Holocaust, Zionism and American Judaism*. Chicago: University of Chicago Press.

Newman, I. and C. Benz. (1998). *Qualitative-quantitative research methodology: Exploring the interactive continuum*. Carbondale, IL: Southern Illinois University Press.

Nickerson, E. (2010). From Books to the Web: A Comparative Analysis of Holocaust Denial in the Internet Age. Honors scholar thesis, University of Connecticut. http://digitalcommons.uconn.edu/srhonors_theses/151 (accessed December 17, 2012)

Nir, H. (1994). How do we tell children about the Holocaust? *Hed haGan* 48(3): 311-315.

Nisan, M. (1992). Beyond intrinsic motivation: Cultivating a sense of the desirable. In: *Effective and responsible teaching*, ed. F. K. Oser, A. Dick and J. L. Patry, 126-138. San Francisco: Jossey-Bass.

Nisan, M. (1993). Balanced identity: Morality and other identity values. In *The Moral Self*, ed. G. Noam, 239-268. Cambridge, MA: MIT Press.

Nora, P. (1989). Between memory and history. *Representations* 26:7-25.

Nora, P. (1998). *Realms of Memory*. New York: Columbia University

Press. [originally published in French as *Les Lieux de Mémoire,* Paris: Gallimard (1984-1992)].

Novick, P. (1999). *The Holocaust in American Life.* Boston: Houghton Mifflin.

Noy, B. (1989). Attitudes towards the Holocaust and the treatment of the subject in the elementary schools in Israel, in the 40s and 50s, as reflected in the recollections of graduates. *Pirsumim, The Journal of the Soldiers and Partizans Museum* 22(70): 259-285.

Observatoire du monde juif. (2001). Liste des incidents dont les communatés juives ont été victimes depuis de début de la deuxième Intifada. *Observatoire du monde juif* 1:2-9.

Ofer, D. (1996). Holocaust survivors as immigrants: The case of Israel and the Cyprus detainees. *Modern Judaism* 16:1-23.

Ofer, D. (2000). The strength of remembrance: Commemorating the Holocaust during the first decade of Israel. *Jewish Social Studies* 6(2): 24-55.

Ofer, D. (2004). History, memory and identity: Perceptions of the Holocaust in Israel. In *Jews in Israel: Contemporary Social and Cultural Patterns*, ed. U. Rebhun and C. Waxman, 394-418. Hanover, NH: University Press of New England.

Ofer, D. (2009). The past that does not pass: Israelis and Holocaust memory. *Israel Studies* 14(1): 1-35.

Ofri, I., Z. Solomon, and H. Dasberg. (1995). Attitudes of therapists toward Holocaust survivors. *Journal of Traumatic Stress* 8(2): 229-242.

Olick, J., V. Vinitzky-Seroussi, and D. Lévy, eds. (2011). *The Collective Memory Reader.* Oxford University Press.

Ophir, A. (2000). The identity of victims and the victims of identity: A critique of Zionist ideology for a post-Zionist age. In *Mapping Jewish Identities*, ed. L. Silberstein, 174-200. New York: New York University Press.

Ouzan, F. (2004). Rebuilding Jewish identities in displaced persons camps in Germany. *Bulletin du centre de recherche français de Jérusalem.* http://bcrfj.revues.org/index269.html (accessed December 17, 2012)

Palgi, Y., A. Shrira, and M. Ben-Ezra. (2011). World assumptions and psychological functioning among ultraorthodox and secular Holocaust survivors. *Traumatology* 17(1): 17-21.

Pappé, I. (2010). Fear, victimhood, self and other: On the road to reconciliation. In *Across the Wall: Narratives of Israeli-Palestinian History,* ed. I. Pappé and J. Hilāl, 75-86. London: I. B. Tauris.

Pappé, I and J. Hilāl, eds. (2010). *Across the Wall: Narratives of Israeli-Palestinian History*. London: I. B. Tauris.

Payne, S. (2008). *Franco and Hitler*. New Haven: Yale University Press.

Peck, J. (2006). *Being Jewish in the New Germany.* New Brunswick, NJ: Rutgers University Press.

Petrie, J. (2009). *The Secular Word "Holocaust": Scholarly Sacralization, Twentieth Century Meanings.* http://www.berkeleyinternet.com/holocaust/ (accessed January 9, 2011).

Pettigrew, A. and S. Foster. (2009). *Teaching About the Holocaust in English Secondary Schools: An Empirical Study of National Trends, Perspectives and Practice.* University of London.

Phillips-Berenstein, M. (2001). Arabs' Stereotypes and Prejudice by Secular Students of Low SES and Religious Students of Middle SES. MA thesis, Tel Aviv University.

Piaget, J. (1932). *The Moral Judgment of the Child.* London: Kegan Paul.

Picheny, M. (2003). A fertile ground: The expansion of Holocaust denial into the Arab world. *Boston College Third World Law Journal* 23(2): 331-358.

Pilch, J., S. Feinstein, and Z. Ury. (1964). The "Shoah" and the Jewish school. *Journal of Jewish Education* 34(3): 162-172.

Pins, A. (1974). *Crisis in Jewish Life: The Aftermath of the Yom Kippur War.* Presented at the Annual Meeting of the National Conference of Jewish Communal Services, San Francisco, California.

Porat, D. (1992). "Amalek's accomplices": Blaming Zionism for the Holocaust; anti-Zionist ultra-orthodoxy in Israel during the 1980s. *Journal of Contemporary History* 27(4): 695-729.

Porat, D. (2004). From the scandal to the Holocaust in Israeli education. *Journal of Contemporary History* 39(4): 619-636.

Ram, U. (2007). The future of the past in Israel: A sociology of knowledge approach. In *Making Israel*, ed. B. Morris, 202-230. Ann Arbor, MI: University of Michigan Press.

Radin, C. (2005). Muslim opens Holocaust museum in Israel. *The Boston Globe*. May 6.

Rauschning, D., K. Wiesbrock, and M. Lailach. (1997). *Key resolutions of the United Nations General Assembly, 1946-1996.* CUP Archive.

Rebhun, U. (2004). Jewish identity in America: structural analysis of attitudes and behaviors. *Review of Religious Research* 46(1): 43-63.

Rein, A. and G. Bensoussan. (2008). *L'historiographie israélienne de la Shoah, 1942-2007. Revue d'histoire de la Shoah,* volume 188. France: Centre de Documentation juive Contemporaine.

Reichmann, E. (1951). *Hostages of Civilization: The Social Sources of National Socialist Anti-Semitism*. Boston: Beacon Press.

Resnik, J. (2003). "Sites of memory" of the Holocaust: Shaping national memory in the education system in Israel. *Nations and Nationalism* 9(2): 297–317.

Rietveld-van Wingerden, M. (2008). Jewish education and identity formation in The Netherlands after the Holocaust. *Journal of Beliefs & Values* 29(2): 185–194.

Riger, E. (1958). *The History of Israel in the New Era, Part 3*. Tel Aviv: Dvir (Hebrew).

Ritchler, Y. (2006). How do we teach children about the Holocaust? *Yad Vashem Yerushalaim* 42:4-5.

Ritterband, P. (1986). Israelis in New York. *Contemporary Jewry* 7(1): 113-126.

Rodman, D. (2007). *Arms Transfers to Israel: The Strategic Logic behind American Military Assistance*. Eastbourne, UK: Sussex Academic Press.

Romi, S. and M. Lev. (2007). Experiential learning of history through youth journeys to Poland: Israeli Jewish youth and the Holocaust. *Research in Education* 78(1): 88-102.

Romi, S. and M. Lev. (2003). Youth and the Holocaust: Changes in knowledge, feelings, and attitudes following the journey to Poland. *Megamot* 42(2): 219-239. (Hebrew).

Rosen, A. (2010). *The Wonder of Their Voices: The 1946 Holocaust Interviews of David Boder*. Oxford: Oxford University Press.

Rosenfeld, A., ed. (1997). *Thinking about the Holocaust after Half a Century*. Bloomington: Indiana University Press.

Rosenfeld, E. (1995). Fatal lessons: United States immigration law during the Holocaust. *UC Davis Journal of International Law and Policy* 249:250-266.

Rosenthal, A. (2002). The Holocaust—History or Education and Ideology? Historiographical approaches to the Holocaust as reflected in textbooks used by Israeli public high schools between the years 1946-1961. MA thesis, Department of Jewish History, Bar-Ilan University (Hebrew).

Rosenthal, G. (1998). *The Holocaust in Three Generations: Families of*

Victims and Perpetrators of the Nazi Regime. London and Washington: Cassell.

Rosenthal, G. (2002). Veiling and denying the past: The dialogue in families of Holocaust survivors and families of Nazi perpetrators. *The History of the Family* 7(2): 225-238.

Rothberg, M. (2009). *Multidirectional Memory: Remembering the Holocaust in the Age of Decolonization*. Stanford, CA: Stanford University Press.

Round, S. (2009). Interview: James Smith. With his brother Stephen, he set up the UK's version of Yad Vashem. *The Jewish Chronicle*. September 2.

Rubenstein, R. (1966). *After Auschwitz*. Baltimore: Johns Hopkins University Press.

Rudge, D. (2005). Arab set up Holocaust teaching center in Nazareth. *Jerusalem Post*. March 18.

Rutland, S. (2010). Creating effective Holocaust education programmes for government schools with large Muslim populations in Sydney. *Propsects* 40(1): 75-91.

Saar, Y. (2011). Experience the Warsaw ghetto. *Ha'aretz*. January 17.

Sagy, S., E. Orr, and D. Bar-On. (1999). Individualism and collectivism in Israeli society: Comparing religious and secular high-school students. *Human Relations* 52(3): 327-348.

Said, E. (2001). *The End of the Peace Process: Oslo and After.* New York: Pantheon Books.

Saraf, M. (1988). *The Hitler Scroll of North Africa: Moroccan and Tunisian Jewish Literature on the Fall of the Nazis.* Lod, Israel: Habermann Institute for Literary Research.

Sarfatti, M. (2006). *The Jews in Mussolini's Italy: From Equality to Persecution*. Madison: University of Wisconsin Press.

Sartre, J.P. (1948). *Anti-Semite and Jew.* Translated by George Becker. New York: Schoken Books.

Schlant, E. (1999). *The Language of Silence: West German Literature and the Holocaust*. London: Routledge.

Schuitema, J., G. Dam, and W. Veugelers. (2008). Teaching strategies for moral education: A review. *Journal of Curriculum Studies* 40(1): 69-89.

Schweber, S. (2006). Holocaust fatigue: Teaching it today. *Social Education,* 7(1): 44-50.

Schweber, S. (2008). "Here there is no why": Holocaust education at a Lubavitch girls' yeshiva. *Jewish Social Studies* 14(2): 156-185.

Schweber, S. (2011). Holocaust education. In *International Handbook of Jewish Education,* volume 5, ed. H. Miller, L. Grant, and A. Pomson, 461-478. New York: Springer.

Segev, T. (2000). *The Seventh Million: The Israelis and the Holocaust.* Translated by Haim Watzman. New York: Henry Holt.

Shafir, M. (2004). Between denial and "comparative trivialization": Holocaust negationism in post-communist East Central Europe. In *The Treatment of the Holocaust in Hungary and Romania during the Post-Communist Era,* ed. R. L. Braham, 43-136. New York: Columbia University Press.

Shandler, J. (2003). The testimony of images: The Allied liberation of Nazi concentration camps in American newsreels. In *Why Didn't the Press Shout? American and International Journalism during the Holocaust,* ed. R. Shapiro, 109-126. Jerusalem: Ktav Publishing House.

Shapira, A. (1997). *Yehudim Hadashim, Yehudim Yeshanim* [New Jews, Old Jews]. Tel Aviv: Am Oved (Hebrew).

Shapira, A., H. Adler, and S. Fire. (1999). *No Need for Nostalgia, Youth Movements Are Here and Now, Though Different: Or Blue Shirt, Green Scarf, Knitted Kipa, Social Profile Of Israeli Youth Movements after Twenty Years.* Ministry of Education and Culture, Tel Aviv University and Hebrew University of Jerusalem (in Hebrew).

Shawn, K. (1995). Current issues in Holocaust education. *Dimensions* 9(2): 15-18.

Shechter, C. (2002). *The Influence of the Journey to Poland on Teenagers' Empathy towards Israeli Arab Suffering.* Haifa: University of Haifa.

Sheramy, R. (2003). Resistance and war: The Holocaust in American Jewish education 1945-1960. *American Jewish History* 91(2): 287-313.

Sheramy, R. (2007). From Auschwitz to Jerusalem: Re-enacting Jewish history on the March of the Living. *Polin* 19:307-326.

Sheramy, R. (2009). The March of the Living: Where is it now? *Jewish Educational Leadership* 8(1): 10-15.

Sheskin, I. and A. Dashefsky. (2011). *Jewish Population in the United States, 2011.* North American Jewish Data Bank.

http://www.jewishdatabank.org/Reports/Jewish_Population_in_the_United_States_2011.pdf (accessed December 17, 2012).

Shitrit, S. (2004). *Oriental Jewry's Struggle in Israel 1948–2000.* Tel-Aviv: Am Oved.

Shoham, E., N. Shiloah, and R. Kalisman. (2003). Arab teachers and Holocaust education: Arab teachers study Holocaust education in Israel. *Teaching and Teacher Education* 19:609–626.

Short, G. (1994). Teaching the Holocaust: The relevance of children's perceptions of Jewish culture and identity. *British Educational Research Journal* 20(4): 393-405.

Short, G. (1995). The Holocaust in the National Curriculum: A survey of teachers' attitudes and practices. *Journal of Holocaust Education* 4:167-188.

Short, G. (2000a). Holocaust education in Ontario high schools: An antidote to racism? *Cambridge Journal of Education* 30(2): 291-305.

Short, G. (2001). Confronting the Holocaust in religious education. *Journal of Beliefs and Values* 22(1): 41-54.

Short, G. and C. Reed. (2004). *Issues in Holocaust Education*. Aldershot, UK: Ashgate.

Short, G., C. Supple, and K. Klinger, eds. (1998). *The Holocaust in the School Curriculum: A European Perspective*. Strasbourg: Council of Europe.

Shtull-Trauring, A. (2011). Professor Asher Cohen to head civics panel at Education Ministry. *Ha'aretz*. June 13.

Shulman, L. (2004). *Teaching as Community Property: Essays on Higher Education*. San Francisco: Jossey-Bass.

Sicron, M. (1957). *Immigration to Israel: 1948-1953*. Jerusalem: Falk Institute (Hebrew).

Simkins, T. (1977). *Non-formal Education and Development*. Manchester: Manchester University Press.

Slonim, S. (1981). President Truman, the State Department and the Palestine question. *The Wiener Library Bulletin* 34(53): 15-29.

Slyomovics, S. (2012). Fatna el Bouih and the work of memory, gender and reparation in Morocco. *Journal of Middle East Women's Studies* 8(1): 37-62.

Smooha, S. (2002). The persistent significance of Jewish ethnicity in Israel. *JCAS Symposium Series* 7:185-212.

Smooha, S. (2004). Jewish ethnicity in Israel: Symbolic or real? In *Jews in Israel: Contemporary Social and Cultural Patterns*, ed. U. Rebhun and C. Waxman, 47-80. Hanover, NH: University Press of New England.

Solomon, Z. (1995). From denial to recognition: Attitudes toward Holocaust survivors from World War II to the present. *Journal of Traumatic Stress* 8(2): 215-228.

Spearman, C. (1904). "General intelligence" objectively determined and measured. *American Journal of Psychology* 14:201-293.

Spearman, C. (1932). *The Abilities of Man*. New York: AMS Press.

Spector, K. (2007). God on the gallows: Reading the Holocaust through narratives of redemption. *Research in the Teaching of English* 42(1): 7-55.

Spolsky, B. and E. Shohamy. (1999). *The Languages of Israel: Policy, Ideology and Practice*. Bristol, UK: Multilingual Matters.

Statham, A., L. Richardson, and J. Cook. (1991). *Gender and University Teaching: A Negotiated Difference*. Albany: SUNY Press.

Stauber, R. (2004). The Jewish response during the Holocaust: The educational debate in Israel in the 1950s. *Shofar: An Interdisciplinary Journal of Jewish Studies* 22(4): 57-66.

Steinberg, B. (1984). The present era in Jewish education: A global comparative perspective. *The Jewish Journal of Sociology* 26(2): 93-109.

Stillman, N. (1991). *The Jews of Arab Lands in Modern Times*. Philadelphia: Jewish Publication Society.

Stone, D. (2000). Day of remembrance or day of forgetting? Or why Britain does not need a Holocaust memorial day. *Patterns of Prejudice* 34(4): 53-59.

Stone, P. (2006). A dark tourism spectrum: Towards a typology of death and macabre related tourist sites, attractions and exhibitions. *Tourism: An Interdisciplinary International Journal* 52(2): 145-160.

Strike, A. (1996). The moral responsibility of education. In *Handbook of Research on Teacher Education* 2nd ed., ed. J. Sikula, T. Buttery, and E. Guyton, 869-892. New York: Macmillan.

Sussman, S. (2010a). Vichy discrimination against Jews in North Africa. *United States Holocaust Memorial Museum Online Encyclopedia*. http://www.ushmm.org/wlc/en/article.php?ModuleId=10007311 (accessed January 22, 2012).

Sussman, S. (2010b). Jews in North Africa: Oppression and resistance. *United States Holocaust Memorial Museum Online Encyclopedia*. http://www.ushmm.org (accessed January 30, 2011).

Szajkowski, Z. (1970). *Jews and the French Revolutions of 1789, 1830 and 1848*. New York: Ktav.

Taum, Y. (2005). Collective Cambodian Memories of the Pol Pot Khmer Rouge Regime. Paper Presented at the Fifth Annual Conference of the Asian Scholarship Foundation. Bangkok, July 25-26.

Tenenbaum, J. (1956). *Race and Reich: The Story of an Epoch*. New York: Twayne.

Thurnell-Read, T. (2009). Engaging Auschwitz: an analysis of young travellers' experiences of Holocaust Tourism. *Journal of Tourism Consumption and Practice* 1(1): 26-52.

Tlalim, A. (1994). *Don't Touch My Holocaust*. (documentary film).

Totten, S. (1998). A Holocaust curriculum evaluation instrument: Admirable aim, poor result. *Journal of Curriculum and Supervision* 13(2): 148-166.

Totten, S. (1999). Should there be Holocaust education for K-4 students? The answer is no. *Social Studies and the Young Learner* 12(1): 36-39.

Totten, S. (2000). Diminishing the complexity and horror of the Holocaust: Using simulations in an attempt to convey historical experiences. *Social Education* 64(3): 65-71.

Totten, S. (2004). *Teaching about Genocide: Issues, Approaches, and Resources*. Greenwich, CT: Information Age Publishing.

Totten, S. and S. Feinberg. (1995). Teaching about the Holocaust: Rationale, content, methodology and resources. *Social Education* 59(6): 323-333.

Trigano, S. (1997). The Jews and the spirit of Europe: A morphological approach. In *Thinking About the Holocaust After Half a Century*, ed. A. Rosenfeld, 300-318. Bloomington: Indiana University Press.

Trunk, I. (1972). *Judenrat: The Jewish Councils in Eastern Europe under Nazi Occupation*. Bison Books Edition, University of Nebraska.

Turner, R. and R. Brown. (2008). Improving children's attitudes toward refugees: An evaluation of a school-based multicultural curriculum and an anti-racist intervention. *Journal of Applied Social Psychology* 38(5): 1295-1328.

Tzimerman, H. (1947). *His Works are Just: Questions and Answers Regarding the Horrific Destruction of Six Million Jews, May God Avenge Their Blood*. Jerusalem: privately published. (Hebrew). http://hebrewbooks.org/pdfpager.aspx?req=37922&st=&pgnum=1&hilite= (accessed December 17, 2012).

UJSF (2002). *Les Antifeujs: Le livre blanc des violences antisémites en France depuis septembre 2000*. Paris: Calmann-Lévy, Union of Jewish Students in France.

USHMM. (2001). *Teaching about the Holocaust: A Resource Book for Educators*. Washington, DC: United States Holocaust Memorial Museum.

USHMM. (2010a). The Farhud. *United States Holocaust Memorial Museum Online Encyclopedia.*

http://www.ushmm.org/wlc/es/article.php?ModuleId=10007277 (accessed January 30, 2011).

Vaknin, R. (1998). *Jewish Identity: A Consideration of the Sources of Israel.* Jerusalem: Touro College. (Hebrew).

van Driel, B. (2003). Some reflections on the connection between Holocaust education and intercultural education. *Intercultural Education* 14(2): 125-137.

Vargen, Y. (2008). *Student Journeys to Poland.* Jerusalem: The Knesset Center for Research and Information.

Velmer, T. (2011). Teachers in civics war: Education Ministry decision to strengthen Jewish identity, patriotism studies in civics classes leads to rift among subject's teachers. *YNet News*. June 30.

Von Hindenberg, H. (2007). *Demonstrating Reconciliation: State and Society in West German Foreign Policy toward Israel, 1952-1965*. Oxford and New York: Berghahn Books.

Waldocks, E. (2008). Rising costs of Poland trips spark concern in Knesset. *Jerusalem Post*. January 30.

Ward, M. (2011). Teaching indigenous American culture and history: Perpetuating knowledge or furthering intellectual colonization? *Journal of Social Sciences* 7(2): 104-112.

Wardekker, W. L. (2001) Schools and moral education: conformism or autonomy? *Journal of Philosophy of Education* 35(1): 101–114.

Wegner, G. (1995). Buchenwald concentration camp and Holocaust education for youth in the new Germany. *Journal of Curriculum and Supervision* 10(2): 171-188.

Weinreich, M. (1946). *Hitler's Professors: The Part of Scholarship in Germany's Crimes against the Jewish People*. New York: YIVO.

Weil, P. (2008). *How to Be French: Nationality in the Making since 1789.* Trans. Catherine Porter. Duke University Press. (originally published in French, Gallimard, 2005).

Weiss, A. (1988). The historiographical controversy concerning the character and functions of the Judenrats. In *The Historiography of the Holocaust Period; Proceedings of the Fifth Yad Vashem International Historical Conference*, ed. Y. Gutman and G. Grief, 679-696. Jerusalem: Yad Vashem.

Weitz, Y. (1994). The Herut movement and the Kasztner trial. *Holocaust and Genocide Studies* 8(3): 349-371.

Weitz, Y. (1996a). The Holocaust on trial: The impact of the Kasztner and Eichmann trials on Israeli society. *Israel Studies* 1(2): 1-26.

Weitz, Y. (1996b). Shaping the Memory of the Holocaust in Israeli Society of the 1950s. In *Major Changes within the Jewish People in the Wake of the Holocaust, Proceedings of the Ninth Yad Vashem International Historical Conference,* ed. Y. Gutman and A. Saf, 497-518. Jerusalem: Yad Vashem.

West, B. (2008). Enchanting pasts: The role of international civil religious pilgrimage in reimagining national collective memory. *Sociological Theory* 26(3): 258-270.

Wettstein, H., ed. (2002). *Diasporas and Exiles: Varieties of Jewish Identity.* Berkeley: University of California Press.

Wicken, S. (2006). Views of the Holocaust in Arab media and public discourse. *Yale Journal of International Affairs* 1(2): 103-115.

Wiesel, E. (1979). *The President's Commission on the Holocaust: Report to the President.* September 27. http://www.ushmm.org/research/library/faq/languages/en/06/01/commission/ (accessed January 23, 2012).

Wiesel, E. (1977). *The Trial of God.* New York: Random House.

Wistrich, R. (1997). Israel and the Holocaust trauma. *Jewish History* 11(2): 13-20.

Wolf, J. (1999). Anne Frank is dead, long live Anne Frank: The Six-Day War and the Holocaust in French public discourse. *History and Memory* 11(1): 104-end.

Worden, J. (2009). *Grief Counseling and Grief Therapy: A Handbook for the Mental Health Practitioner, 4th edition.* New York: Springer.

Worth, R. (2005). *Elisabeth Kübler-Ross: Encountering Death and Dying.* Philadelphia: Chelsea House.

Wyman, D. (1984). *The Abandonment of the Jews: America and the Holocaust, 1941-1945.* New York: Pantheon Press.

Yablonka, H. (1994). *Estranged Brothers: Holocaust Survivors in the State of Israel: 1948-1952.* Jerusalem: Yad Izhak Ben-Zvi Press. (in Hebrew).

Yablonka, H. (2008). *Off the Beaten Track: The Mizrahim and the Shoah.* Tel Aviv: Miskal–Yedioth Aharonot Books and Chemed Books. (Hebrew).

Yablonka, H. (2009). Oriental Jewry and the Holocaust: A tri-generational perspective. *Israel Studies* 14(1): 94-122.

Yad Vashem. (2006). Events at the International School for Holocaust

Studies. *Yad Vashem Quarterly Magazine* 41:9.

Yad Vashem. (2010). The outbreak of World War II and anti-Jewish policy: North Africa and the Middle East. www.yadvashem.org (accessed January 31, 2011).

Yagil, D. and A. Rattner. (2002). Between commandments and laws: Religiosity, political ideology, and legal obedience in Israel. *Crime, Law & Social Change* 38:185–209.

Young, J. (1990). *Writing and Rewriting the Holocaust: Narrative and the Consequences of Interpretation*. Bloomington: Indiana University Press.

Young, J. (2004). When a day remembers: A performative history of Yom Hashoah. In: *Textures and Meaning: Thirty Years of Judaic Studies at the University of Massachusetts Amherst,* ed. L. Ehrlich et al., 436-452. Amherst: University of Massachusetts.

Zarchin, T. (2008, December 11). Who benefits from Holocaust victims' money? Majority of heirs of Holocaust victim still have not received restitution from state body. *Ha'aretz*.

Zertal, I. (1998). *From Catastrophe to Power: Holocaust Survivors and the Emergence of Israel*. Berkeley: University of California Press.

Zertal, I. (2005). *Israel's Holocaust and the Politics of Nationhood*. Trans. Chaya Galai. Cambridge: Cambridge University Press (original in Hebrew, 2002).

Zohar, Z. (2005). *Sephardic and Mizrahi Jewry: From the Golden Age of Spain to Modern Times*. New York: New York University Press.

Zuccotti, S. (1987). *The Italians and the Holocaust: Persecution, Rescue, and Survival*. New York: Basic Books.

Zuckerman, M. (1993). *Shoa in the Sealed Room: The Holocaust in the Israeli Press during the Gulf War*. Tel Aviv: Hamechaver Publishing. (Hebrew).

Zuckerman, M. (2010). The Shoah on trial: Aspects of the Holocaust in Israeli political culture. In *Across the Wall: Narratives of Israeli-Palestinian History,* edited by I. Pappé and J. Hilāl, 75-86. London: I. B. Tauris.

Index of Names

CPSIA information can be obtained at www.ICGtesting.com
Printed in the USA
BVOW001613100713

325499BV00004B/22/P

9 781936 235810